Simple Pleasures

EMMA FONTANELLA

Simple Pleasures

EASY RECIPES FOR EVERYDAY INDULGENCE

Publisher Mike Sanders
Art & Design Director William Thomas
Editorial Director Ann Barton
Senior Designer Jessica Lee
Photographer and Stylist Emma Fontanella
Recipe Tester Julie Harrington
Proofreaders Jean Bissell, Mira Park
Indexer Celia McCoy

First American Edition, 2023
Published in the United States by DK Publishing
1745 Broadway, 20th Floor, New York, NY 10019

The authorized representative in the EEA is Dorling Kindersley Verlag GmbH.
Arnulfstr. 124, 80636 Munich, Germany

Text and photographs copyright © 2023 by Emma Fontanella
DK, a Division of Penguin Random House LLC
23 24 25 26 27   10 9 8 7 6 5 4 3 2 1
001-333384-OCT2023

A catalog record for this book
is available from the Library of Congress.
ISBN 978-0-7440-6619-7

DK books are available at special discounts when purchased
in bulk for sales promotions, premiums, fundraising, or educational use.
For details, contact SpecialSales@dk.com

Printed and bound in China

For the curious
www.dk.com

MIX
Paper | Supporting
responsible forestry
FSC™ C018179

This book was made with Forest
Stewardship Council ™ certified
paper – one small step in DK's
commitment to a sustainable future.
For more information go to
www.dk.com/our-green-pledge

To my mom and dad, who instilled in me
a passion for food and cooking. You've
always supported me, no matter what.
I love you very much.

Contents

Introduction

REDISCOVERING THE JOY OF COOKING AND EATING SIMPLE FOOD, DONE WELL

When I was thinking about writing this book, I wanted to address some of the things that have frustrated me about cookbooks over the years. For me, too many cookbooks are filled with recipes I don't want to make. They include "unusual" twists on dishes using unfamiliar, hard-to-find ingredients or unnecessarily complicated recipes that aren't practical to tackle at home. While I do love twists and experimenting with new ingredients, most of the time when I'm craving something delicious and comforting, I find myself leaning toward something simple and familiar. I think it's time we rediscovered the pleasure to be found in cooking simple food and then, of course, eating it!

For me, the most amazing food isn't complicated. Yet often, I've found myself flipping through cookbooks that offer versions of recipes far away from what I picture in my mind. When I'm craving a cinnamon roll, I'm thinking thick, fluffy, gooey, delicious classic cinnamon rolls. Now imagine opening a cookbook to find "matcha green tea and lavender" cinnamon rolls. Who has a bag of lavender lying around in their cupboard?! Whenever I see a recipe like that, I ask myself, "Do I really want to hunt down an entire bag of that unusual ingredient? Will it end up unused after that one recipe?". While that twist on a cinnamon roll might be delicious, I really just want a great, classic cinnamon roll!

I'm guessing I'm not the only one to feel this way. In my career as a chef in restaurants, bakeries, and hotels, when designing menus, I've had to learn to predict what most people will order. When I was running a bakery in Rome, it was the classic chocolate and vanilla cupcakes that were always the first to go! And you know what happened to all the unusual flavors? No one bought them, and the chefs ended up having to take them home. It couldn't be more clear—it's the classics that most people really love.

That's how the idea for *Simple Pleasures* was born. I wanted to offer amazing recipes for simple versions of classic dishes that you can easily master, all using familiar ingredients. Then, when you've nailed those, provide ideas for how to change things up so you'll want to make these dishes again and again. I want you to be able to pick up this book whenever you're craving a comforting treat and find a dish that appeals, whether it's breakfast, dinner, delicious snacks, or celebration baking. With these recipes, I never compromise on the quality of the result, but I've simplified them to make the recipes approachable. Wherever it makes sense, I've given you instructions for how to make ahead and freeze the dishes (along with easy reheating guidance) and given ideas for using up leftovers in interesting ways. Every recipe is a proven crowd-pleaser. I hope when you flip through the pages of this cookbook, you'll find yourself thinking, "Yes! I think I'd like to eat that!" much more often than wondering, "Who is ever going to make that?!"

LESS IS OFTEN MORE

In my opinion, too many of us have forgotten about the simple pleasures of cooking with family and friends using staple ingredients we're already familiar with. When I was a kid, on Sundays, my mom and I would dedicate the day to cooking. She'd open her cupboard, take out some pantry staples, and we'd start making something simple but delicious. I think it's important to remind ourselves that real cooking doesn't need to be elaborate—often, less is more.

Simplicity is famously a hallmark of Italian cuisine, but across cultures, some of the best foods have only a few ingredients. Bread is a great example—what you can do with just flour, water, yeast, and salt is incredible! The amount of variation you can achieve by varying flours, hydration levels, fermentation, and methods of working doughs never ceases to amaze me. There are several bread recipes in this book, but there's one that's particularly personal to me—my **Mom's Focaccia** (page 144). Focaccia is one of Italy's most popular breads. If you're a foodie, no matter where in the world you live, you'll likely have heard of it. There are many vastly different versions of focaccia across Italy. I might be biased, but I think my mom's version is even more

delicious than the commonly exported versions. The dough incorporates potato as well as flour, which gives an incredible texture to the bread.

IN DEFENSE OF SHORTCUTS

I think cookbooks should focus on solving problems for people. Of course, everyone has their own unique challenges they need to solve, whether cooking for themselves or for families and friends. It often comes down to not having much time and wanting easy dishes that satisfy. Over the last ten years, through the magical interactivity of social media, I've enjoyed getting to know all kinds of home cooks, from busy parents trying to feed their families, to young people just starting to experiment in the kitchen, to grandparents wanting to bake with their grandkids. This book is for anyone who seeks the comforting indulgence of a homemade cookie

or a cozy bowl of pasta—but needs a recipe that will come together quickly and yield consistent results.

Making recipes approachable was one of my top priorities when writing this book. Often, this meant taking some shortcuts compared to traditional methods. Many people have told me that they think shortcuts aren't "real recipes" or aren't "real cooking." Whenever they say that it makes me smile. Try telling that to a professional chef! Probably every professional chef—from the most junior to the most senior—has developed shortcuts for getting their work done right, but quickly.

Now, if you love shortcuts as much as I do, then you won't need convincing about how great they can be. However, if you're one of those who thinks they're not real cooking, let's talk about the shortcuts I've included in this book! From a culinary perspective, I put as

much effort into developing shortcuts as I do into more complex recipes to make sure the quality stays high. In fact, many of my shortcuts are designed to make dishes *better*, with some being inspired by advanced techniques used in Michelin-star restaurant kitchens. So, think of learning and understanding these shortcuts as a way of improving your cooking skills.

Let's take my **Instant DIY McFlurry** (page 222). If you've ever made homemade ice cream, you'll know that once it's frozen, it soon turns into a solid block of ice. It's very different from the soft ice cream texture you get in restaurants. The reason this happens is due to the way domestic freezers work and their frequent freeze-thaw cycles. I developed a solution for this problem that's super simple and gives you creamy, soft ice cream within seconds. However, the idea behind it is identical to the way high-end restaurants create individual portions of ice creams and sorbets to order, each with a perfect soft texture. The difference is that my method uses an inexpensive food processor rather than the $5,000 piece of equipment that high-end restaurants use. (By the way, my method is more reliable because food processors aren't prone to breaking—those expensive ice cream machines always break!)

Or take my quick **Three-Ingredient Fettucine Alfredo** (page 106). The method allows you to make the whole Alfredo dish, including the sauce, in one pan. Now, the big benefit of this technique is that it uses just one pan and one burner. I hope the benefits speak for themselves in terms of simplicity, cost, and easy cleanup. However, the precise details of the method are worth thinking about if you're an advanced home cook. At the very highest level of pasta cooking, it turns out there's a problem cooking pasta in the traditional way, using lots of heavily salted water. You see, you often want the pasta water to serve two different purposes: first, to season the pasta as it cooks; and second, to use the starchy water to emulsify the sauce you're making for the pasta. The problem is—the traditional method doesn't really work. If you add enough salt to season the pasta correctly, the water will be far too salty to use in making the sauce; and the large volume of water makes the starch too dilute to emulsify the sauce easily. Now,

in a high-end restaurant kitchen, there are ways to solve this; but we need a simple solution in the home. In my recipe, you use a small, precise volume of water to cook the pasta in, and season it precisely (it's a myth that you need to use lots of water to cook pasta). When the pasta is cooked, you're left with appropriately seasoned pasta, and correctly seasoned, super-starchy water that will emulsify sauces fantastically. I also use a variation on this method for my **One-Pot Mac & Cheese** (page 98).

Sometimes, my shortcut recipes are designed to up the quality compared to similar recipes you'll find elsewhere. My **One-Minute Microwave Mug Cakes** (page 80) are a great example. Before I developed my own recipes, I tried popular recipes I found online and sadly found they produced some horrible, rubbery cakes. After some experimenting, I figured out it was the eggs that were causing the problem. In a conventional oven, eggs have almost magical properties for cake texture, but it turns out things go horribly wrong in a microwave! So I developed an egg-less recipe that gives delicious results.

All this is to say, if you're someone who thinks shortcut recipes aren't "real cooking," my message is they take lots of testing and developing—so give them a try. There's more to them than you think, and you might be surprised at the results you get!

FINAL THOUGHTS

In writing this book, I wanted to create a place you can go any time you're craving some amazing comfort food, where you can trust you'll always get great results. It has easy recipes for when you need something in a hurry, and recipes for those times when you want to spend a little more time making something special. The recipes reflect my background growing up and living in both the United States and Italy. It's filled with classic dishes from both cultures, and ideas for variations that will keep the recipes fresh, and hopefully spark your own creativity. If you love comfort food, this book is for you. I hope you'll love it as much as I loved writing it for you.

Foundations & Techniques

Cakes

CAKE SIZES

The layer cakes you'll find in this book have been developed for two or three 7-inch (18cm) diameter round cake pans. Seven-inch cake pans are inexpensive and readily available online. However, I know not everyone will want to buy 7-inch cake pans; and sometimes, you'll simply want to make larger cakes if you're feeding a larger crowd.

To scale a recipe from 7-inch (18cm) to 8-inch (20cm) or 9-inch (23cm) cakes, simply multiply all the ingredient amounts by 1½. To scale from 7-inch (18cm) to 10-inch (25cm) cakes, multiply all the ingredient amounts by 2.

Baking times will vary for different size and shape cakes, but use the toothpick test (page 15), and you'll never under- or overbake a cake again.

STORING CAKES

Many people instinctively think the best way to store a cake is to put it in the fridge, but most of the time, that will do your cake more harm than good.

Whether you're storing your cake in the fridge or on your countertop, you need to cover it. My top tip is to put your frosted cake on a cutting board and cover it with an upside-down pot. Alternatively, you can cover an unfrosted cake tightly with plastic wrap. Most cakes—including those frosted with buttercream, ganache, or sugar glaze—can be stored covered on the countertop for 2 to 3 days.

Now let's deal with the few times when you need to refrigerate a cake: 1) if it's a really hot day; 2) if the cake has a filling or frosting that will go bad easily, such as fresh whipped cream, fresh fruit, pastry cream, cream cheese frosting, or anything else perishable. My tip here is to make sure to take your cake out of the fridge at least 30 minutes before serving to allow the cake to soften. If you don't, the cake will taste hard, as if it's gone stale. Cakes stored in the fridge, covered, will keep for 4 to 5 days.

MAKING AHEAD & FREEZING

Any cake layer can be made ahead and frozen, but I'm going to share with you a pastry chef secret that can give you even better results than using a freshly baked cake right away! Allow your cakes to cool completely, then brush them with 3 to 4 tablespoons of milk. Cover the cakes in plastic wrap and ideally put the wrapped cakes in a resealable freezer bag. Store in the freezer for up to 1 month (for the best flavor and texture, it's preferable to use them within 2 to 3 weeks). Before serving the cake, defrost it in the fridge overnight. The tiny crystals of frozen milk from the milk bath you added before freezing will slowly melt as the cake defrosts, reviving its soft cake texture! BOOM—you've got yourself a cake that's *better* than new!

Some fully assembled cakes freeze well and will keep for up to a month. You always need to cover cakes when you freeze them, but how do you cover a freshly frosted cake? The trick is to put the cake in the freezer for 1 to 2 hours *uncovered*, until the outer frosting is frozen. Then you can cover the cake with an upside-down container without risking damaging the frosting. The best fillings and frostings for freezing are buttercreams, jams, and ganache. Cakes with cream cheese frosting and sweetened whipped cream also freeze well (unsweetened whipped cream does not freeze well, however). Make sure to defrost fully assembled cakes slowly in the fridge overnight. If you're planning on freezing a fully assembled cake, make sure to use the milk bath method above on the unfrosted cake layers.

AVOIDING UNWANTED DOMING, CRACKING, & CARAMELIZATION

Do you find that your cakes dome, crack, or turn dark brown? If you do, that means you're overbaking your cakes. Now, I can hear you saying, "But Emma, I followed your recipe timings exactly!" This is down to your oven. The chances are your oven was too hot or the cake was too near to the heat source. There's an easy solution—turn the oven temperature down. Did you know you can bake cakes with the oven at just 220°F (100°C)? Yes, they will take longer to bake at such low temperatures, but they will cook gently. Over the years,

I've found that 320°F (160°C) is the ideal temperature for baking most cakes. At this temperature, the cakes will remain super soft, with no doming, no cracks, and no caramelized surfaces will form that need trimming. It's also important to avoid placing your cakes close to the heat sources in your oven—this can cause cakes to overbake or even burn. Place your cake pans in the middle shelf of your oven.

Now, sometimes, you *want* your cakes to dome and crack, and to have caramelized surfaces (e.g., loaf cakes). In fact, cakes made that way can be delicious. But if you want a level cake, instead of trimming off huge amounts of unwanted doming, cracking, or dark edges, simply bake your cakes at a lower temperature.

HOW TO RESCUE AN OVERBAKED CAKE

When baking at home, I've lost count of the number of times I've put a cake in the oven and then promptly forgotten all about it. It happens to us all. There's no need to throw out a dried out, maybe even slightly burnt cake, though. While the cake is still hot, brush all the hard surfaces with milk (about 3 to 4 tablespoons), and let it soak until the cake has cooled completely. The dry cake will absorb the milk. If any of the edges are really burnt, trim them off once the cake is cool. No one will ever know anything went wrong!

THE GOLDEN RULE FOR CAKE BATTERS

There are many ways to get great results when making batters for cakes. Sometimes recipes call for melted butter or oil, sometimes they call for softened butter. Sometimes you can make the batter by hand, sometimes it's better to use a mixer. Some recipes call for sifting the dry ingredients, some don't. Every recipe is different. There's just one golden rule that applies to all cake recipes: add the flour last, and only mix until there are no more spots of flour left. If you overmix cake batter after you've added the flour, you risk making your cake gummy or chewy due to unwanted gluten—and no one wants a chewy cake! There's so much butter or oil in cakes, though, that you don't have to be too careful (the fat slows down gluten development). Make sure you mix just enough that there are no lumps of flour left.

THE TOOTHPICK TEST

Every oven is different, so any cake recipe (including the ones in this book) can only offer a guideline for baking time. When people start baking, they want to know how long a cake will take to bake. The truth is, it's done when it's done! The best way to tell when a cake is ready to come out of the oven is the "toothpick test."

To do the toothpick test, simply insert a toothpick into a few places in the cake. As soon as the toothpick comes out clean, with no batter on it, the cake is ready. If using the toothpick test for brownies, you want a little bit of wet crumb left on the toothpick.

For the recipes in this book, do the toothpick test at the first point when the recipe says the cake might be ready. For example, if the recipe says the cooking time is 18 to 22 minutes, do the first check after 18 minutes. Also, don't stress if it's not baked when the guidelines say it should be—just leave it in the oven longer, checking every few minutes until the toothpick comes out clean.

Underbaked

Perfect for brownies; underbaked for cakes

Perfect for cakes; overbaked for brownies

 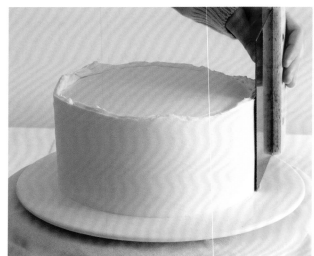

BAKE CAKE LAYERS SEPARATELY

In my recipes for layer cakes, which are mainly in the Birthday Cakes chapter (page 177), you will see that I specify baking each cake layer in a separate pan. If you only have one cake pan, please don't be tempted to bake a larger cake and cut it into two or three layers. Instead, bake the layers individually one after the other in the same pan—you'll get much better results. If you have multiple cake pans, you can bake the layers all at the same time. When you bake cake layers in their own pans, you will find it easy to produce tender, moist, perfectly baked cakes every single time.

CRUMB COAT

Applying a "crumb coat" is the first step in decorating a cake. The idea is to apply a thin layer of frosting to catch any crumbs on the surface of your cake and form a barrier so that your final layer of frosting will be free of crumbs. It couldn't be easier to do. Assemble your cake with all its fillings. Then, apply a layer of frosting to the top and the sides, completely covering the cake. Now, using a cake scraper, carefully remove most of the frosting, to leave a very thin layer of frosting. Put the crumb-coated cake in the freezer for 15 minutes (or 30 minutes in the fridge), then take it out and proceed to put your final frosting layer on the cake.

FROSTING TECHNIQUE & STYLES

People always ask me how I get my final layers of frosting looking so smooth and even. It's not as hard as you might think, but it does take practice. So don't worry if you're not there yet—for baking at home, cakes really don't have to look perfect! In fact, a rustic look can be just what you want.

If you want to aim for a perfectly smooth surface, though, here are my top tips.

- Make sure your cake is secure so it won't move around while frosting. Apply a dollop of frosting to your cake board or serving plate and place your cake on that.

- Make sure your frosting is the right consistency—it should be loose enough that it's easy to spread, but stiff enough that it doesn't collapse under its own weight. Also make sure your cake is completely cool so that it doesn't change the consistency of the frosting. You'll never get a good result if your frosting is too runny or your cake is still warm.

- Frost the cake starting with the sides before moving to the top. By starting with the sides, you will seal in any fillings, so they won't move around when you frost the top of the cake.

- A cake scraper is the most important tool for getting a good result. Use a cake scraper to gently smooth out the frosting and remove any excess. Take your time. If you go wrong, you can always remove the frosting and redo it.

- If you're aiming for perfection, a sturdy cake turntable is invaluable. You can spin the turntable while holding the cake scraper still and achieve a smooth finish in seconds.

- Finally, for a truly professionally look, warm your cake scraper in hot water, dry it off, and use the warm cake scraper to create a super-smooth look.

When frosting a cake, you may also see terms like "nude" or "naked" and "semi-nude" or "semi-naked." These terms can be confusing, but it's actually very simple. A nude or naked cake has no frosting on the sides of the cake but can have frosting on the top. A semi-nude or semi-naked cake has minimal frosting applied to the sides, or in other words, it's just crumb-coated. (See the White Christmas Cake as an example, opposite page.) Of course, you should decorate cakes however you like—there's no right or wrong, there's only what you prefer. In this book, I've usually chosen to apply a full coat of frosting to the cake—either in a smooth style or a rustic style with lots of swirls to give texture. That's only a guide, though. If you like the idea of making semi-nude or fully nude versions, you should absolutely feel free to do that!

Yeast-Raised Doughs

DRIED YEAST & FRESH YEAST

Dried yeast comes in powdered form and is great to use in all yeast-based doughs. I always recommend people use dried yeast instead of fresh yeast—dried is so much easier to work with, it's shelf-stable, and the results are just as good as using fresh. The thing to remember about all yeast (fresh and dried) is that yeasts are living, growing organisms. Unlike baking soda or baking powder, the exact quantity you use in a recipe really isn't important. If you don't have as much yeast as a recipe calls for, just add less. Even if you use only a fraction of a teaspoon of yeast it will still grow, and your dough will rise just fine. Just remember, it will take longer to rise if you start with a tiny amount. While you can always add less dried yeast than a recipe recommends, it's usually not a great idea to add more. (There's more about this in Doubling Recipes, see page 23.)

When you go to buy dried yeast at the supermarket, the array of products on offer can be confusing, even for professional bakers. So, which dried yeast should you be using? Well, the answer is—it doesn't much matter, as long as you know what you're using. Feel free to use whatever dried yeast you can get a hold of. Despite the many products on sale, there are only two fundamental types—active and instant—and they're used slightly differently.

Active dry yeast. This is probably the most common form of dried yeast sold in supermarkets. It's the original dried yeast. The important thing to know about this kind of yeast is that you often have to "wake it up," or activate it, before adding it to the rest of your dough ingredients. You do this by mixing it with a little warm water and a teaspoon of sugar, giving it a stir, and leaving it for 10 minutes. (That's not always the case, though, because some newer formulations of active dry yeast have smaller particle sizes which will work well without this step).

Instant dry yeast. Instant yeast is a more modern dried yeast product. It's sometimes marketed as "quick rise" or "rapid rise." The big benefit is that you don't need to bother with the step of activating the yeast in warm water. Instead, you can simply add the dry powder directly into the rest of the ingredients. Instant yeast products are designed to allow the yeast to find its way through your dough quickly, and to make it rise faster. In fact, instant dry yeast is so effective, you sometimes don't need to allow your dough to rise twice.

In this book, though, I've assumed you might not know which type of dried yeast you're using, so to make sure the recipes work for any kind of dried yeast, I always give instructions to wake the yeast up in warm water. However, if you know you're using instant dry yeast, or if you know you're using an active dry yeast that can be added directly to ingredients, feel free to skip this step.

Fresh Yeast. While I recommend dried yeast for baking, of course you can get great results using fresh yeast. Like with active dry yeast, before incorporating it into your doughs, you must always wake up the yeast using warm water and sugar. For the recipes in this book, if you want to use fresh yeast, triple the amounts you use compared to the dried yeast. My mom doesn't believe me when I say dried yeast is best, so she always uses fresh in her baking! Her top tip for using fresh is to store it in the freezer. It keeps beautifully for up to six months.

MAKE AHEAD & FOOLPROOF DOUGH PREPARATION FOR BEGINNERS

This is a foolproof technique to use if you're a beginner and you aren't confident kneading doughs, or you don't have a stand mixer, or you don't have the strength to knead the dough by hand. It's also the way to make your dough ahead of time.

If you want to make a dough the day before, or you don't want to knead your dough, here's what to do. Add half of the yeast called for in the standard recipe and roughly bring your dough together so that there are no dry patches of flour. There's no need knead it because the resting step in the fridge will do all the work for you. (The gluten, which is developed during kneading, will develop by itself with the extra time in the fridge.)

Allow the dough to rest at room temperature for 2 hours covered, then put it in the fridge in a covered container. The cold temperatures in the fridge will slow down the growth of the yeast. (This is called "retarding the dough.") The next day, when you want to use the dough, take it out of the fridge and knock the air out. You can then use the dough as normal. The dough will be cold to the touch, but soft enough to shape easily; and you can let it rise at room temperature as required. If you're using a bread dough enriched with butter, though, you will need to let it rest at room temperature for around 30 minutes to allow the butter in the dough to soften before using.

KNEADING TECHNIQUE

Kneading dough by hand takes a lot of effort—many people don't realize just how much energy you need to put into kneading. The precise technique doesn't matter. Just move the dough around, stretching it out and bringing it back together. As you work the dough, it will become more elastic and won't break when you stretch it. If you don't have the strength in your arms to knead a big ball of dough all at once, a good tip is to split the dough in half and knead the two halves separately. Another tip, once you've roughly formed your dough, is to let it rest covered for around 20 minutes at room temperature, which will make it easier to knead.

ADJUSTING WATER QUANTITY FOR DIFFERENT FLOURS

Different flours will absorb different amounts of water to create a dough of a given consistency. If, when you've brought your dough together, it seems too stiff, don't be afraid to add a little more water. Add water or flour half a tablespoon at a time—small changes in water or flour content can have a big effect on the dough.

For making dough, I really recommend using a scale. For a general standard bread dough using all-purpose flour, I typically use about 60 percent hydration (that's 60 grams water for every 100 grams flour). If I'm using a strong bread flour, then I'll use about 70 percent hydration (that's 70 grams water for every 100 grams flour). For doughs made with these ratios, don't add

extra flour when kneading or bringing the dough together—as the dough forms, it will have the perfect consistency. Adding extra flour will make it too dry.

For the recipes in this book, I've developed all the bread recipes to use all-purpose flour, because it's what everyone usually has easily available.

CHEF'S SECRET FOR DONUTS, BAGELS, & PRETZELS

When you have soft, delicate doughs, like donuts (pages 118 and 126), pretzels (page 142) or bagels (page 122) that need to be manipulated when raw, it can be tricky to avoid messing them up when you move them. Donuts need to be lowered into hot oil, and bagels need to be lowered into boiling water. A great tip is to put the shaped dough onto small squares of parchment paper before their final rise. That way, you can pick up the parchment paper rather than handling the light, airy dough directly. Drop the whole thing into the oil or water. The parchment paper will quickly detach from the dough. Using tongs, carefully remove the parchment paper from the oil or water as soon as it's separated. This way, your donuts and bagels will keep their even shapes beautifully.

ROLLING AND RE-ROLLING DOUGHS

When you're rolling out a dough to cut out shapes, such as for donuts or bagels, you'll be left with "scraps" of unused dough. Often, you'll be told that you'll get bad results if you re-roll the scraps, but that's a myth. There are two tricks you need to know to get good results.

Use as little extra flour as possible. Brush off any excess flour and gather all your scraps together and form them firmly into a ball. Because you didn't use too much flour initially, the scraps will come together well when you press them together, allowing a new dough ball to form just as good as the original.

Allow the newly formed dough ball to rest before re-rolling. This allows time for any excess flour to hydrate, and for newly formed dough to relax. Cover the dough ball tightly with plastic wrap and allow to rest on the counter for 15 to 20 minutes before re-rolling.

PROOFING TEMPERATURES

People often worry about what temperature they should keep their dough at while it's rising. For almost all situations, it doesn't matter. Modern yeasts grow strongly at room temperature and even in the fridge (see Make Ahead & Foolproof Dough Preparation for Beginners, page 18). However, if you have very cold winters, this will slow down the growth of the yeast at room temperature, meaning that your dough might take a long time to rise. In this case, what I like to do is to preheat my oven to its lowest temperature for 5 minutes. For my oven, that's 100°F (50°C). Then switch the oven off and allow your dough to rise in the middle of the very slightly warmed oven. That way, your dough will rise reasonably quickly.

DIFFERENT PIZZA DOUGHS

If you're a pizza geek, please avert your eyes now. You see, truly hardcore pizza fans love nothing more than measuring their yeast and salt to the nearest tenth of a gram and measuring their water and specially imported Italian flour to the nearest gram. They ferment their dough on a precise schedule and will only cook their pizza in a wood-fired oven. "Italians would be offended by any lesser treatment of pizza," they say.

Now, there's mostly nothing wrong with all that—it's exactly the right way to make the best-quality pizza. The only thing that's wrong is that great Italian home cooks don't do any of those things—to this day, I've never met an Italian who has their own wood-fired oven—and they certainly aren't the least little bit offended by pizza made in all sorts of different ways. Did you know that in Italy, we even have a version of pizza called *pizzette* that uses puff pastry for the base? Shock and horror! And sometimes, we even deep-fry our pizza—it's a popular street food in Naples!

All of this is to say, this book includes recipes for a few different pizza doughs and ways of making pizza, each designed to fit various needs and different lifestyles of home cooks. Whether it's a quick no-yeast pizza (page 104), a microwavable pizza (page 90), or an authentic pizza margherita (page 100), I'm here to tell you—they're all real pizza, and they're all delicious!

Pasta

DON'T ADD OIL TO PASTA WATER

I want to scream every time I see chefs telling people to add oil to their pasta water to "stop the pasta sticking." It doesn't! It's just a waste of oil. You'll remember from school science class that oil and water don't mix—it just floats on the surface of the pasta water doing absolutely nothing. So skip the oil. Instead, stir your pasta, especially during the first minutes of cooking when the starch first starts to leach out from the pasta. It won't stick to the pan or to itself.

COOKING PASTA IN SMALL AMOUNTS OF WATER

The traditional method of cooking pasta is to use lots of heavily salted boiling water. Many people think you must do this to get good results. However, it's a myth. You can cook pasta in a small amount of water just fine, and the extra starchy water you get from cooking pasta this way is perfect for emulsifying sauces. Food writer Harold McGee was the first to write about this in 2009. In this book, I've refined the method to make an entire pasta dish in one pan (page 106). This not only makes for a great shortcut, but also gives *better* results than you would achieve using traditional methods. This method is especially great for recipes which call for adding pasta water to the sauce, such as creamy Alfredo sauce or carbonara.

FRESH VS. DRIED PASTA

Outside Italy, the chilled sections of supermarket aisles are stocked with so-called "fresh" pasta. It's marketed as being a premium product compared to dried pasta, but it's not. Even the cheapest dried pasta is a far superior product to the expensive fresh pasta supermarkets sell. So please leave it in the chilled cabinet and pick up some dried pasta instead. Aside from anything else, you can't achieve the iconic *al dente* texture we want when cooking pasta unless you use dried pasta. Homemade fresh pasta is an entirely different thing—that's especially great for making homemade filled pastas like ravioli or tortellini.

COOKING PASTA AL DENTE

You've probably seen people talk about cooking pasta to the *al dente* stage, but what does it mean? Well, it's easy—you cook dried pasta until it's almost fully cooked all the way through, leaving just a tiny fraction in the middle slightly undercooked. This gives the pasta a great bite when you eat it. How best to achieve it? The best way is to test the pasta about 2 minutes before you reach the stated cooking time on the pasta packet. When it has a texture you like, remove the pasta from the water. If you want to be fancy, it's best to take it out *before* it reaches the perfect *al dente* stage and add the pasta to your sauce where it will continue to cook for a minute or so while you mix the pasta and sauce.

REHEATING LEFTOVER PASTA

This is a great tip for dealing with leftover pasta and sauce. Almost every Italian does this. Simply heat a little olive oil in a frying pan over a medium high heat. Add your leftover pasta and sauce, and fry until it reaches the stage you like—it's delicious to fry it until the pasta becomes a little bit crispy. This works for lasagna too. Cut a slice of cold leftover lasagna and fry the slice on both sides until crispy. Delicious!

General Techniques

APPLIANCES USED IN THE BOOK

In this book, I've stuck to using cooking appliances that are common in home kitchens: a conventional oven, a stovetop, and a microwave oven. For some recipes, like the Melt-In-Your Mouth Glazed Donuts (page 118), I give a variation for using an air fryer, an appliance now popular with home cooks in many parts of the world. I have chosen not to include recipes that make use of precision ovens that control humidity or immersion circulators for low-temperature sous vide cooking. While these are fantastic and growing in popularity, they're quite specialized and not yet widely adopted by most home cooks. In a nutshell, for all the recipes in this book, you've probably already got what you need to make everything!

Some recipes use appliances that make life easier: a fridge, a freezer, a stand mixer, a food processor, a handheld mixer, and a blender. In fact, a few recipes are explicitly designed to use a blender (see pages 72, 156, and 163) because it can save you so much time. Using the appliances that I recommend in a particular recipe will make it much easier for you to get good results. Of course, it's possible to do everything by hand, so don't worry if you don't have a particular appliance. It will take some effort, but that's okay—the exercise is good for burning off those extra carbs!

There's one other appliance I really recommend people invest in—a digital scale. They're quite inexpensive, and they really do make your life easier, especially for baking. Of course, I've designed all the recipes in the book to give you great results when you use cups to measure out ingredients. I promise you, though, it's easier and more consistent to use a scale. If I still haven't convinced you—there's also much less washing up to do when you use a scale instead of measuring cups!

GET TO KNOW YOUR OVEN

In recipes that make use of an oven, I give you a temperature setting to use. However, the truth is that every oven is different. So, think of the temperature settings I give as guides. You might well need to use a higher or lower temperature setting on your oven to get good results.

Because every oven is so different, I really recommend getting to know your own oven well. An awesome way to do this is by baking cookies. The great thing about cookies is you can bake them one at time and they're small—unlike a cake or loaf of bread—so it doesn't matter if some go wrong! Have fun experimenting with different timings and temperatures to get the cookies exactly how you like them—gooey, soft, or crispy! If the cookie isn't gooey enough, leave it in for less time (it might even look uncooked when it comes out of the oven). If it's not crispy enough, leave it in longer.

MEASURING INGREDIENTS

In baking, the easiest (and best) way to get consistent results is to use a digital scale for both solid and liquid ingredients, but I know many of you prefer to use cups to measure out ingredients.

When you're using light, powdery ingredients like flour, powdered sugar, or cocoa powder, make sure to break up any lumps before measuring. It's also important to spoon those ingredients into the measuring cup—don't use the cup as a scoop—and level everything off with the back of a knife.

As an illustration of how measuring techniques affect ingredient amounts, you will see that in this book, I'm telling you that 1 cup of all-purpose flour weighs 140 grams. If you look on the Internet, you will see different amounts depending on where you look. This is largely due to differences in technique for loading up the measuring cups. When it comes to "bigger" ingredients, like oats, blueberries, or chopped chocolate, variation in sizes affects the packing density in cups so much that we're well into approximate territory. Don't worry about this kind of thing too much, though—this is home cooking and we're not looking for perfection. If you feel you want more accuracy and reproducibility, a digital scale is your best friend.

For brown sugar, pack it tightly into the cup to get the right amount. Press the sugar down in the cup with the back of a spoon and add more to get it level with the top of the cup.

For liquids, use a liquid measuring cup rather than the cups used for measuring dry ingredients like flour. When you're looking at the amount of liquid in a measuring cup, you need to bend down to see the mark on the cup at eye level. If you look at the level from above, you'll get the amount completely wrong.

When using spoons to measure out ingredients, always use actual measuring spoons rather than spoons used for eating. This will give you much more consistent results. Note that in the context of spoon measurements, in the recipes in this book, I always use fine table salt, which packs differently in spoons compared to coarser types of salt, such as kosher salt.

Finally, when it comes to other ingredients, you might see that the amounts specified in the book don't convert exactly among ounces, grams, and cups. Often, this is because I want you to be able to use a whole package of an ingredient, and package sizes are slightly different when packaged in ounces versus grams. Don't worry though—the recipes in the book have been designed and tested to make sure they give great results, no matter whether you're working in cups/ounces or in grams.

DOUBLING RECIPES

For most recipes in the book, if you want to make a bigger amount, you can just double the amounts of the ingredients to make double the recipe. That applies to flour, sugar, eggs, vanilla extract, etc. However, there are a couple of exceptions. Don't double the salt. If you're doubling the recipe, multiply the salt amount by about 1½. For example, if a recipe calls for 1 teaspoon of salt, use 1½ teaspoons, not 2, when doubling. (This applies especially to savory dishes and is less important for baked goods.) For recipes that use yeast, don't double it. Just use the same amount as in the original recipe. The yeast will grow quickly. (See page 18.)

Doubled recipes can result in different cooking times. For anything that you're cooking "bigger" like a cake or a pie, the cooking time can be longer when you double the recipe. Don't be afraid to keep testing to know when your doubled recipe is ready. The cooking time won't change if you're cooking more of the same size things; for example, if you double a cookie recipe, you're just making more cookies. The cookies themselves are the same, so they'll take the same amount of time to cook.

WHIPPING EGG WHITES

The most important thing when whipping egg whites is to use a *clean* glass or metal bowl. You may have heard that if you get a spot of egg yolk in your egg whites, they won't whip up and you have to throw them out and start again. That's a myth. A little bit of egg yolk won't stop the egg whites whipping up if it's only a small amount. Adding a little cream of tartar, lemon juice, or vinegar will help the egg whites whip more easily.

There are three stages of whipped egg whites: soft peaks, medium/firm peaks, and stiff peaks. With soft peaks, the peaks are just starting to hold, but will quickly sink back into the mixture. With medium or firm peaks, the peaks will hold, but the tips of the peaks will fold over back onto themselves. With stiff peaks, the tips of the peaks will stay in place.

WHIPPING CREAM

When whipping cream, it's the amount of butterfat in the cream that determines how well the cream will whip up. In the United States, any product sold as "heavy cream" or "heavy whipping cream" must have at least 36% milkfat, which is perfect. Products labeled "light whipping cream" have a lower fat content, about 30% milkfat, and won't always work as well. Stick to the higher fat version, and you'll always get great results.

Always use cold cream straight from the fridge because it whips more easily, and it will form a more stable foam. Use the soft peak, firm peak, stiff peak guide previously covered for egg whites to know which stage you're at. Unlike with egg whites, with cream there's not much margin of error between perfectly whipped and badly overwhipped. Always take care not to overwhip cream—just one or two additional movements of a whisk can be the difference between perfectly whipped and overwhipped.

If you want to make your whipped cream more stable, add a dollop or two of cold mascarpone. This will help the cream hold longer.

FOLDING

When you've whipped your egg whites or cream, recipes often call for folding in the whipped ingredient. When you're folding in an ingredient, you're aiming to retain as much air in the final mixture as you can. It's easy to do but requires some care. (See photos, opposite page.)

To start with, sacrifice a little of your whipped ingredient to loosen the mixture you're working with. Add a few tablespoons of the whipped ingredient, and incorporate it well, not worrying too much about losing air. The reason is, the more similar in consistency two ingredients are, the easier they are to mix. Then add the rest of the whipped ingredient carefully and with light movements, gently fold it in. You're cutting one into the other rather than stirring vigorously. As soon as they're combined, stop folding, because even the gentlest folding process loses air.

USING A MICROWAVE

Many people look down on microwaves and don't think of them as "good" cooking appliances. That's a mistake. They are genuinely useful in the kitchen. In this book, I use the microwave in a couple of different ways.

For melting butter and chocolate: The microwave is the best way to melt butter and chocolate (and the best way to heat up milk). There are a couple of tricks to keep in mind. First, cut up the butter or chocolate into small pieces. This will help them melt much more evenly and quickly. Second, heat ingredients in 30 second bursts, stirring after each 30 seconds. This will stop super-heated spots from forming, which can cause the ingredients to splatter all over the microwave. The other benefit of melting the ingredients as quickly as possible is it stops your bowl from heating up.

For making baked goods: You can get great results for baked goods using a microwave. Everything cooks super quickly, much faster than in a regular oven. However, you can't just use a recipe designed for conventional baking and microwave it—some ingredients really don't give good results in a microwave. This book includes a whole chapter on fast microwave recipes (page 78), which I've designed to give delicious results. When making these recipes, please bear in mind that the timings really are approximate. Every microwave cooks food at different rates, so experiment with timings on your own microwave to get the best results—always be careful not to overcook when using a microwave. When making the microwave recipes, because they use such small quantities, it's important to be as accurate and precise as possible measuring out ingredients. There's a big difference between making a small error in measuring out a cup of flour for a traditional recipe versus measuring out 2 tablespoons for a microwave recipe. For these recipes, I *always* use a digital scale.

BROWNING BUTTER

Brown butter is delicious in cakes and in cookies. It's also great as a garnish for pasta dishes. It's easy to make. My top tip is to use an aluminum saucepan so you can see the color of the butter as it browns. If you use a dark, nonstick saucepan, it's hard to judge when the butter is at the right stage.

To make the brown butter, simply add the butter to a saucepan over medium heat. Gently melt it. When it's completely melted, turn the heat up a little. The butter will start to bubble as the water boils off. When it stops bubbling, continue heating, swirling the butter in the pan. You will see solid particles in the butter begin to turn brown, and the butter itself will also turn brown. Take the pan off the heat when the solid particles in the butter have reached a medium brown color, and well before they burn. You will smell a delicious, nutty aroma. That's your brown butter made. Depending on the recipe, you can use it immediately, or store it covered in the fridge.

DEEP FRYING

People often worry about what oil they should use for frying, but usually the best answer is whatever you have on hand. For most of the recipes in this book, any unscented, unflavored oil will be fine. Vegetable, canola, peanut, sunflower, or grapeseed oil are all great choices. You may have heard that you shouldn't use olive oil for frying because it has a low smoke point, but this is nonsense. The smoke point of extra virgin olive oil can range from 350°F (180°C) to 410°F (210°C), which is appropriate for frying. However, olive oil does impart a stronger flavor and it is more expensive than other oils, so it may not be the best choice for every recipe.

I have a couple of simple tips for getting good results when deep frying. First, if you find that your food is browned and crispy on the outside but undercooked on the inside, the issue is simple—you've just been using too high a temperature. So, lower the heat. My second tip is to heat the oil a little higher than you want it initially. The temperature will drop when you add the food. As soon as you've added the food, lower the heat to maintain a consistent temperature while frying and stop it from overheating. Unlike with boiling water, it's easy for the temperature of oil to go too high. The oil is hot enough when you see bubbles coming out of the food (this is water in the food boiling off).

EVENLY BROWNED PANCAKES

Browning and caramelization is what gives pancakes their amazing flavor. To get even browning when frying, the food must have even contact with the bottom of the pan, and no parts can be heated more quickly than others. The secret for pancakes is to use a nonstick pan over a medium-low heat and add a little butter or oil. When the butter or oil has heated, wipe the pan with a paper towel to remove almost all the fat and distribute the small amount of oil or butter remaining evenly. If you leave too much fat, it will pool and create hot spots that will prevent even browning. At this point, add your pancake batter to the pan. You should find the pancakes brown beautifully and evenly.

Baking Substitutions

We've all been there—you're craving a particular dish and you're just about to bake it only to find you've run out of one of the ingredients. Don't worry—it doesn't mean you can't satisfy that craving! Often, you'll have something that can act as a pretty good substitute. This is your guide to understanding how to bake with the ingredients you have. You won't get *exactly* the same results, but using these substitutions, the recipes will almost always work out just fine. Your friend in substituting ingredients is a scale—you will often get much better results substituting by weight than you will using cups or spoons to measure.

FLOUR

I developed all the recipes in this book to use all-purpose flour (also known as plain flour), because that's the easiest flour for everyone to find. I didn't want you to have to search out lots of types of flour to make any of the recipes in this book. However, if you've run out of all-purpose flour and have some other kinds of flour, here's how to substitute them.

If you have self-raising / self-rising flour, and the recipe calls for all-purpose flour plus a raising agent like baking soda or baking powder, then you can simply use the self-rising flour and omit the raising agents (baking soda or baking powder) specified in the recipe. Please note, this doesn't work for yeast-raised doughs.

If you have a gluten-free flour designed for baking, it will work well as a substitute in cookies and cakes. It won't work for breads, where gluten is critical.

If you have bread flour, you can substitute it 1:1 in most bread recipes. Bear in mind that you might need to add a little extra liquid because bread flour tends to absorb more liquid than all-purpose flour. The texture will be a little different, but the recipe will work.

RAISING AGENTS

Baking soda and baking powder do similar jobs in recipes. When you've run out of one or the other, here's how to substitute them.

Baking soda. If you've run out of baking soda, for every teaspoon of baking soda in a recipe, use 3 teaspoons of baking powder. This works well for cakes, but for cookies the texture will be affected.

Baking powder. If you've run out of baking powder, for every teaspoon of baking powder in a recipe, use ⅓ teaspoon of baking soda plus 1 teaspoon of lemon juice or vinegar.

SUGAR

Powdered sugar and granulated white sugar do similar jobs in recipes. If you measure by weight using a scale (not by cups or spoons), you can substitute one for the other. (Frostings are the exception.)

Making your own powdered sugar. The one time you really need powdered sugar is when making frostings. If you've run out, you can make your own from granulated sugar. To a high-powered blender, add 1 cup of white granulated sugar and 1 tablespoon of cornstarch. Blend until it forms a fine powder.

Brown sugar. If a recipe calls for brown sugar, if you're using a scale to weigh your ingredients, you can substitute it 1:1 for white granulated sugar. Maybe the exception here is chocolate chip cookies—if you've run out of brown sugar, I'd hold off making those until you have some in your cupboard!

BUTTER & OIL

Butter and oil can usually be substituted for each other in recipes. If you're looking to replace butter, coconut oil makes a particularly good substitute because it's a soft solid at room temperature. If you don't like coconut flavor, refined coconut oil has no flavor.

You can also use products like margarines or baking spreads, just don't use low-fat versions of these—the fat is what's required for the recipe to work. You need at least 80% fat content for these products to work.

EGGS

For cookies, pastry, or bread, you can use use 2 to 3 tablespoons of milk in place of each egg. Please note, this doesn't work for cakes! If you want to bake a cake and you've run out of eggs, try one of my microwave cake recipes (pages 80 and 86), which are eggless.

DAIRY MILK & PLANT-BASED MILKS

The recipes in this book call for whole milk, which will deliver the most reliable outcome. If you prefer to use a plant-based milk, you can substitute at a 1:1 ratio, but it's imporant to keep a few things in mind:

- The milk proteins in dairy milk play several significant roles in baked goods that affect the texture and browning. Using a plant-based milk instead of dairy milk might result in a final product that is less tender or evenly browned.

- Use an unsweetened version of plant-based milk to avoid altering the overall sweetness of a recipe too much.

- Choose a plant-based product with a similar consistency to dairy milk—different amounts of water in the different products can affect the final texture of a dish.

Feel free to experiment with plant-based milks in your cooking and baking—with a bit of practice, you will find lots of ways to achieve delicious results.

CHOCOLATE CHIPS

If you've run out of chocolate chips, but you have some chocolate in the form of bars, then you can chop the chocolate into small pieces. The chopped-up chocolate will melt a bit differently to the chocolate chips, but the results will be equally, if not even more, delicious.

FRESH FRUIT

For recipes that call for fresh berries, such as strawberries, raspberries, or blueberries, you can often substitute frozen berries. If you're cooking the fruit as a bulk ingredient, you can use the frozen berries as a straight 1:1 substitution and cook them directly from frozen. If you're including the berries individually in the recipe, such as in a muffin or cake batter, I recommend defrosting the berries and patting dry before using.

Grab & Go Breakfasts

From easy to grab-and-go, there's a breakfast here for everybody. Can you guess which breakfast dish is my favorite? (It's pancakes!)

The Fluffiest Make-Ahead Pancakes

PREP: 10 minutes // **COOK:** 10 minutes // **YIELD:** 10 to 12 pancakes

INGREDIENTS

1¼ cups (300g) whole milk

1 tsp lemon juice

1¾ cups (250g) all-purpose flour

¼ cup (50g) granulated white sugar

1 tsp baking powder

½ tsp baking soda

¼ tsp salt

2 large eggs

4 tbsp (½ stick / 60g) unsalted butter, melted, plus more for cooking

Maple syrup, to serve

I don't know about you, but first thing in the morning, all I want is coffee and food. I don't want to think about cracking eggs or weighing out flour—which is where these pancakes come in. This batter can be prepared in advance if needed, and the pancakes freeze and reheat beautifully, making them a super quick weekday breakfast. Make these on a lazy Sunday morning and you'll have pancakes to eat all week!

1. **Make the "buttermilk."** In a small bowl or large liquid measuring cup, whisk together the milk and lemon juice. Set aside for 5 minutes to allow the milk to thicken. If it curdles or splits, don't worry.

2. **Make the batter.** In a medium bowl, whisk together the flour, sugar, baking powder, baking soda, and salt. To the milk/lemon juice mixture, add the eggs and melted butter, and whisk to incorporate. Then add the milk/egg mixture to the flour mixture, and whisk to incorporate. Stop mixing when there are no lumps of flour.

3. **Make the pancakes in batches.** Place a large skillet over medium heat, and very lightly grease with butter. Wipe away excess fat from the pan (see page 26). Gently spoon the batter into the pan to create 3 or 4 pancakes per batch. The pancakes will spread during cooking. Cook the pancakes for 1 to 2 minutes, or until bubbles start to form on the surface and the edges begin to look dry. Flip and cook for 1 minute more, or until the other side has browned.

4. **Serve.** Serve these pancakes in a stack, drenched with maple syrup.

> **MAKE AHEAD & FREEZE**
>
> To make ahead, prepare the batter in the evening, cover the bowl, and refrigerate overnight. In the morning, give the batter a quick whisk just before you use it.
>
> To freeze, arrange the pancakes in a single layer on a parchment-lined baking sheet and put them in the freezer for 30 minutes. Transfer to a zip-top freezer bag and freeze for up to 2 months.
>
> To reheat, arrange the frozen pancakes in a single layer on a microwave-safe plate. Microwave on high for 1 minute or until hot.

Crispy Waffles

PREP: 10 minutes // **COOK:** 10 minutes // **YIELD:** 2 large or 8 to 10 small waffles

INGREDIENTS

¾ cup (180g) whole milk

½ tsp lemon juice

1 cup (140g) all-purpose flour

4 tbsp (60g) granulated white sugar

1 tsp baking powder

¼ tsp baking soda

¼ tsp salt

1 medium egg, at room temperature

2 tbsp (25g) unsalted butter, melted, plus more for cooking

Maple syrup, to serve

SPECIAL EQUIPMENT

Waffle iron (any type)

// SUGGESTED TOPPINGS

Sweet: maple syrup; fresh fruit (bananas, strawberries, blueberries); fruit compote; sautéed apples with cinnamon and sugar; yogurt; nuts

Savory: fried egg; crispy bacon; fried chicken

With their deep pockets, fluffy interiors, and crispy edges, what's not to love about waffles? If you're making these for a crowd, double or triple the recipe.

1. **Make the "buttermilk."** In a small bowl or large liquid measuring cup, whisk together the milk and lemon juice. Set aside for 5 minutes to allow the milk to thicken.

2. **Make the batter.** In a medium bowl, whisk together the flour, sugar, baking powder, baking soda, and salt. To the milk/lemon juice mixture, add the egg and the melted butter, and whisk to incorporate. Add the milk mixture to the flour mixture, and gently whisk to incorporate. Stop mixing when there are no lumps of flour.

3. **Make the waffles.** Grease the waffle iron with a little butter, then preheat the waffle iron. (A big factor in how crispy your waffles will turn out is how hot your waffle iron is, so be sure to preheat it well.) Pour the batter into the center of the waffle iron, spreading the batter so it leaves about a ½ inch (1.5cm) border at the edge of the waffle iron to prevent the batter from overflowing when you close it. Cook for 3 to 5 minutes or until the waffles are crispy and golden.

4. **Serve.** Serve the waffles immediately, drenched with maple syrup or any other toppings of your choice.

MAKE AHEAD & FREEZE

To make ahead, prepare the batter in the evening, cover the bowl, and refrigerate overnight. In the morning, give the batter a quick whisk just before you use it.

If you want to make a batch for freezing, I recommend doubling or tripling the recipe so you have plenty to store. To freeze cooled waffles, place in a zip-top freezer bag, with the waffles separated by pieces of parchment paper.

To serve, pop the frozen waffles in your toaster to reheat and crisp up.

Homemade Sausage & Egg McMuffin

PREP: 5 minutes // **COOK:** 10 minutes // **YIELD:** 1 sandwich

INGREDIENTS

1 English muffin (homemade, page 140, or store-bought)

2½oz (70g) uncooked breakfast sausage, casing removed

Oil or butter, for greasing

1 large egg

1 slice American cheese

Salt and pepper, to taste

SPECIAL EQUIPMENT

3- to 4-inch (8–10cm) round cookie or biscuit cutter

VARIATIONS

Adjust the recipe to your taste by adding extra cheese, swapping out the sausage patty for bacon, or leaving out the meat entirely.

The McDonald's Egg McMuffin is possibly the most iconic grab-and-go breakfast. This homemade version is absolutely delicious. It's also super quick—and with the make-ahead-and-freeze technique, you can have a hot breakfast ready to eat in just two minutes. Now that's what I call fast food! If you want to really kick this up a notch, why not make your own English muffins?

1. **Toast the English muffin.** Split the English muffin in half and toast. Set aside.

2. **Prepare the sausage patty.** Using your hands, form the loose sausage meat into a patty a little larger in diameter than the English muffin. (It will shrink during cooking.) In a lightly greased nonstick skillet, cook the patty over medium-high heat until cooked through and browned and crispy on both sides (a few minutes each side). Set aside.

3. **Cook the egg.** (If you intend to freeze your sandwich, follow the instructions for cooking the egg in the Make Ahead & Freeze section—the method is different.) In the same skillet, fry the egg to your liking. (I like a runny yolk.) Using a round cookie or biscuit cutter, cut out a circular piece of egg. Season the egg with salt and pepper.

4. **Assemble the sandwich.** Onto the base of the English muffin, place a slice of American cheese. Then, add the sausage patty and the egg. (If you like, you can add the scraps of egg white to the sandwich.) Add the top of the muffin.

5. **Serve.** Enjoy immediately or wrap it in parchment paper and eat it on the go.

MAKE AHEAD & FREEZE

Cooked egg white doesn't thaw well (it becomes watery), so to make the sandwich freezer friendly, you need to adjust the preparation of the egg. Instead of frying the egg, whisk together the yolk and white, and cook them as if you're making a small omelet. Assemble as directed, and wrap the sandwich well in parchment paper and then in aluminum foil. Pop into a zip-top freezer bag. It will freeze beautifully.

To reheat, take the sandwich out of the freezer bag and remove the foil, but leave the parchment paper. Refrigerate overnight to defrost. With the parchment paper in place, heat in the microwave for 1 minute 30 seconds. It should be piping hot all the way through. If it's not, heat for 30 seconds more or until it's hot.

Cheese Quesadillas

PREP: 2 minutes // **COOK:** 3 minutes // **YIELD:** 1 quesadilla

INGREDIENTS

1 tbsp cooking oil (any type)

1 garlic clove, peeled and smashed

1 large flour tortilla (homemade, page 152, or store-bought)

1oz (30g) shredded melting cheese (I like a mix of mozzarella and Cheddar)

¼ tsp dried oregano (optional)

Finely sliced jalapeño pepper (optional), to taste

Finely sliced fresh herbs (optional), to garnish

Quesadillas make a quick and easy breakfast, but these crispy, gooey creations are great any time of day. You can make these with store-bought corn or flour tortillas and they'll be delicious (I prefer flour for this recipe), but honestly, they're 10 times better if you make the tortillas yourself. I like to infuse the cooking oil with garlic to scent the tortillas as the quesadilla cooks, which reminds me of cheesy garlic bread! Make as many of these as you need—one or two at a time—to feed a crowd.

1. **Infuse the oil.** In a large skillet, heat the oil over medium heat. Add the garlic and sauté for 1 to 2 minutes to infuse some garlic flavor. Remove and discard the garlic.

2. **Cook the quesadilla.** Add the tortilla to the pan. Scatter the cheese over half the tortilla, leaving the other half without fillings. Top the cheese with the oregano and jalapeño (if using). Fold the tortilla half without fillings over the cheese side to create a semicircular sandwich. Cook for 90 seconds. Flip the quesadilla and cook for 90 seconds more or until the cheese has melted and the tortilla is golden brown.

3. **Serve.** Cut into wedges and serve immediately. If desired, garnish with finely sliced fresh herbs, such as cilantro, basil, mint, oregano, or epazote.

VARIATIONS

Add whatever fillings you like—shredded chicken or pork work well, as do chopped mushrooms. For ingredients like these that should be cooked, cook them before assembling the quesadilla. Typically, I use equal amounts of cheese and other fillings—you need the melty cheese to bind all the ingredients together. If you want an authentic Mexican touch—and you can get them—add a couple squash blossoms with the stems cut off. (Roughly chop the blossoms and sauté with a little garlic.) Whatever fillings you use, add them sparingly. If you're using more than 2 to 3 heaping tablespoons of filling, it's probably too much.

Make-Ahead Crêpes

PREP: 5 minutes, plus 30 minutes to rest // **COOK:** 20 minutes // **YIELD:** 12 crêpes

INGREDIENTS

1 cup (150g) all-purpose flour

¼ tsp salt

1 large egg

1¼ cups (300g) whole milk

1 tbsp unsalted butter, melted, plus more for frying

// SUGGESTED FILLINGS

Sweet: Nutella; any jams, jellies, or curds of your choice; fresh fruit of your choice (strawberries, blueberries, raspberries, banana), optionally sweetened with powdered sugar; sweetened ricotta cheese.

Savory: scrambled eggs; bacon; sausage; ham; cheeses; smoked salmon; cream cheese; sautéed veggies such as onions, mushrooms, and bell peppers. Don't forget to season the fillings with salt and pepper as needed. Often, a squeeze of fresh lemon juice will make the fillings really pop.

VARIATIONS

You can add flavorings to the batter. For sweet crêpes, try finely grated citrus zest or spices, such as cinnamon or vanilla. For savory crêpes, add chopped soft herbs of your choice, such as fresh dill, basil, or chives.

Crêpes are a crowd-pleaser! They freeze beautifully, so they're a great option for make-ahead breakfasts. When you need a quick breakfast, simply reheat a crêpe, add the fillings of your choice, and you're ready to go. If you want to meal prep filled crêpes, you can store them in the fridge for a few days and grab a couple whenever you want. Have fun experimenting with combinations of fillings. There are no rules here—there's only what you like!

1. **Make the batter.** In a medium bowl, combine the flour and salt. In a large liquid measuring cup or small bowl, whisk the egg and milk together. Whisking continuously, gradually add the milk/egg mixture to the flour. When all the ingredients are incorporated and there are no lumps of flour, stop mixing. Cover and set aside at room temperature for 30 minutes to give the flour time to fully hydrate. After 30 minutes, whisk the melted butter into the batter.

2. **Make the crêpes.** Heat a medium nonstick skillet over medium heat. Lightly grease the skillet with butter. Add ¼ cup of batter to the skillet and swirl it around, coating the base evenly. You should add just enough batter to create a thin, lacey crêpe about 8 inches (20cm) in diameter. Cook for 45 seconds on the first side or until the top surface looks like it's dried. At this point, if the heat is high enough, the bottom of the crêpe should be a light golden color. Flip and cook for 30 seconds more. Transfer to a plate. Repeat the process with the remaining batter, stacking the finished crêpes on top of each other. (Stacking the crêpes keeps them soft.)

3. **Fill the crêpes.** Add your choice of filling to a crêpe, then roll or fold it up so you can eat it with your hands.

MAKE AHEAD & FREEZE

Freeze stacks of cooled crêpes, separated by pieces of parchment paper, in large zip-top bags. When ready to use, defrost in the microwave or in a hot skillet on the stovetop for a few seconds. Add your fillings and you're good to go.

Filled crêpes can be refrigerated in an airtight container for as long as the fillings and the crêpes stay fresh, usually 1 to 3 days.

Freezer-Friendly Breakfast Burritos

PREP: 10 minutes // **COOK:** 5 minutes // **YIELD:** 1 burrito

INGREDIENTS

Butter or oil, for greasing

2 large eggs, beaten

Salt and pepper, to taste

1 large flour tortilla
(homemade, page 152,
or store-bought)

1½ tbsp cream cheese

3 tbsp shredded cheese
of choice or 1 slice
American cheese

3–4 cherry tomatoes

¼ medium red onion,
finely chopped

VARIATIONS

Any low-water content
fillings will work well for
these burritos. Try chopped
bell peppers or cooked ham,
turkey, or sausage. If you want
to use high-water content
fillings, like mushrooms, you
can—just make sure to cook
them first.

Quick, easy, and comforting, these breakfast burritos take only a few minutes to put together. With the make-ahead-and-freeze method, they'll quickly become one of your favorite grab-and-go breakfasts! If you're making these to freeze, it's easy to triple or quadruple the recipe to freeze a bunch in one go. To make these extra delicious, I recommend making your own flour tortillas.

1. **Cook the eggs.** In a lightly greased nonstick skillet over low to medium heat, lightly scramble the eggs. Season with salt and pepper to taste. Set aside.

2. **Warm the tortilla.** Wipe out the pan and heat the tortilla in the dry pan for 10 to 15 seconds to soften. Then remove it from the pan and place on a clean work surface.

3. **Fill the burrito.** Spread the cream cheese on the tortilla. Add the eggs and top them with the cheese. Halve the cherry tomatoes, squeeze all the liquid out, and roughly chop. Place the tomatoes and onion atop the cheese.

4. **Fold and cook.** Fold the burrito and cook in a dry pan for about 2 minutes on each side or until toasty and brown.

5. **Serve.** Serve immediately.

MAKE AHEAD & FREEZE

Prepare as directed, but omit the tomatoes. Wrap the burrito in parchment paper and then tightly in aluminum foil. Place in a zip-top freezer bag before popping in the freezer.

The night before, take the burrito out of the freezer, remove the bag and foil (leave the parchment paper), and defrost overnight in the fridge. In the morning, reheat the burrito still in its parchment paper in the microwave for 1 to 2 minutes or until hot all the way through. (Or, if you prefer, reheat in a dry skillet over medium heat.) Don't overdo the reheating; otherwise, the eggs will overcook and expel water.

Blender Banana Pancakes

PREP: 5 minutes // **COOK:** 5 minutes // **YIELD:** 4 medium or 6 small pancakes

INGREDIENTS

1 small ripe banana (about 3½oz / 100g), cut into large chunks

1 large egg

½ cup (120g) whole milk

1 tsp vanilla extract

¾ cup (110g) all-purpose flour

1 tsp baking powder

1 tbsp unsalted butter

Maple syrup, to serve

Toppings of choice, such as sliced banana and chocolate chips

SPECIAL EQUIPMENT

Small blender or food processor

Who wants to eat lumps of cooked banana in pancakes? Not me! The beauty of this method is you get the smooth, fluffy texture of traditional pancakes along with a sweet banana flavor—and no chunks of mashed banana. Did I mention the batter comes together in a few seconds?

1. **Make the batter.** In a blender or food processor, combine the banana, egg, milk, and vanilla. Pulse the mixture until smooth. Add the flour and baking powder. Pulse on and off again for 5 seconds more. Don't blend more than this. If any flour sticks to the sides, incorporate it using a rubber spatula.

2. **Cook the pancakes.** In a large skillet over medium heat, melt the butter until it begins to foam. Wipe away excess fat from the pan (see page 26). Working in batches if needed, spoon about a quarter of the batter into the skillet for each pancake. Cook for about 2 to 3 minutes or until bubbles appear on the surface of the pancakes and the bottoms are golden brown. Flip and cook for 1 to 2 minutes more.

3. **Serve.** Serve immediately with maple syrup and other toppings of your choice. (I like to add a sliced banana and a handful of chocolate chips.)

Light & Fluffy Oatmeal Pancakes

PREP: 5 minutes // **COOK:** 5 minutes // **YIELD:** 3 or 4 medium pancakes

INGREDIENTS

2oz (60g) instant oats or 2 packets plain instant oatmeal

¼ cup (60g) whole milk

3 tbsp (50g) plain Greek yogurt

1 medium egg

1 tsp vanilla extract

1 tsp baking powder

1 tbsp (15g) granulated white sugar

Oil or butter, for cooking

Maple syrup, to serve

Toppings of choice, such as fresh fruit

SPECIAL EQUIPMENT

Small blender or food processor

Most oatmeal pancakes are dense and heavy—but not these! These taste just like regular pancakes, and you can whip them up in your blender or food processor in less than a minute. If you're tired of oatmeal, or if you're looking to cut down on flour, these are a fantastic option. They're also the perfect way to make gluten-free pancakes (if the oats are certified gluten-free).

1. **Make the batter.** To a small blender or food processor, add the oats, milk, yogurt, egg, vanilla, baking powder, and sugar. Process until smooth. Scrape the bottom and sides of the blender and then process for 5 to 10 seconds more. Make sure to blend the batter well to ensure the oats hydrate properly. If the mixture seems loose, allow it to sit for a few minutes to thicken up.

2. **Cook the pancakes.** In a large skillet, heat a little oil or butter over medium heat. If you're using butter, heat until the butter is melted and beginning to foam. Wipe away excess fat from the pan (see page 26). Spoon the batter into the skillet to make 3 or 4 pancakes. Cook for 2 to 3 minutes or until bubbles appear on the surface and the edges begin to look dry. Flip and cook on the opposite side until golden brown.

3. **Serve.** Serve with maple syrup and toppings of your choice.

Chocolate Chip Granola Bars

PREP: 10 minutes // **COOK:** 12 minutes, plus 1 hour to cool // **YIELD:** 8 granola bars

INGREDIENTS

3 tbsp (50g) peanut butter or other nut butter, softened

½ cup (150g) honey

1½ cups (180g) old-fashioned oats

¼ tsp salt

4 tbsp mini chocolate chips

SPECIAL EQUIPMENT

8-inch (20cm) square baking pan

VARIATIONS

Experiment by replacing the chocolate chips with your favorite chopped dried fruit and/or nuts. As a guide, you usually want 4 tablespoons of finely chopped "mix-ins." If you want to add sprinkles, use about 1 tablespoon.

These granola bars are soft, chewy, and just the right balance of sweet and wholesome. I usually make these on Sunday and have them throughout out the week. The variations are endless, so have fun experimenting! Once you try these, you'll never go back to the store-bought ones.

1. **Preheat the oven and prepare the pan.** Preheat the oven to 350°F (180°C). Line an 8-inch (20cm) pan with parchment paper, leaving a 2-inch (5cm) overhang on two sides of the pan. Lightly grease the parchment paper so the mixture doesn't stick to the paper.

2. **Mix the ingredients.** In a large bowl, roughly mix the softened (or, even better, melted) peanut butter and honey. Add the oats and salt, and mix well to combine. Take your time with this—the mixture will be sticky, but it's important to coat each oat grain well, so every part of the mixture sticks together. Stir in the chocolate chips.

3. **Press the mixture into the pan.** Transfer the mixture to the prepared pan. Using wet hands, press the mixture firmly into the pan. The more firmly you press, the better the bars will hold their shape after baking.

4. **Bake the bars.** Bake for about 12 minutes, or until the edges turn a light golden color. Remove the pan from the oven and cool for 30 minutes to set. Then lift the baked granola out of the pan using the parchment paper overhang and allow to cool completely. Cut into 8 bars. Don't cut into bars until the baked granola has cooled.

MAKE AHEAD
Store the bars at room temperature in an airtight container for up to 10 days. In warm weather, store them in the fridge.

Easy Breakfast Cookies

PREP: 10 minutes // **COOK:** 15 minutes, plus 30 minutes to cool // **YIELD:** 12 small cookies

INGREDIENTS

1 small ripe banana

1 cup (100g) old-fashioned oats

3 tbsp (60g) peanut butter or another nut butter, softened

1½ tbsp (30g) honey

¼ tsp salt

⅓ cup (40g) dried cranberries

Cookies are the number one breakfast food in Italy, so I had to include my version in this book. People outside Italy are often surprised by the idea of eating cookies for breakfast, but Italian breakfast cookies are delicious! Unlike the traditional crispy versions you find in Italian stores, these are soft and chewy, and they're just a little bit healthier.

1. **Preheat the oven and prepare the baking sheet.** Preheat the oven to 320°F (160°C). Line a baking sheet with parchment paper. Lightly grease the parchment paper to make sure the cookies don't stick.

2. **Combine the ingredients.** In a large bowl, use a fork to mash the banana well. Add the oats, softened peanut butter, honey, and salt. Mix well to make sure all the oats are coated with honey, peanut butter, and banana. Stir in the dried cranberries and mix until evenly distributed.

3. **Form the cookies.** Divide the mixture into 12 equal portions. With wet hands, lightly press the portions into small cookie shapes and place on the prepared baking sheet. You can place the cookies close together because they won't spread during baking.

4. **Bake the cookies.** Bake for 10 to 15 minutes. (The cooking time will depend on the size of the banana.) The cookies will be very soft once done. Remove the sheet from the oven and allow the cookies to cool for 5 to 10 minutes on the baking sheet. Then gently remove them from the parchment paper and transfer to a wire rack to allow them to cool completely. These cookies will be deliciously soft and chewy.

MAKE AHEAD
Store at room temperature in an airtight container for up to 3 to 5 days. In warm weather, store in the fridge.

French Toast Two Ways

PREP: 10 minutes // **COOK:** 10 minutes // **YIELD:** 4 slices of French toast per method

Everybody loves French toast—it's so good, I had to give you two versions! First up are what I call "Lazy Pancakes." I make this when I'm craving the comfort and fluffiness of pancakes but don't want to get out the measuring cups or kitchen scale. The second version is my indulgent French toast, which I save for the occasional Sunday morning breakfast when I want something special.

"LAZY PANCAKES" FRENCH TOAST

INGREDIENTS

1 large egg

½ cup (120g) whole milk

1 tbsp granulated white sugar

1 tsp vanilla extract

1 tbsp butter

½ tbsp vegetable oil

4 slices pre-sliced white sandwich bread

1. **Make the soaking bath.** In a large shallow bowl, whisk together the egg, milk, sugar, and vanilla. Set aside.

2. **Heat the skillet.** In a large skillet, heat the butter and oil over medium heat. (The combination of butter and oil will prevent the butter from burning).

3. **Coat the bread.** Dip the slices of bread into the egg mixture, making sure both sides are well covered.

4. **Cook.** Fry the bread for 2 to 3 minutes per side, or until golden brown. (If all the bread doesn't fit in the skillet, dip the bread just before cooking in batches.)

5. **Serve.** Add your toppings of choice (I like lots of maple syrup), and serve immediately.

INDULGENT FRENCH TOAST

INGREDIENTS

4 slices white bread, cut from a whole loaf in thick ¾-inch (2cm) slices (Any bread will do, but I like to use brioche.)

3 large eggs

¾ cup (180g) heavy cream

1 tsp vanilla extract

1 tbsp butter

½ tbsp vegetable oil

1. **Prepare the bread.** Arrange the thickly sliced bread in a single layer in a large, shallow dish. Set aside.

2. **Make the soaking bath.** In a medium bowl, whisk together the eggs, cream, and vanilla.

3. **Soak the bread.** Pour the cream mixture over the bread and let sit for 5 minutes to allow the bread to soak up the mixture. Flip over each slice of bread and allow to sit for another 5 minutes.

4. **Cook.** In a large skillet, heat the butter and oil over medium heat. Fry the slices of bread for 2 or 3 minutes per side, until golden brown.

5. **Serve.** Dust with powdered sugar and add your choice of toppings. Sometimes, I just want maple syrup; other times, I'm in the mood to go to town.

// SUGGESTED TOPPINGS

Powdered sugar, maple syrup, sliced fresh fruit (strawberries, bananas, peaches), chopped nuts (pecans, walnuts, hazelnuts), ground cinnamon

VARIATIONS

To make it festive during the holidays, add 1 to 2 tablespoons of bourbon, rum, or Cognac to the milk or cream mixture. This makes it a kind of eggnog French toast.

French toast doesn't have to be sweet (just leave out the sugar and vanilla extract). It's amazing with crispy bacon and a tomato sauce made with fresh tomatoes cooked until they're completely broken down, with a little garlic and a good handful of fresh basil.

Afternoon Treats

From brownies and cookies to banana bread and instant donuts (yes, *instant* donuts), these classic treats will keep you going between meals. In fact, why not skip breakfast or lunch and have more cookies instead?

Perfect Chocolate Chip Cookies

PREP: 30 minutes // **COOK:** 10 minutes, plus 3 minutes to cool // **YIELD:** 8 to 10 cookies

INGREDIENTS

1⅓ cups (185g) all-purpose flour

½ tsp baking soda

¼ tsp salt

8 tbsp (1 stick / 115g) unsalted butter, melted

⅓ cup + 1 tbsp (75g) brown sugar (light or dark), packed

⅓ cup + 1 tbsp (75g) granulated white sugar

1 tsp vanilla extract

1 medium egg, at room temperature

5½oz (150g) good-quality chocolate, chopped into small chunks

VARIATIONS

Crispy cookies. For a crispy chocolate chip cookie, leave them in the oven a little longer. Every oven is different, so experiment with the timings to get the texture you want. (See page 21.)

Brown butter cookies. Instead of regular butter, use an equal amount of delicious brown butter (page 25). It's worth the little extra effort—trust me!

Change up your mix-ins. You can add ½ cup of any chopped nuts of your choice. Use chocolate chips rather than chopping up your own chocolate. This will give you more defined chips that aren't as melty as your own chocolate chunks.

Chocolate chip cookies are very special to me—they were the first cookies I tried when I moved to the United States. At that time, we only had crunchy cookies in Italy. I didn't know cookies could be soft and gooey in the middle and have crispy edges. So, these cookies are exactly that.

1. **Prepare the baking sheet.** Line a baking sheet with parchment paper.

2. **Mix the dry ingredients.** In a large bowl, whisk together the flour, baking soda, and salt until combined. Set aside.

3. **Mix the wet ingredients.** In another large bowl, whisk together the melted butter, brown sugar, granulated sugar, and vanilla. Mix until combined and emulsified. (The texture should be smooth and creamy.) Whisk in the egg until fully incorporated.

4. **Mix the wet ingredients into the dry.** Using a rubber spatula, combine the flour mixture with the butter mixture, and mix until the dough is well combined and there are no visible spots of flour. Stir in the chocolate chunks.

5. **Prepare the cookies.** Using a large ice cream scoop, scoop 8 to 10 balls of dough onto a plate. Place in the fridge for 10 minutes.

6. **Preheat the oven.** Preheat the oven to 350°F (180°C).

7. **Bake the cookies.** Transfer the cookies to the prepared baking sheet, leaving about 4 inches (10cm) between each cookie. Bake for 10 to 12 minutes. They will seem slightly underbaked. Bang the baking sheet on the kitchen counter to make the cookies crinkle.

8. **Serve.** Allow the cookies to sit on the cookie sheet for 3 minutes to set up a little, then enjoy warm!

MAKE AHEAD & FREEZE

When cool, store the cookies in an airtight container at room temperature for up to 5 days.

To freeze, prepare the cookies as directed, but press the cookie balls down slightly. Place the cookies on a baking sheet and freeze. When frozen, transfer the cookies to a zip-top freezer bag and store in the freezer for up to 1 month. To bake, place the frozen cookies onto a baking sheet lined with parchment paper and bake at 350°F (180°C) for 13 minutes.

Chewy Vanilla Sugar Cookies

PREP: 30 minutes // **COOK:** 8 minutes, plus 3 minutes to cool // **YIELD:** 9 to 10 cookies

INGREDIENTS

8 tbsp (1 stick / 115g) unsalted butter

1¼ cups (175g) all-purpose flour

½ tsp baking soda

¼ tsp baking powder

¼ tsp salt

½ cup (100g) granulated white sugar

1 tsp vanilla extract

2 egg yolks, at room temperature

1–2 tbsp sprinkles (optional)

These sugar cookies stay soft and chewy for days. If you're a sugar cookie fan, you'll absolutely love these!

1. **Preheat the oven and prepare the baking sheet.** Preheat the oven to 350°F (180°C) Line two baking sheets with parchment paper.

2. **Melt the butter.** Melt the butter in a large bowl in the microwave (see page 25) or in a small saucepan over low heat. If using a saucepan, transfer the butter to a large bowl and allow to cool slightly, about 5 to 10 minutes, while you prepare the rest of the ingredients.

3. **Mix the dry ingredients.** In a large bowl, whisk together the flour, baking soda, baking powder, and salt. Set aside.

4. **Mix the wet ingredients.** To the bowl with the melted butter, add the sugar and vanilla, and mix until combined and emulsified. Add the egg yolks and whisk until completely incorporated.

5. **Mix the wet ingredients into the dry.** Using a rubber spatula, combine the butter mixture with the flour mixture and mix until the dough is well combined and there are no more visible spots of flour. Stir in the sprinkles, if using.

6. **Bake the cookies.** Using a medium ice cream scoop, place 9 to 10 balls of dough onto the prepared baking sheets. Leave at least 3 inches (7.5cm) between each cookie because they will spread out in the oven. Bake the cookies for 8 to 10 minutes. Do not overbake. The cookies will seem underdone, but they will set up as they cool.

7. **Serve.** Allow the cookies to sit on the baking sheets for 5 minutes to set up a little, then enjoy!

MAKE AHEAD & FREEZE

When cool, store the cookies in an airtight container at room temperature for up to 5 days.

To freeze, prepare the cookies as directed, but press the cookie balls down slightly. Don't flatten them completely—leave them a little over 1 inch (2.5cm) tall. Place the cookies on a small baking sheet and freeze. When frozen, transfer the cookies to a zip-top freezer bag and store in the freezer for up to 1 month. To bake from frozen, place on a parchment-lined baking sheet and bake at 350°F (180°C) for 10 to 12 minutes.

Fudge Brownie Cookies

PREP: 30 minutes // **COOK:** 8 minutes, plus 10 minutes to cool // **YIELD:** 8 large cookies

INGREDIENTS

4 tbsp (½ stick / 60g) unsalted butter, cut into small pieces

3½oz (100g) 50–70% cocoa chocolate, cut into small pieces

1 medium egg, at room temperature

⅓ cup (75g) granulated white sugar

3 tbsp (25g) all-purpose flour

¼ tsp baking powder

¼ tsp salt

SPECIAL EQUIPMENT

Handheld mixer or stand mixer

Piping bag

TROUBLESHOOTING

Cookies turn out thin.
Either you didn't incorporate enough air when you beat the egg mixture (step 3); or you knocked all the air out of the batter when folding the ingredients together (step 4); or your oven wasn't hot enough, causing the cookies to spread before setting.

Cookies have height, but no cracked tops. Your oven might be too hot, causing the cookies to set before they spread and crack. Or you didn't rest the batter for long enough. Or you changed the recipe in some way (e.g., cut the amount of sugar).

These incredible cookies are the perfect cross between fudge brownies and soft chocolate cookies. The secret to success lies in the whipping of the eggs and your folding technique. Once you've mastered these methods, you'll be able to whip up batches in no time!

1. **Prepare the baking sheet.** Line the baking sheet with parchment paper.

2. **Melt the butter and chocolate.** In a medium bowl, melt together the butter and chocolate. If you're using a microwave, stir the mixture every 30 seconds (see page 25). If you're using a double boiler, gently mix the butter and chocolate until fully melted. Allow the bowl to cool slightly, about 5 to 10 minutes.

3. **Beat the egg and sugar.** In a clean glass or metal bowl, using a mixer on its highest setting, beat the egg and sugar together until the mixture has tripled in volume and become a light mayonnaise color, about 3 minutes. (This step is critical because the aerated beaten egg/sugar mixture will give structure to the cookie. If you don't incorporate enough air at this stage, the cookies will turn out flat with no crinkles.)

4. **Fold the ingredients together.** The folding technique you use for this stage is important (see page 25) to ensure you don't knock out the air you've just incorporated. Gently fold in the chocolate and butter. Then, sift the flour, baking powder, and salt into the mixture, and fold them in. Be careful to not overmix—once the flour has been incorporated, stop folding. The batter should look soft and loose but still retain a somewhat airy texture.

5. **Rest the batter.** Cover the batter and set aside for 10 to 15 minutes. Don't rest the batter for any longer than this; otherwise, you will start to lose air from the mixture.

6. **Preheat the oven.** Preheat the oven to 350°F (180°C).

7. **Prepare the cookies.** Transfer the mixture to a piping bag. Cut a small opening and pipe 8 cookies onto the prepared baking sheet, leaving at least 2 inches (5cm) between the cookies. These will spread out, so work quickly and try to pipe them as "high" as you can.

8. **Bake the cookies.** Bake for 8 to 10 minutes. The crinkles will form toward the very end of baking, so don't panic when you don't see the cracks.

9. **Serve.** Allow the cookies to sit on the cookie sheet for 10 minutes to set. Then very gently remove them from the parchment paper (be careful not to break the cookies—they will be lightly stuck to the paper) and enjoy!

> **MAKE AHEAD**
> When cool, cookies can be stored in an airtight container at room temperature for up to 5 days.

Crackly Top Fudge Brownies

PREP: 20 minutes // **COOK:** 35 minutes, plus 45 minutes to cool // **YIELD:** 16 brownies

INGREDIENTS

2¼ sticks (250g) unsalted butter, cut into small pieces, plus more for greasing

13oz (350g) 70% cocoa chocolate, chopped into small pieces

2 cups (400g) granulated white sugar

4 large eggs, at room temperature

1 cup (140g) all-purpose flour

3 tbsp (25g) unsweetened cocoa powder

½ tsp salt

1 tbsp freshly brewed coffee or 1 tsp instant coffee dissolved in 1 tbsp hot water

SPECIAL EQUIPMENT

Handheld mixer or stand mixer

9 × 13-inch (23 × 33cm) baking dish

These brownies are fudgy, amazing, and so easy to make! This foolproof method will deliver that iconic crackly top every single time.

1. **Prepare the dish and preheat the oven.** Butter the baking dish and line with parchment, leaving a 2-inch (5cm) overhang on two sides of the dish. Then lightly butter the parchment paper. Preheat the oven to 350°F (180°C).

2. **Melt the butter and chocolate.** In a large glass bowl, melt together the butter and chocolate. If you're using a microwave, stir the mixture every 30 seconds (see page 25). If you're using a double boiler, gently mix the butter and chocolate until fully melted. Set aside.

3. **Beat the eggs and sugar.** In another bowl, using a mixer, beat the eggs and sugar together until the sugar has dissolved and the mixture has lightened in color, about 3 minutes.

4. **Add the butter and chocolate.** Add the melted butter and chocolate mixture to the eggs and sugar, and quickly mix to combine.

5. **Add the dry ingredients and coffee.** Add the flour, cocoa powder, and salt to the chocolate mixture, and using a rubber spatula, mix until the batter is well combined and there are no more visible spots of flour. Add the coffee and mix to combine.

6. **Bake the brownies.** Transfer the batter into the prepared baking dish and bake for 35 minutes. To test when they're done, insert a toothpick into the middle of the dish. The toothpick should have some wet crumbs on it (see page 15).

7. **Serve.** Allow the brownies to cool for at least 45 minutes in the baking dish. Using the edges of the parchment paper, remove the brownies from the baking dish and cut into bars.

MAKE AHEAD
When cool, store the brownies in an airtight container at room temperature for up to 5 days.

Double Chocolate Muffins

PREP: 10 minutes // **COOK:** 18 minutes, plus 10 minutes to cool // **YIELD:** 12 muffins

INGREDIENTS

10 tbsp (1¼ stick / 140g) unsalted butter, cut into small pieces

1½ cups (210g) all-purpose flour

¾ cup (150g) granulated white sugar

½ cup (50g) unsweetened cocoa powder

1 tsp baking soda

½ tsp baking powder

¼ tsp salt

1 medium egg, at room temperature

1¼ cups (300g) buttermilk, at room temperature

¾ cup chocolate chips, lightly dusted in flour to prevent them from sinking

SPECIAL EQUIPMENT

12-cup muffin tin

Paper liners

These chocolate muffins are fluffy, moist, and loaded with chocolate chips in each bite. They're irresistible!

1. **Prepare the pan and preheat the oven.** Line a muffin tin with paper liners. Preheat the oven to 400°F (200°C).

2. **Melt the butter.** In a large heat-safe bowl, melt the butter in the microwave (see page 25). Set aside.

3. **Mix the dry ingredients.** In another large bowl, whisk together the flour, sugar, cocoa powder, baking soda, baking powder, and salt. Set aside.

4. **Mix the wet ingredients.** To the warm, melted butter, add the egg and buttermilk. Mix until well combined.

5. **Mix the wet ingredients into the dry.** Combine the wet ingredients with the dry ingredients and mix well. Look for a smooth batter, but don't overmix. Scrape the bottom and sides of the bowl, and stir in the chocolate chips.

6. **Bake the muffins.** Transfer the muffin batter into the prepared muffin tin. Make sure to fill the liners all the way to the top—that will result in the best doming. Bake for 5 minutes. Then lower the temperature to 320°F (160°C) and continue baking for 13 to 15 minutes more. The total baking time for the muffins should be 18 to 20 minutes—be careful not to overbake them! Do the toothpick test (see page 15). If the toothpick comes out clean, the muffins are ready.

7. **Serve.** Allow muffins to sit in the pan for about 2 minutes, then carefully remove them from the pan and allow to cool on a wire rack. Enjoy them warm or at room temperature.

MAKE AHEAD
When cool, store in an airtight container for 4 to 5 days.

Instant Donuts

PREP: 5 minutes // **COOK:** 3 minutes per batch, plus 2 minutes to cool // **YIELD:** About 30 donut holes

INGREDIENTS

FOR THE CINNAMON SUGAR COATING

⅓ cup (70g) granulated white sugar

1 tsp ground cinnamon, plus more to taste

FOR THE DONUTS

1 cup (140g) all-purpose flour

1½ tsp baking powder

¼ tsp salt

¾ cup (190g) plain yogurt

Vegetable oil, for frying

Melted chocolate (optional), for drizzling

SPECIAL EQUIPMENT

Dutch oven or heavy pot

Instant-read thermometer

Sturdy piping bag (Double them up if your bags are flimsy.)

Craving donuts but don't want the fuss of making a yeast dough? These donuts are almost identical in texture to yeast-raised donuts, but you can whip these up in two minutes. That's right—you can make these faster than going to your local donut shop, and they're amazing!

1. **Make the cinnamon sugar coating.** In a large bowl, toss together the sugar and cinnamon. Set aside.

2. **Prepare the dough.** In a large bowl, mix the flour, baking powder, salt, and yogurt until well combined. The dough should be soft and sticky. If it seems dry, add an extra tablespoon of yogurt. Transfer the sticky mixture into a piping bag. Do not add extra flour.

3. **Fry the donuts.** Fill a large Dutch oven or heavy-bottomed pot with vegetable oil to a depth of at least 2 inches (5cm). Heat the oil over medium heat until it reaches 340°F (170°C). Cut a ½-inch (1.3cm) opening at the bottom of the piping bag, and gently pipe 1-inch (2.5cm) pieces of dough into the oil. Cut the dough into the oil using kitchen scissors. Fry the donut holes in batches until golden, a few minutes per batch. (The precise timing will depend on the type of yogurt used.)

4. **Serve.** Using a slotted spoon, remove the donuts from the oil and drain briefly on paper towels. Toss immediately in the cinnamon sugar and, if desired, drizzle with melted chocolate. Enjoy warm!

Melt-In-Your-Mouth Lemon Cookies

PREP: 45 minutes // **COOK:** 12 minutes, plus 5 minutes to cool // **YIELD:** 10 to 12 small cookies

INGREDIENTS

1 cup (150g) all-purpose flour

½ tsp baking powder

¼ tsp salt

5 tbsp (70g) unsalted butter, at room temperature

½ cup (100g) granulated white sugar

1 tsp vanilla extract

Gel-based yellow food coloring (optional)

2 lemons

1 medium egg, at room temperature

Powdered sugar, for coating the cookies

If you're a die-hard fan of lemon desserts like me, you have to add these heavenly soft lemon cookies to your collection. They'll be a big hit with everyone who tries them—they won't be able to resist asking you for the recipe!

1. **Mix the dry ingredients.** In a large bowl, whisk together the flour, baking powder, and salt. Set aside.

2. **Mix the wet ingredients.** In another large bowl, cream together the softened butter, granulated sugar, and vanilla until combined. Add a drop of yellow food coloring, if using. Finely grate the zest of the 2 lemons directly over the softened butter mixture and mix to combine. Mix in the egg until completely incorporated.

3. **Juice a lemon.** Cut 1 lemon in half and juice it into a small bowl. Remove the seeds if necessary. You will need 1½ tablespoons of lemon juice.

4. **Mix the dry ingredients into the wet.** Add the flour mixture to the butter mixture along with the 1½ tablespoons of lemon juice. (Don't worry if the mixture curdles—the flour will bring it together.) Using a rubber spatula, mix until the dough is well combined and there are no visible spots of flour. (The dough might be loose—don't be tempted to add extra flour. Instead, put the dough in the fridge for 30 minutes to firm up a little.)

5. **Prepare the cookies.** Using a medium ice cream scoop, portion out 10 to 12 cookies onto a small tray lined with parchment paper. Freeze the cookies for 30 minutes.

6. **Prepare the baking sheet and preheat the oven.** Line a baking sheet with parchment paper. Preheat the oven to 350°F (180°C).

7. **Bake the cookies.** Transfer the cookies from the freezer onto the prepared baking sheet, leaving about 4 inches (10cm) between each cookie. Bake for 12 to 13 minutes. Don't overbake them—there should be no browning on top of the cookies!

8. **Toss the cookies in sugar.** Take the cookies out of the oven. They should still be soft, and the bottoms of the cookies should be a light golden color. Allow them to sit on the cookie sheet for 3 to 5 minutes to set up. While they're still warm, gently toss them in powdered sugar. (The cookies are delicate, so be careful not to break them).

9. **Serve.** Enjoy the cookies warm or allow them to cool completely.

MAKE AHEAD
When cool, the cookies can be stored in an airtight container at room temperature for up to 5 days.

Chewy Oatmeal Cookies

PREP: 15 minutes // **COOK:** 10 minutes, plus 5 minutes to cool // **YIELD:** 9 to 12 cookies

INGREDIENTS

1 cup (140g) all-purpose
flour

1 cup (110g) old-fashioned
oats

½ tsp baking soda

¼ tsp salt

¼ tsp ground cinnamon

8 tbsp (1 stick / 115g)
unsalted butter, melted

⅓ cup + 1 tbsp (75g) brown
sugar (light or dark)

⅓ cup + 1 tbsp (75g)
granulated white sugar

1 tsp vanilla extract

2 egg yolks, at room
temperature

VARIATIONS

If you like, you can add
¾ cup of chopped nuts,
raisins, or dried cranberries
(or try a mixture). I really
recommend making these
with dried cranberries!

Oatmeal cookies deserve so much more appreciation than they get. I really recommend you try these—you won't be disappointed.

1. **Preheat the oven and prepare the baking sheet.** Line a baking sheet with parchment paper. Preheat the oven to 350°F (180°C).

2. **Mix the dry ingredients.** In a large bowl, whisk together the flour, oats, baking soda, salt, and cinnamon. Set aside.

3. **Mix the wet ingredients.** In another large bowl, combine the melted butter, brown sugar, granulated sugar, and vanilla. Mix until combined and emulsified. (It's important that you can't see any separated melted butter.) The texture should be smooth and creamy. Whisk in the egg yolks and mix until completely incorporated.

4. **Mix the wet ingredients into the dry.** Using a rubber spatula, combine the flour/oat mixture with the butter mixture, and mix until the dough is well combined and there are no more visible spots of flour.

5. **Prepare the cookies.** Using a medium to large ice cream scoop, form 9 to 12 balls of dough and lightly sprinkle some extra oats on top. (This gives the cookies a beautiful look and makes them stand out against other oatmeal cookies.) Gently press them down. Don't flatten them completely—they should be about 1 inch (2.5cm) tall. Place the cookies on the prepared baking sheet. Leave plenty of space between each ball of dough because these cookies will spread out in the oven.

6. **Bake the cookies.** Bake for 10 to 12 minutes. The cookies will seem soft and underdone. It's important to not overbake them, so remove them at this stage. They will continue to bake on the sheet.

7. **Serve.** Allow the cookies to sit on the cookie sheet for 5 to 10 minutes to set up a little, then enjoy!

> **MAKE AHEAD & FREEZE**
>
> When cool, store the cookies in an airtight container at room temperature for up to 5 days.
>
> To freeze, place the unbaked cookies in the freezer on a baking sheet. Once frozen, transfer the cookies to a zip-top freezer bag and store in the freezer for up to 1 month. To bake from frozen, place on a parchment-lined baking sheet and bake at 350°F (180°C) for 10 to 12 minutes.

Easy Muffins

ONE RECIPE—ENDLESS FLAVORS

PREP: 10 minutes // **COOK:** 15 minutes, plus 20 minutes to cool // **YIELD:** 12 muffins

INGREDIENTS

2½ cups (350g) all-purpose flour

¾ cup (150g) granulated white sugar

3 tsp baking powder

¼ tsp salt

12 tbsp (1½ sticks / 180g) unsalted butter, melted

2 medium eggs, at room temperature

1 cup (240g) whole milk, at room temperature

2 tsp vanilla extract

SPECIAL EQUIPMENT

12-cup muffin tin

Paper liners

Let me tell you a secret about the muffins you buy from bakeries. They sell endless different flavors, but the truth is they're mostly based on one base recipe. This is my base vanilla muffin recipe and a few of my favorite variations to get you started—the only limit here is your imagination!

1. **Preheat the oven and prepare the pan.** Preheat the oven to 400°F (200°C). Line the cups of the muffin tin with paper liners.

2. **Mix the dry ingredients.** In a large bowl, whisk together the flour, sugar, baking powder, and salt. Set aside.

3. **Mix the wet ingredients.** In another large bowl, whisk together the warm melted butter, eggs, milk, and vanilla. Mix until well combined.

4. **Make the batter.** Combine the wet ingredients with the dry ingredients and mix well. Look for a smooth batter, but don't overmix. Transfer the batter into the prepared muffin pan, dividing it evenly among the cups. Make sure to fill the paper liners all the way to the top to get that signature "muffin top."

5. **Bake the muffins.** Bake for 5 minutes and then lower the oven temperature to 320°F (160°C). Continue baking for 10 to 15 minutes more. The total baking time for the muffins will be 15 to 20 minutes—be careful not to overbake them. Do the toothpick test (see page 15). If the toothpick comes out clean, the muffins are ready.

6. **Serve.** Allow the muffins to sit in the pan for about 2 minutes, then carefully remove them from the pan and allow to cool on a wire rack for at least 20 minutes or the paper liners will stick to the muffins. Enjoy warm or at room temperature.

VARIATIONS

Chocolate chip muffins: Dust 7 ounces (200g) of chocolate chips in 1 teaspoon of all-purpose flour. After combining the wet and dry ingredients in step 4, add the chocolate chips to the batter, and mix gently to distribute them.

Lemon blueberry muffins: Add the finely grated zest of 2 lemons to the wet ingredients in step 3. Dust 1½ cups (200g) of fresh blueberries with 1 teaspoon of flour to prevent them from sinking to the bottom of the muffins. After combining the wet and dry ingredients in step 4, add the blueberries to the batter and mix gently to distribute them.

Cinnamon streusel muffins: Add ½ tablespoon of ground cinnamon to the dry ingredients in step 2. Before baking, top the muffins with a streusel topping. To make the topping, in a medium bowl, combine ¾ cup (115g) all-purpose flour, ½ cup (100g) granulated white sugar, 1 teaspoon ground cinnamon, and ½ teaspoon salt. Add 6 tablespoons (85g) cold butter, cut into small pieces. Using your fingers, rub this mixture between your hands until crumbs form. Distribute the topping evenly over the muffins before baking.

> **MAKE AHEAD**
> When cool, store the muffins in an airtight container at room temperature for up to 5 days.

Moist Blender Banana Bread

PREP: 5 minutes // **COOK:** 50 minutes, plus 1 hour to cool // **YIELD:** 1 loaf; serves 12

INGREDIENTS

7 tbsp (100g) unsalted
butter

2 medium ripe bananas,
about 8oz (220g) in total

1 (5oz / 140g) container
plain Greek yogurt

1 tsp vanilla extract

2 large eggs, at room
temperature

¾ cup (150g) granulated
white sugar

1½ cups (200g) all-purpose
flour, sifted

1 tsp baking soda

½ tsp salt

SPECIAL EQUIPMENT

8 × 4-inch (20 × 10cm)
loaf pan

Large blender

Banana bread is a true crowd-pleaser. My method uses a blender. It's easy, quick, and has little clean up—plus, you won't be left with any small pieces of banana that result in black dots in the final cake! (By the way, just to set the record straight, banana "bread" is in fact a cake.)

1. **Preheat the oven and prepare the pan.** Preheat the oven to 340°F (170°C). Grease and line the loaf pan with parchment paper, leaving about 1 inch (2.5cm) of overhang at the ends of the pan.

2. **Melt the butter.** In a large bowl, melt the butter in the microwave (see page 25). Allow the butter to cool for 5 to 10 minutes before proceeding with the recipe.

3. **Blend the wet ingredients.** To a large blender, add in this exact order: bananas, yogurt, butter, vanilla, and eggs. Blend on high for 8 to 10 seconds or until smooth. As soon as it's smooth, stop mixing; otherwise, the cake will collapse once baked. It's important to use a large blender because of the large volume of batter in the recipe.

4. **Blend the dry ingredients into the wet ingredients.** Add the sugar, flour, baking soda, and salt. Pulse the blender on and off at medium-high speed for 5 to 8 seconds (no more than this). At this point, you'll most likely have some unmixed ingredients on the sides or bottom of the blender jug, but don't continue to blend. Instead, using a spatula, scrape the sides and bottom of the blender jug to finish combining all the ingredients. It's important not to overblend the batter at this stage; otherwise, your banana bread will have gluey streaks.

5. **Bake the banana bread.** Pour the batter into the prepared loaf pan and bake for 50 to 60 minutes. If the banana bread starts to darken too much, you can cover it with some foil.

6. **Serve.** Allow the banana bread to cool for 10 minutes in the pan, then remove it from the pan using the parchment paper and allow to cool completely.

MAKE AHEAD & FREEZE
When cool, store the banana bread in an airtight container or zip-top bag at room temperature for up to 3 days.

To freeze, wrap the cooled banana bread tightly in plastic wrap and freeze for up to 1 month (see page 14).

Soft Peanut Butter Cookies

PREP: 10 minutes // **COOK:** 13 minutes, plus 3 minutes to cool // **YIELD:** 14 to 16 cookies

INGREDIENTS

1 cup (140g) all-purpose flour

½ tsp baking soda

½ tsp baking powder

¼ tsp salt

8 tbsp (1 stick / 115g) unsalted butter, at room temperature

½ cup (130g) peanut butter (smooth or crunchy), at room temperature

¾ cup (150g) granulated white sugar

1 tsp vanilla extract

1 medium egg, at room temperature

SPECIAL EQUIPMENT

Handheld mixer or stand mixer

Irresistibly soft, with a sweet and salty flavor, these chewy peanut butter cookies are very different from the "crisscross" version you might be familiar with. Once you try these, there's no going back!

1. **Preheat the oven and prepare the baking sheets.** Preheat the oven to 350°F (180°C). Line two baking sheets with parchment paper.

2. **Mix the dry ingredients.** In a large bowl, whisk together the flour, baking soda, baking powder, and salt. Set aside.

3. **Mix the wet ingredients.** In a stand mixer with a paddle attachment (or in another large bowl, if using a handheld mixer), beat the butter, peanut butter, sugar, and vanilla until combined. Add the egg and beat until completely incorporated.

4. **Mix the dry ingredients into the wet.** Using a rubber spatula, combine the flour mixture with the butter mixture, and mix until the dough is combined and there are no more visible spots of flour.

5. **Prepare the cookies.** Using a medium ice cream scoop, spoon 14 to 16 balls of dough onto the prepared baking sheets. Leave about 4 inches (10cm) between the cookies because they will spread in the oven.

6. **Bake the cookies.** Bake one cookie sheet at a time for 13 minutes. They will look a little underbaked at this stage, but they will set as they cool.

7. **Serve.** Allow the cookies to sit on the cookie sheet for 3 minutes, then enjoy!

> **MAKE AHEAD & FREEZE**
> When cool, store the cookies in an airtight container at room temperature for up to 5 days.
>
> To freeze, place the unbaked cookies in the freezer on a baking sheet. Once frozen, transfer the cookies to a zip-top freezer bag and store in the freezer for up to 1 month. To bake from frozen, place on a parchment-lined baking sheet and bake at 350°F (180°C) for 13 to 14 minutes.

French Macarons

PREP: 1 hour // **COOK:** 10 minutes, plus 30 minutes to cool // **YIELD:** 25 to 30 macarons

INGREDIENTS

FOR THE COOKIES

1 cup (110g) super finely ground almond flour (It's best to weigh this if possible.)

1⅔ cups (200g) powdered sugar

¼ tsp salt

2 large egg whites, at room temperature

4 tbsp (50g) granulated white sugar

¼ tsp cream of tartar (optional)

Gel-based food coloring (optional)

FOR THE FILLING

½ cup (100g) filling of your choice, such as Dark Chocolate Ganache (page 211), Cream Cheese Frosting (page 209), American Buttercream (page 208), or store-bought jams, curds, and jellies

SPECIAL EQUIPMENT

Piping bag with ¼-inch (6mm) round tip

MAKE AHEAD

Once cool, the plain, un-sandwiched cookies can be kept in an airtight container at room temperature for up to 10 days. Ideally, fill the cookies the night before you want to serve them, and rest overnight in the fridge.

Macarons are super easy to make when you know how, but they do require a little practice. So don't be discouraged if they don't come out magazine-perfect on the first try! The secret to making them successfully is all about the folding technique, and ideally, it's best to use grams for accurate results.

1. **Prepare the baking sheet.** Lightly grease the baking sheet and line it with parchment paper. (This will prevent the parchment from moving while piping the macarons.)

2. **Prepare the flour.** Sift the almond flour, powdered sugar, and salt into a medium bowl and set aside. Discard any chunks of almond flour that remain in the sieve.

3. **Whip the egg whites.** In a large, clean glass or metal bowl, whip the egg whites until frothy. Gradually add the granulated sugar and cream of tartar and continue whipping until glossy, stiff peaks form (see page 23). Add a few drops of food coloring, if using, and mix just until combined.

4. **Mix in the dry ingredients.** Now re-sift the almond flour mixture directly over the whipped egg whites. Gently fold together the egg whites and the almond flour mixture (see page 25). Take your time with this. The final batter should look like flowing molten lava and form ribbons.

5. **Prepare the cookies.** Transfer the mixture into a piping bag fitted with a round tip and pipe 50 to 60 cookies (to make 25 to 30 sandwiched macarons) onto the prepared baking sheet. Tap the sheet on the counter to even out the cookies. Allow the cookies to dry at room temperature for 30 to 45 minutes. They should be dry to the touch. High humidity will affect the cookies, so ideally leave the cookies to set in a dry room.

6. **Preheat the oven.** Preheat the oven to 280°F (140°C).

7. **Bake the cookies.** Bake one sheet at a time for 10 to 13 minutes. When the macarons are ready, they should have formed bubbly-looking feet, and when you touch the top of a macaron, the cookie should not move at all.

8. **Assemble the macarons.** Allow the cookies to cool completely (about 30 minutes) and then assemble with the filling of your choice.

9. **Serve.** Enjoy the macarons right away, or refrigerate overnight for best texture.

TROUBLESHOOTING

Batter is too stiff to pipe easily. You likely used too much almond flour or it's undermixed.

Batter is gritty. The almond flour was too coarse. You can make it finer using a food processor and then passing through a fine sieve.

Cookies spread out too much. You likely overmixed the batter and knocked out all the air when folding in the dry ingredients.

Cookies have sticky bottoms. You didn't bake the cookies long enough.

Cookies crack. The oven temperature was too high.

Superfast Snacks

When you're craving a treat and just can't wait, these snacks come together in minutes. They make for great midnight snacks or emergency after-school snacks for kids—all you need is a microwave!

One-Minute Mug Cakes

PREP: 2 minutes // **COOK:** 1 minute // **YIELD:** 1 small mug cake per flavor

Mug cakes are my ultimate quick snack—they're delicious, and they come together in an instant. Whether you're craving a slice of cake or seeking a sweet midnight snack, a mug cake is the perfect quick fix. Try all three variations!

CHOCOLATE MUG CAKE

INGREDIENTS

1 tbsp (13g) unsalted butter

2 tbsp (12g) cocoa powder

2 tbsp (30g) granulated white sugar

2 tbsp (30g) whole milk

¼ tsp vanilla extract

2 tbsp (20g) all-purpose flour

¼ tsp baking powder

Nutella (optional), for frosting, or 2 tbsp mini chocolate chips, to add to the batter

1. **Combine the ingredients.** In a small mug (about 6oz / 170ml), melt the butter in the microwave. Add the cocoa powder, and mix well with a fork until there are no lumps of cocoa powder left. Add the sugar, milk, and vanilla, and mix well. Add the flour and baking powder, and give everything a good mix until a smooth batter forms. Using a rubber spatula, scrape the bottom and sides of the mug.

2. **Cook the mug cake.** Make sure there are no lumps of flour at the bottom of the mug. Wipe clean the sides of the mug, and give it a good tap on the countertop to make sure there are no air pockets in the batter. If you're not frosting with Nutella, stir 2 tablespoons of mini chocolate chips into the batter. Microwave on high for 50 seconds to 1 minute and 15 seconds (see page 25).

3. **Decorate and serve.** Frost with Nutella, if using. Allow to cool for 2 minutes before serving warm.

VANILLA OR CHOCOLATE CHIP MUG CAKE

INGREDIENTS

1 tbsp (13g) unsalted butter

1 tbsp (15g) granulated white sugar (for vanilla cake) or light brown sugar (for chocolate chip cake)

2 tbsp (30g) whole milk

¼ tsp vanilla extract

3 tbsp (30g) all-purpose flour

¼ tsp baking powder

1 tbsp sprinkles (for vanilla cake; optional) or 2 tbsp mini chocolate chips (for chocolate chip cake)

1. **Combine the ingredients.** In a small mug (about 6oz / 170ml), melt the butter in the microwave. Add the sugar, milk, and vanilla, and stir well using a fork. Add the flour and baking powder, and give everything a good mix until a smooth batter forms. Using a rubber spatula, scrape the bottom and sides of the mug.

2. **Add mix-ins.** For a vanilla mug cake, stir the sprinkles into the batter, if using. For a chocolate chip mug cake, stir the chocolate chips into the batter.

3. **Cook the mug cake.** Make sure there are no lumps of flour at the bottom of the mug. Wipe clean the sides of the mug, and give it a good tap on the countertop to make sure there are no air pockets in the batter. Microwave on high for 50 seconds to 1 minute and 15 seconds (see page 25).

4. **Serve.** Allow to cool for 2 minutes before serving warm.

One-Minute Mug Pancake

PREP: 1 minute // COOK: 1 minute // YIELD: 1 mug pancake

INGREDIENTS

1 tbsp (13g) unsalted butter, plus more for serving

¾ tbsp (10g) granulated white sugar

2 tbsp (30g) whole milk

3 tbsp (30g) all-purpose flour

¼ tsp baking powder

Maple syrup, to serve

This mug pancake is so fluffy and comforting, it's every bit as delicious as a regular stack of pancakes—except made in a fraction of the time. It's perfect for a quick breakfast or as a midnight snack. You won't believe how good this is!

1. **Combine the ingredients.** In a small mug (about 6oz / 170ml), melt the butter in the microwave. Add the sugar and milk, and stir well using a fork. Add the flour and baking powder, and give everything a good mix with the fork until a smooth batter forms. Using a rubber spatula, scrape the bottom and sides of the mug.

2. **Cook the mug pancake.** Make sure there are no lumps of flour at the bottom of the mug. Clean the sides of the mug, and give it a good tap on the countertop to make sure there are no air pockets in the batter. Microwave on high for 50 seconds to 1 minute (see page 25). The mug pancake won't brown like a regular pancake, but the taste and texture are amazing!

3. **Serve.** Serve immediately, topped with butter and a good drizzle of maple syrup. I like to swirl the maple syrup around on top of the pancake, which will warm it up and melt the butter into the pancake.

One-Minute Microwave Brownie

PREP: 2 minutes // **COOK:** 1 minute // **YIELD:** 1 brownie

INGREDIENTS

1½ tbsp (20g) unsalted butter

2oz (60g) 70% cocoa dark chocolate, chopped into small pieces, divided

2 tbsp (30g) whole milk

2 tbsp (30g) superfine white sugar

½ tbsp (4g) unsweetened cocoa powder

Pinch of salt

4 tbsp (40g) all-purpose flour

SPECIAL EQUIPMENT

4-inch (10cm) square microwave-safe container

Fudgy and delicious, this brownie cooks in just one minute in the microwave. It's a treat on its own and even better served with ice cream.

1. **Prepare the container.** Line a 4-inch (10cm) square microwave-safe container with parchment paper, leaving a 1-inch (2.5cm) overhang at opposite ends of the container.

2. **Melt the butter and chocolate with the milk.** To a small microwave-safe bowl, add the butter, 1 ounce (30g) chopped dark chocolate, and milk. Microwave for 30 to 40 seconds (see page 25) or until the butter and chocolate are mostly melted. Give the mixture a good stir to finish melting the chocolate and butter.

3. **Add the other ingredients.** Add the sugar, cocoa powder, and salt, and incorporate into the mixture using a fork or small whisk. Mix well until a smooth batter forms with the sugar completely dissolved. Add the flour and, using a rubber spatula, mix until fully incorporated.

4. **Add the topping and microwave.** Transfer the batter into the prepared square container. Top with the remaining 1 ounce (30g) chopped dark chocolate. Microwave on high for 50 seconds to 1 minute 15 seconds, depending on your microwave. (See page 25.)

5. **Serve.** You can serve this right away and eat it with a spoon—it will be very soft. Or cool for 15 minutes if you want to be able to pick it up with your hands and eat it like a regular brownie.

One-Minute Cupcakes

PREP: 5 minutes // **COOK:** 1 minute // **YIELD:** 2 cupcakes per flavor

INGREDIENTS

FOR THE CHOCOLATE CUPCAKES

1 tbsp (13g) unsalted butter, melted

2 tbsp (12g) unsweetened cocoa powder

3 tbsp (40g) whole milk

2 tbsp (30g) granulated white sugar

2 tbsp (20g) all-purpose flour

¼ tsp baking powder

Pinch of salt

FOR THE VANILLA CUPCAKES

1 tbsp (13g) unsalted butter, melted

2 tbsp (25g) whole milk

1 tbsp (15g) granulated white sugar

¼ tsp vanilla extract

3 tbsp (30g) all-purpose flour

¼ tsp baking powder

Pinch of salt

FOR THE CHOCOLATE TOPPING

1½ tbsp Nutella

4 tbsp heavy cream, cold

Sprinkles (optional)

FOR THE VANILLA TOPPING

2 tbsp Cool Whip or marshmallow fluff

Sprinkles

SPECIAL EQUIPMENT

2 silicone cupcake liners or 6 sturdy paper liners

Handheld mixer (optional; for the chocolate topping)

If you're craving cupcakes but don't want to cook a whole batch, this is the recipe for you. This quick recipe makes two at a time because you won't be able to stop at one—they're just so fluffy and comforting. Choose either chocolate or vanilla cupcakes—or make both varieties!

1. **Prepare the cupcake liners.** For best results, use silicone liners. If you're using paper liners, triple them up so you have two stacks of three liners—this will ensure they're strong enough to hold the cupcakes as they cook. The outer liners won't go to waste; once the cupcakes have baked, remove them to reuse at another time.

2. **Prepare the batter.** Follow the instructions for your flavor of choice.

   For chocolate cupcakes. In a small bowl, stir together the melted butter and cocoa powder using a rubber spatula until the mixture is smooth and there are no lumps. Stir in the milk and sugar and roughly mix. Add the flour, baking powder, and salt, and mix until combined.

   For vanilla cupcakes. In a small bowl, stir together the melted butter, milk, sugar, and vanilla using a rubber spatula. Add the flour, baking powder, and salt and mix until combined.

3. **Microwave the cupcakes.** Divide the batter evenly between the prepared cupcake liners. The batter should go about halfway up the liners. These cupcakes will expand a lot as they bake, so don't over fill them. Microwave the cupcakes one at a time, about 30 to 45 seconds per cupcake. (Be careful not to overcook them; see page 25.) The cupcakes will be super soft when they're baked, so treat them gently when you're taking them out of the microwave. Allow the cupcakes to cool before adding toppings.

4. **Make the chocolate topping (optional).** Using a mixer, in a small bowl, beat the Nutella and cold heavy cream until they form a chocolate mousse consistency.

5. **Add toppings (optional).** Once the cupcakes are completely cool, put a dollop of chocolate or vanilla topping on each cupcake with a spoon (or use a piping bag, if you're feeling fancy). Top with sprinkles, if desired.

6. **Serve.** You can serve these immediately or wait for them to cool and have them with toppings.

Microwave Hot Chocolate

PREP: 1 minute // **COOK:** 3 minutes // **YIELD:** 1 serving

INGREDIENTS

1 tbsp (15g) white granulated sugar

1 tbsp (8g) unsweetened cocoa powder

½ tbsp (4g) cornstarch

⅔ cup (160g) whole milk

1½oz (50g) 70% cocoa dark chocolate, chopped into very small pieces

Mini marshmallows (optional), to serve

Whipped cream (optional), to serve

When you want a single serving of hot chocolate, this is the way to do it. You can make this from scratch in about the same time it would take to use some instant hot chocolate mix. This version is much more delicious!

1. **Prepare the hot chocolate mix.** To a large liquid measuring cup or a tall microwave-safe container, add the sugar, cocoa powder, cornstarch, and half the milk. (You can't make this directly in your drinking mug because the mixture will boil over). Using a fork or mini whisk, stir to break up the cocoa lumps as best as you can. Then add the remaining milk and stir to fully incorporate the ingredients.

2. **Heat in the microwave.** Microwave the mixture for 1 minute 30 seconds or until it's hot. If you're happy with the texture at this point, it's ready. If you would like a creamier texture, stir the mixture well, then microwave again for an additional 1 to 2 minutes or until it boils.

3. **Add the chocolate.** Add the chopped chocolate and stir until fully melted.

4. **Serve.** Serve immediately with your preferred toppings, such as mini marshmallows or whipped cream.

Microwave Snack Pizza

PREP: 3 minutes // COOK: 1 minute 20 seconds // YIELD: 1 snack-size pizza

INGREDIENTS

FOR THE DOUGH

⅓ cup (50g) all-purpose
    flour

½ tsp baking powder

Pinch of salt

2 tbsp (30g) whole milk

FOR THE TOPPING

1 tbsp seasoned pizza sauce

2–3 tbsp shredded cheese
    (mozzarella recommended)

½ tbsp grated
    Parmesan cheese

5 slices of mini pepperoni
    (optional)

¼ tsp dried oregano
    (optional)

Don't knock it 'til you try it! Of course, this isn't anything like an authentic pizza, but it's delicious! It's perfect for when kids get home from school in urgent need of a snack. Kids can also have fun making this themselves.

1. **Make the pizza dough.** In a small bowl, mix the flour, baking powder, and salt until well combined. Add the milk and give it a good stir to form the dough. If the dough seems dry, add additional milk 1 teaspoon a time until it comes together.

2. **Roll out the dough.** Using a rolling pin, roll out the dough on a piece of parchment paper. It should be roughly 5 inches (12–13cm) across. Poke some holes in the rolled-out dough with a fork. The dough will look thin, but it will puff up in the microwave.

3. **Par-bake the crust.** Place the dough along with the parchment paper on a microwave-safe plate. Top the dough with the pizza sauce, spreading it right to the edges of the crust, and microwave on high for 40 seconds.

4. **Add the pizza toppings.** Add the shredded cheese and Parmesan along with the oregano and pepperoni, if using, or any other toppings you like. Microwave again for 30 to 40 seconds or until the cheese has melted. (Because it's cooked in the microwave, the crust won't brown, so I like to spread the toppings right to the edge of the pizza.)

5. **Serve.** Serve immediately.

Edible Cookie Doughs

PREP: 5 minutes // **COOK:** 1 minute // **YIELD:** 2 servings per flavor

INGREDIENTS

FOR THE CHOCOLATE CHIP COOKIE DOUGH

6 tbsp (50g) all-purpose flour

1½ tbsp (30g) unsalted butter

2 tbsp (30g) granulated white sugar

1 tbsp (15g) brown sugar (light or dark)

2 tbsp (30g) whole milk

⅛ tsp salt

2 tbsp mini chocolate chips

FOR THE SUGAR COOKIE DOUGH

6 tbsp (50g) all-purpose flour

1½ tbsp (30g) unsalted butter

2 tbsp (30g) granulated white sugar

2 tbsp (30g) whole milk

½ tsp vanilla extract

⅛ tsp salt

1 tbsp sprinkles

FOR THE DOUBLE CHOCOLATE CHIP COOKIE DOUGH

5 tbsp (40g) all-purpose flour

1½ tbsp (30g) unsalted butter

2 tbsp (30g) granulated white sugar

1 tbsp (15g) brown sugar (light or dark)

1½ tbsp (10g) unsweetened cocoa powder

2 tbsp (30g) whole milk

⅛ tsp salt

2 tbsp mini chocolate chips

Everybody loves cookie dough! This egg-free version is super quick to make because the flour is heat-treated using the microwave. Try all three varieties—they're delicious on their own or as a topping for ice cream.

1. **Heat-treat the flour.** For each batch of cookie dough, in a medium microwave-safe bowl, microwave the flour on high for 1 minute. Heat-treating the flour kills bacteria and cooks out the raw flour taste. You'll notice the flour will have formed clumps—this is because of water in the flour boiling off as the flour heats. Break up the clumps using a spatula and allow the flour to cool down. (To speed things up, I place the bowl in the freezer for 5 minutes.)

2. **Melt the butter.** For each batch of cookie dough, in a small microwave-safe bowl, microwave the butter for 20 to 30 seconds or until melted (see page 25). Allow the butter to cool for a few minutes, to prevent the chocolate chips from melting later.

3. **Make the cookie dough.** Follow the instructions for your flavor of choice.

   Chocolate chip: To the heat-treated flour, add the melted butter, granulated sugar, brown sugar, milk, and salt. Mix well to form the cookie dough. Stir in the chocolate chips until evenly incorporated.

   Sugar cookie: To the heat-treated flour, add the melted butter, granulated sugar, milk, vanilla, and salt. Mix well to form the cookie dough. Stir in the sprinkles until evenly incorporated.

   Double chocolate chip: To the heat-treated flour, add the melted butter, granulated sugar, brown sugar, cocoa powder, milk, and salt. Mix well to form the cookie dough. Stir in the chocolate chips until evenly incorporated.

4. **Serve.** You can serve the cookie dough right away if you like a soft texture. If you prefer a firmer texture, pop the cookie dough in the fridge for 1 hour to set up.

MAKE AHEAD
The cookie dough can be wrapped tightly in plastic wrap and refrigerated for up to 2 days.

Cozy, Comforting Dinners

This chapter features crowd-pleasing, comforting, cozy meals. Yes, that means carbs—from pizza and pasta to potatoes. Several of these are family recipes I loved as a kid and have refined as an adult to make them even faster and easier to prepare.

One-Pan Oven Spaghetti

PREP: 10 minutes // **COOK:** 25 minutes // **YIELD:** 6 servings

INGREDIENTS

Olive oil, as needed

1 (14½oz / 400g) can
crushed tomatoes

1lb (500g) spaghetti

Dried oregano

1 small potato, thinly sliced
(Yukon gold or similar)

6oz (180g) freshly grated
Parmesan or pecorino
cheese, plus more to serve

Salt, to taste

6–8 cherry tomatoes, halved

4 cups (1 liter) vegetable or
chicken stock

SPECIAL EQUIPMENT

9 × 13-inch (23 × 33cm)
baking dish, about
3 inches (7.5cm) deep

Sometimes, even Italians want shortcuts for making pasta dishes! This recipe is my mom's and it's become a family classic. It yields perfectly cooked spaghetti bathed in a rich, savory tomato sauce, all with minimal effort. This recipe not only delivers on taste but also makes cleanup a breeze.

1. **Preheat the oven and prepare the baking dish.** Preheat the oven to 430°F (220°C). Generously grease the bottom and sides of the baking dish with olive oil.

2. **Assemble the dish.** To the bottom of the baking dish, add a thin layer of crushed tomatoes. On top of the crushed tomatoes, scatter one-third of the spaghetti. Add 1 tablespoon olive oil, a pinch of oregano, a few slices of potatoes, a pinch of salt, and one-third of the Parmesan and crushed tomatoes. Repeat these layers until you've used all the ingredients. Scatter the cherry tomatoes over the top. The layers don't have to be precise—everything will be mixed up in the end.

3. **Boil the stock.** In a saucepan, bring the stock to a boil over medium heat.

4. **Bake the pasta.** Place the baking dish in the oven, and using a ladle, cover the spaghetti with the boiling stock. Bake uncovered for 10 minutes. Using tongs, give the spaghetti a stir and continue cooking for 10 to 15 minutes more or until the broth is mostly absorbed into the pasta. Taste the spaghetti to make sure it's cooked. If it's not, give it a few more minutes. If necessary, adjust the seasoning and stir well.

5. **Serve.** Add more grated cheese and serve with a mixed salad.

> **MAKE AHEAD**
> This dish can be prepared in advance through step 2 and covered with foil. When you're ready to bake, add the boiling stock and follow the recipe as directed.
>
> If you have leftovers, you can make a delicious dish by reheating in a pan with a little olive oil (see page 21).

One-Pot Mac & Cheese

PREP: 5 minutes // **COOK:** 15 minutes // **YIELD:** 2 servings

INGREDIENTS

7oz (200g) dried cavatappi
  or elbow macaroni

½ tsp salt

2½ cups (600g) water

½ cup (120g) whole milk

3½oz (100g) shredded
  Cheddar cheese

2 slices (40g) American
  cheese, torn into
  small pieces

¼ cup (30g) grated
  Parmesan cheese

This homemade mac and cheese is super creamy and comes together quickly and easily in one pot, so there's not much cleanup. Now there's no excuse to make the boxed version!

1. **Boil the pasta.** In a large saucepan over medium-high heat, combine the pasta, salt, and water, which should be enough to just cover the pasta. (You won't drain the macaroni, so don't add more water than necessary.) Stir continuously until the water comes to a boil. Once the mixture begins to boil, partially cover the saucepan with a lid. Cook for 6 to 7 minutes or until the water is almost completely absorbed and the macaroni is close to fully cooked, stirring every 30 to 40 seconds. Once the pasta is cooked, there might be some water left in the pan. Remove the lid, increase the heat to high, and reduce the water until there's no more than ¼ inch (6mm) remaining. This won't take more than 1 to 2 minutes.

2. **Add the milk and cheese.** With the burner still on high, add the milk and bring to a boil, stirring continuously. As soon as the milk begins to boil, add the Cheddar, American, and Parmesan cheeses. Continue to cook until the sauce has reduced slightly. (Don't let it reduce too much or it will split.) Reduce the heat to low and mix well using a rubber spatula to scrape the bottom and sides of the pan until the cheese has fully melted and the sauce thickens slightly. Turn off the heat. The sauce will continue to thicken as it cools.

3. **Serve.** Taste and adjust the seasoning. Serve immediately.

VARIATIONS

The Cheddar cheese can be swapped out for any melty cheese you like. Similarly, you can swap out the Parmesan for any strongly flavored cheese you prefer. However, you must include the American cheese, which has ingredients that help keep the sauce creamy and emulsified.

Authentic 24-Hour Pizza Margherita

PREP: 30 minutes, plus overnight to rest the dough // **COOK:** 25 minutes // **YIELD:** 4 medium pizzas

INGREDIENTS

FOR THE DOUGH

1¾ cups (400g) warm water

2 tsp (7g) active dry yeast

2 tbsp extra virgin olive oil, plus more for greasing

4½ cups (630g) all-purpose flour

3 tsp (12g) salt

Fine cornmeal, for sprinkling on the baking sheets

FOR THE SAUCE

2 cloves garlic, minced

1½ tbsp extra virgin olive oil

18oz (500g) puréed tomato sauce (passata) or finely crushed tomatoes

Salt, to taste

Large handful of fresh basil

(You will have sauce left over. It freezes beautifully.)

FOR THE TOPPINGS

Low-moisture mozzarella, sliced

A few fresh basil leaves

SPECIAL EQUIPMENT

Stand mixer with dough hook attachment

Pizza stone (optional)

VARIATION

Pizza bianca. Pizza bianca is popular in Rome. It's delicious and couldn't be easier to make. Instead of the quick tomato sauce, simply top the pizza with olive oil, rosemary, and salt. Bake as directed.

Every Italian family has their own amazing pizza recipe, and this is ours. Crispy, comforting, and such a crowd-pleaser. You can use this base recipe to create any pizza with whatever toppings you love. Ideally, make the dough the day before baking so it can slowly ferment in the fridge.

1. **Activate the yeast.** In a small bowl, combine the warm water and yeast. Stir in the olive oil. Set aside for 5 minutes.

2. **Make the dough.** To the bowl of a stand mixer with a dough hook attachment, add the yeast mixture, flour, and salt. Stir to combine. Mix on medium-high for 8 to 10 minutes or until the dough is smooth. The dough might be sticky—don't worry if it seems hard to handle at this stage. (To make the dough by hand, see page 18).

3. **Let the dough rise.** Transfer the dough to a greased bowl. Cover with plastic wrap or a damp kitchen towel, and let the dough rise for 2 to 3 hours or until tripled in size. Transfer the dough to a floured work surface, press the dough to remove the air, and divide into 4 equal portions. Shape the portions into balls.

4. **Refrigerate the dough.** Place the dough balls onto lightly floured baking sheets and cover well with plastic wrap. Make sure the covering is airtight, otherwise the dough will dry out in the fridge. Refrigerate for 24 hours to slowly rise. (If you don't want to wait 24 hours, then at this stage, allow the dough balls to rise again, covered, for 1 hour at room temperature.)

5. **Make the sauce.** In a medium saucepan, heat the olive oil and garlic over very low heat for 3 minutes. Increase the heat to medium, add the tomatoes, salt, and basil, and cook for 5 minutes more. Set aside to cool.

6. **Preheat the oven and prepare the baking sheets.** Preheat the oven to 480°F (250°C). Sprinkle a little cornmeal onto the baking sheets to prevent the pizza from sticking.

7. **Shape the dough.** Form each dough ball into a circle about 10 inches (26cm) in diameter. Do not use a rolling pin for this—you've waited a day to create an aerated texture in the crust! Using a rolling pin will knock all the air out. Instead, dip the dough ball into a small pile of flour and gently stretch out the dough with your hands. Push the air to the edges, forming a thicker crust. The dough in middle of the pizza should be thin (as thin as you can make it).

8. **Add toppings.** Carefully transfer the shaped dough to the prepared baking sheets. Top the pizzas with a little tomato sauce and some slices of mozzarella. Brush the crusts with a little olive oil, so they brown in the oven.

9. **Bake.** Bake for 10 to 15 minutes. If you want, you can place the baking sheet on the stovetop over medium-high heat for a few minutes to get the bottoms browned and crispy before baking. Alternatively, transfer the pizzas to a preheated pizza stone.

10. **Serve.** Top with a few leaves of fresh basil when the pizzas come out of the oven.

Easy Cheesy Pasta Bake

PREP: 5 minutes // **COOK:** 30 minutes // **YIELD:** 1 pasta bake; serves 6

INGREDIENTS

FOR THE PASTA

2 tbsp salt

1lb (500g) tube-shaped pasta, such as penne, tortiglioni, or rigatoni

FOR THE SAUCE

2 cloves garlic, minced

1 small to medium white onion, finely chopped

3 tbsp extra virgin olive oil

1 (25oz / 700g) jar plain puréed tomato sauce (passata)

2 tsp salt

5–6 fresh basil leaves

⅓ cup (75g) cream cheese or ricotta

6 tbsp freshly grated Parmesan cheese, divided

9oz (250g) low-moisture mozzarella, ⅔ cut into tiny pieces and ⅓ shredded, divided

SPECIAL EQUIPMENT

9 × 13-inch (23 × 33cm) baking dish

Pasta bakes are a family favorite—they're comforting and delicious, and everyone loves them! This version comes together quickly on a weeknight, makes great leftovers, and is perfect for feeding a crowd. I've also given you suggestions for great additions in the variations.

1. **Preheat the oven and prepare the baking dish.** Preheat the oven to 400°F (200°C). Generously grease a baking dish with a little olive oil.

2. **Parboil the pasta.** In a large pot, bring 2½ quarts water and the salt to a boil. Add the pasta and cook for 2 minutes less than the recommended timing on the package. You want the pasta slightly undercooked because it will continue to cook in the oven.

3. **Prepare the sauce.** While the pasta is boiling, prepare the sauce. In a large, deep saucepan, heat the garlic, onion, and olive oil over low heat for about 3 minutes or until fragrant. Stir in the tomato sauce. Add ¼ cup water to the now-empty jar, shake to dislodge any remaining sauce, and add the liquid to the pan. Stir in the salt and the basil, cover with a lid, and allow the sauce to simmer for 8 minutes or until the pasta has finished cooking. Turn off the heat and add the cream cheese and 2 tablespoons grated Parmesan. Taste and adjust the seasoning.

4. **Add the pasta to the sauce.** Drain the pasta and immediately mix it into the sauce. Make sure to coat the pasta completely. Add the mozzarella that's cut into tiny pieces and stir that through.

5. **Assemble the dish.** Transfer the pasta to the prepared baking dish and top with the remaining shredded mozzarella and 4 tablespoons of grated Parmesan.

6. **Bake.** Bake for 15 to 20 minutes or until the top is golden.

VARIATIONS

You can add crumbled sausage, ground beef, cubed eggplant, or mushrooms. Add any of these to the sauce after you've sautéed the onion and garlic, and cook for about 10 minutes to get some color. Then proceed with the recipe.

Superfast No-Yeast Pizza

PREP: 10 minutes // **COOK:** 15 minutes // **YIELD:** 1 large pizza

INGREDIENTS

FOR THE DOUGH

1 cup (140g) all-purpose flour

1½ tsp baking powder

½ tsp salt

½ cup + 2 tbsp (140g) plain yogurt

Olive oil, for greasing

FOR THE TOPPINGS

Seasoned pizza sauce

Shredded mozzarella cheese

Thinly sliced bell pepper (optional)

Halved black olives (optional)

Any other toppings of choice

SPECIAL EQUIPMENT

Large oven-safe skillet, 10 to 12 inches (26–30cm) in diameter

// NOTE

If you want to make two smaller pizzas, you can do so. Divide the dough in half and prepare as directed using two smaller oven-safe skillets.

When you need to get dinner on the table quickly and you need a true crowd-pleaser, this is the recipe you turn to. There's no need to wait for the dough to rise, the pizza comes together quickly, and you can use whatever you have in the fridge as toppings. Of course, it's not the same as yeast-raised pizza, but it's a hundred times more delicious than a frozen supermarket pizza!

1. **Make the dough.** In a large bowl, combine the flour, baking powder, salt, and yogurt, mixing with a spoon until a rough dough forms. Transfer the dough onto a lightly floured surface and knead for a few minutes. Cover with plastic wrap and allow to sit for 5 to 10 minutes while you prepare the toppings. (This gives time for the flour to hydrate.)

2. **Preheat the oven.** Preheat the oven to 400°F (200°C).

3. **Brown the bottom of the crust.** Using a rolling pin, form the pizza crust by rolling out the dough to the size of your oven-safe skillet. Grease the skillet with a little olive oil and add the pizza crust to the skillet. Cook over medium-high heat for 2 minutes or until the bottom has turned a golden brown color.

4. **Par-bake the crust.** Place the skillet in the oven for 5 minutes or until the edges of the crust have started to turn golden brown.

5. **Add the toppings and finish cooking.** Take the skillet out of the oven, brush the crust with olive oil, and add the pizza sauce, shredded cheese, and the other toppings of your choice. Make sure the sauce and toppings go right to the edge of the crust. Return the pizza to the oven to bake for about 5 minutes or until the cheese has melted and is bubbling.

6. **Serve.** Serve immediately.

Three-Ingredient Fettuccine Alfredo

PREP: 5 minutes // **COOK:** 15 minutes // **YIELD:** 2 to 3 servings

INGREDIENTS

2½ cups (600g) water

7oz (200g) dried fettuccine pasta nests (ideally egg fettucine)

½ tsp salt

½ cup (60g) grated Parmesan cheese

2 tbsp (30g) butter

Handful of roughly chopped flat leaf parsley (optional)

This dish originated more than 100 years ago in Rome, Italy, when chef Alfredo Di Lelio wanted to create a comforting dish for his wife, who had just given birth to their son. To this day in Rome, what we call *burro e parmigiano* is still a favorite comfort food, especially among kids. This version is super creamy and comes together in 10 minutes, all in one pan. Many fettuccine Alfredo recipes call for heavy cream, but no cream is used in the real Italian dish. Instead, the creaminess comes from the emulsified sauce made with butter, Parmesan cheese, and starchy pasta water.

1. **Prepare the pasta for cooking.** To a large saucepan, add the water, pasta, and salt. Please be precise about the amounts. This is not the usual way of cooking pasta; you won't be draining it. Instead, you're using a small amount of water and a precise amount of salt to cook the pasta. This creates a super starchy liquid with which to emulsify the Alfredo sauce. Put the pan on high heat, and place a lid on the pan halfway, so there's some space for steam to escape. Bring the water to a boil.

2. **Cook the pasta.** When the water is boiling, lower the heat to medium and stir the noodles gently, making sure to not break them. Cover again and cook for 7 to 8 minutes, stirring every 1 to 2 minutes. This will ensure the pasta doesn't stick to the pan, it cooks evenly, and that the water doesn't boil over.

3. **Finish cooking and stir in remaining ingredients.** After 7 minutes, remove the lid and taste the pasta; it should be almost cooked. Look to see how much water is left in the bottom of the pan. If there's more than an inch of water, increase the heat to high and boil until an inch of water remains. Then reduce the heat to low, and add the Parmesan and butter. Stir for 1 to 2 minutes to make a creamy Alfredo sauce. Stir in the parsley, if desired.

4. **Serve.** Taste and adjust for seasoning and serve immediately.

VARIATIONS

These variations aren't authentically Italian (did you know many Italians hate the idea of chicken with pasta?), but they're delicious!

Chicken Alfredo. Before you cook the pasta, cut 2 boneless, skinless chicken thighs into rough ¾-inch (2cm) cubes. Finely slice 1 clove of garlic. In a medium skillet, heat 1 tablespoon olive oil over medium-high heat and fry the chicken for about 10 minutes or until cooked through. Add the garlic about 7 minutes into the cooking process. Season with salt and pepper, cover to keep warm, and set aside. Prepare the fettucine Alfredo directed. Add the cooked chicken pieces and garlic at the end when the Alfredo sauce has just formed and stir through for about 1 minute.

Shrimp Alfredo. Before you cook the pasta, devein 18 large raw shrimp. Finely slice 1 clove of garlic. In a medium skillet, heat 1 tablespoon olive oil and the garlic over medium-high heat. Fry for 1 minute, then add the shrimp and cook for 1 to 2 minutes per side (no more than this), or until they have some color. Season with salt and pepper, cover to keep warm, and set aside. Prepare the fettucine Alfredo as directed. Add the cooked shrimp and garlic at the end when the Alfredo sauce has just formed and stir through for about 1 minute.

Ultimate Easy Lasagna

PREP: 30 minutes // **COOK:** 2½ hours, plus 30 minutes to rest // **YIELD:** 1 lasagna; serves 8 to 10

INGREDIENTS

FOR THE RAGU

1 large white onion, roughly chopped

2 medium carrots, roughly chopped

2 celery stalks, roughly chopped

3 tbsp olive oil

2 tbsp tomato paste

1lb (450g) 90% lean ground beef

½ cup (120g) dry white wine

45oz (1.3kg) puréed tomato sauce (passata)

Salt and pepper, to taste

FOR THE BÉCHAMEL

2 tbsp (30g) unsalted butter

3 tbsp (30g) all-purpose flour

2 cups (470g) whole milk

½ tsp freshly grated nutmeg

Salt and pepper, to taste

TO ASSEMBLE

10½oz (300g) low-moisture mozzarella cheese, diced into small cubes

3½oz (100g) freshly grated Parmesan cheese

1 (1lb / 500g) package oven-ready lasagna sheets (You'll probably use about half the package; it depends on the size and depth of your dish.)

SPECIAL EQUIPMENT

9 × 13-inch (23 × 33cm) baking dish, at least 3 inches (7cm) deep

Lasagna is truly amazing, but the traditional method of preparation requires many hours of slow cooking. In real life, Italians mostly reserve slow-cooked versions for the holidays. My mom's version has a few tricks that help to develop flavor quickly, delivering a rich ragu layered with pasta, a delicious béchamel, and cheese. Give it a try—it might be the best lasagna you've ever had!

Making a truly great lasagna is a bit of a project, even with the time-saving tricks in this recipe. Plan to begin prepping about 3½ to 4 hours before you want to serve the lasagna. Don't be daunted by the time, though—it's easy to put this together.

MAKE THE RAGU

1. **Prepare the onion, carrot, and celery.** In a food processor, pulse the onions, carrots, and celery until everything is finely chopped. To a large saucepan over medium heat, add the olive oil. Add the chopped vegetables to the pan and cook for about 10 minutes, stirring frequently, until the vegetables have softened and released their liquid. Don't allow them to become too brown.

2. **Assemble the ragu.** Add the tomato paste and sauté for 2 minutes. Add the beef and cook until well browned. (The timing here depends on your pan and your stovetop.) Add the wine, scraping any remaining brown bits from the bottom of the pan to deglaze it, and cook for 2 or 3 minutes or until the wine has almost disappeared. Add the tomato sauce. Add a little water to the empty tomato sauce jar or cans, swirl around to rinse out any residual sauce, and add to the pan.

3. **Cook the ragu.** Bring the ragu to a boil. Cover, leaving the lid slightly ajar, and reduce the heat to low. Simmer for 2 hours, stirring occasionally. If the ragu seems dry, add some water. Adjust the seasoning with salt and pepper. (The ragu might need more salt than you think it will.) If some fat rises to the top of the ragu during cooking, just stir it back in. When done, set aside or refrigerate until ready to assemble the lasagna.

MAKE THE BÉCHAMEL

When the ragu is done and you're ready to assemble the lasagna, make the béchamel. (You want to make this at the last minute to avoid it thickening too much.)

1. **Make the roux.** In a large saucepan, melt the butter over medium-high heat. When the butter has melted, add the flour. Cook for 5 minutes, stirring constantly. Make sure to scrape the edges of the pan so none of the roux sticks and burns.

2. **Make the sauce.** Gradually begin adding the milk, a little at time, stirring vigorously after each addition to remove any lumps. Once you've added about a quarter of the milk, add the remaining milk all in one go. Cook until the sauce thickens slightly, stirring continuously. The sauce should have a smooth, runny consistency that just coats the back of a spoon. Stir in the nutmeg. Turn off the heat.

3. **Adjust the seasoning.** The sauce might need more salt than you think—add enough so that the sauce tastes savory rather than "milky."

>> Recipe continues on next page.

ASSEMBLE THE LASAGNA

1. **Preheat the oven.** Preheat the oven to 350°F (180°C).

2. **Start the first pasta layer.** Place a 9 × 13-inch (23 × 33cm) baking dish on a baking sheet. (The baking sheet will catch any spills as the lasagna cooks.) We're aiming for a total of four layers of pasta in the lasagna. Add a couple of spoonfuls of ragu to the baking dish and spread evenly over the bottom of the dish in a thin layer. Drizzle in a little béchamel. Add a layer of pasta, overlapping the sheets slightly. You can use some broken bits to fill in any gaps at the edges of the dish. (Use more or less as needed, according to the size of your pasta sheets.)

3. **Create the main layers.** Add enough ragu to just cover the pasta. Drizzle in enough béchamel to form a thin layer with some gaps. Scatter one-quarter of the mozzarella over the béchamel. Scatter a little under a quarter of the Parmesan over the béchamel. Add another layer of pasta. Repeat this process twice more. You should now have four layers of pasta. If your dish is deep and you have leftover ingredients, you can add an extra layer. Top the final layer of pasta with ragu and béchamel, completely covering the pasta, and scatter over the remaining mozzarella and Parmesan.

4. **Bake the lasagna.** Transfer the lasagna dish on its baking sheet to the preheated oven. Cook for 30 minutes. After 30 minutes, the top of the lasagna should be bubbling and well-browned. If it's not, cook for up to 10 minutes more or until the lasagna is browned.

5. **Serve.** Allow the lasagna to rest for a good 30 minutes before cutting into it with a knife and serving. Serve with a crisp mixed salad, if desired.

MAKE AHEAD & FREEZE

The ragu can be prepared a day ahead and refrigerated overnight. This will give the ragu greater depth of flavor. Leftover ragu also freezes beautifully and can be used as a quick pasta sauce.

The assembled lasagna can be made a day ahead, covered with pastlic wrap, and refrigerated overnight or frozen. Bake as directed. If you're baking the lasagna from frozen, it will take extra time to cook.

Grilled Cheese & Tomato Soup

ITALIAN VS. AMERICAN

PREP: 15 minutes // **COOK:** 45 minutes // **YIELD:** 3 to 4 servings of soup; 1 American and 1 Italian sandwich

INGREDIENTS

FOR THE TOMATO SOUP

16oz (450g) cherry tomatoes

2 tbsp extra virgin olive oil, divided, plus more for serving

1 medium to large yellow onion, finely chopped

1 tbsp (15g) unsalted butter

2 cloves garlic, finely chopped

1 small to medium potato (about 5oz / 150g), peeled and thinly sliced

1 (15oz / 430g) can whole tomatoes in juice

2 cups (450g) water

3–4 fresh basil leaves

Salt and pepper, to taste

1–3 tsp granulated white sugar, as needed

Finely grated Parmesan cheese, to taste

SPECIAL EQUIPMENT

Air fryer (for the tomato soup; optional)

Blender

// NOTE

I prefer to roast the cherry tomatoes in an air fryer because it's a quick way of doing it, but you can roast them in a regular oven on a baking sheet if you don't have an air fryer.

A grilled cheese with tomato soup is one of the most iconic pairings for comfort food. I grew up eating both American grilled cheese and the Italian version, called *mozzarella in carrozza*. They're quite different from each other but equally delicious, so I'm giving you both versions here. (I couldn't resist adding a little Italian flare to the American version, which increases the cheesy flavor.) The rich tomato flavor in this homemade soup is a million miles away from canned. It's important to follow all the steps in the recipe, which build layer upon layer of deep tomato flavor, so there's no need for cream or broth.

TOMATO SOUP

1. **Roast the tomatoes.** Grease the air fryer basket and scatter the whole cherry tomatoes in the basket. Drizzle with 1 tablespoon of olive oil. Cook at 400°F (200°C) for 10 to 15 minutes until the tomatoes shrink in size and the skins become wrinkled with brown spots. Remove from the air fryer and set aside.

2. **Make the soup.** In a large saucepan, cook the onion with the butter and remaining 1 tablespoon of olive oil over low heat for 10 minutes, stirring continuously to avoid burning. Add the garlic, and sauté for 2 minutes more. Add the potato and cook for 5 minutes more. Add the roasted cherry tomatoes, canned whole tomatoes (including the juice), and the water. Increase the heat and bring to a boil. When boiling, lower the heat and simmer for 8 to 10 minutes. Finally, add the basil, bring to a boil, cover with a lid, and simmer gently for 20 minutes. Continue simmering until the potato is fully cooked (taste a piece to check). Remove from the heat.

3. **Blend the soup.** Carefully transfer the soup to a blender, and blend until creamy and completely smooth. (A high-powered blender will give the best texture.) Be careful blending the hot soup—don't use a tight-fitting lid and make sure not to splash hot soup on yourself. I like to use a clean kitchen towel to cover the lid of the blender.

4. **Finish the soup.** Pour the soup back in the pan and adjust the salt to taste. If the soup seems too acidic, add some sugar to balance the flavors. I typically add 1 to 3 teaspoons of sugar. Add a little at a time until you get the balance you like.

5. **Serve.** Before serving, top each bowl with a few extra basil leaves, a drizzle of olive oil, and grated Parmesan.

AMERICAN GRILLED CHEESE

2 slices sandwich bread

1 slice American cheese

3 tbsp freshly grated sharp Cheddar cheese

2 tbsp mayonnaise

1oz (30g) freshly grated Parmesan cheese

1 tbsp unsalted butter, for frying

1. **Assemble the sandwich.** To one slice of bread, add the slice of American cheese and the freshly shredded Cheddar cheese. Close the sandwich and spread the top of the outside of the sandwich with mayonnaise. Add the Parmesan cheese, and pack it well so it adheres to the bread—the mayo will act like glue.

2. **Cook the sandwich.** In a large nonstick skillet, melt the butter over medium-low heat. Place the sandwich in the pan, Parmesan side down. Now, with the sandwich in the pan, spread the remaining top side of the sandwich with mayonnaise and add Parmesan as you did for the first side. Fry until the bottom side of the sandwich is crispy and deep golden-brown. This will take a few minutes. Flip the sandwich over and cook on the final side until brown. Remove from the skillet.

3. **Serve.** Cut diagonally into triangles and serve immediately with a bowl of hot tomato soup.

ITALIAN GRILLED CHEESE

1 large egg, beaten

4 tbsp breadcrumbs

Salt and pepper, to taste

Olive oil, for frying

2 slices sandwich bread, with the crusts removed

2 slices low-moisture mozzarella, sliced to the same thickness as the bread

1. **Prepare your ingredients.** Arrange two shallow bowls on your work surface: to one, add the beaten egg; to the other, add the breadcrumbs. Season the breadcrumbs with salt and pepper and give them a stir to mix.

2. **Heat the oil.** In a large skillet, heat ¼ inch (6mm) of oil over medium heat.

3. **Assemble the sandwich.** Sandwich the mozzarella slices between the two slices of bread, pressing down the edges of the bread to seal the mozzarella inside.

4. **Coat the sandwich.** Dip the sandwich in the beaten egg, being sure to coat all the sides and edges. Then, dip the sandwich into the breadcrumbs, making sure it's completely covered in breadcrumbs.

5. **Fry the sandwich.** Fry the sandwich in the hot olive oil, flipping once or twice until the coating has turned a golden-brown color. Drain the sandwich on paper towels to remove any excess oil.

6. **Serve.** Serve immediately with a bowl of hot tomato soup.

Dad's Potato-Cheese Pie

PREP: 15 minutes // **COOK:** 1 hour // **YIELD:** 1 pie; serves 6

INGREDIENTS

2lb (1kg) high-starch, floury potatoes such as russets, Yukon Golds, or Maris Pipers, peeled and halved

2 tsp salt, plus more to taste

6 tbsp (80g) butter, cut into thin slices, plus more for greasing

1 cup (240g) whole milk

Freshly ground black pepper, to taste

3 medium eggs, beaten

8½oz (240g) shredded sharp Cheddar cheese, divided

3½oz (100g) grated Parmesan cheese, divided

6 scallions, finely sliced

SPECIAL EQUIPMENT

8-inch (20cm) round or square baking dish

Potato ricer, food mill, or potato masher

One of my dad's specialties is a potato-cheese pie. I love making it with him, so this recipe is very dear to me. This is comfort food at its best: mashed potatoes loaded with cheese and baked until golden. I hope it will quickly become a favorite in your family, as it is in mine.

1. **Cook the potatoes.** To a large saucepan, add the potatoes and salt. Add cold water to cover. Bring to a boil over high heat. Reduce the heat to medium so the water is just boiling and cook for 20 minutes or until the potatoes are cooked through. Drain the potatoes and set aside for 5 minutes to allow the steam to escape.

2. **Preheat the oven and prepare the pan.** Preheat the oven to 350°F (180°C). Grease the baking dish well with butter.

3. **Mash the potatoes.** In a large bowl, mash the potatoes. (I like to use a food mill for this because it makes such quick work of mashing the potatoes.) Add the butter and mix to incorporate. (The residual heat in the potatoes will quickly melt the butter.) Add the milk and mix until you have fluffy mashed potatoes. Taste and adjust the seasoning to your liking with salt and pepper.

4. **Add the remaining ingredients.** Add the beaten eggs, three-quarters of the cheeses (hold back one-quarter each of the Cheddar and Parmesan), and the scallions. Mix to combine.

5. **Prepare the pie.** Transfer the potato mixture to the prepared baking dish. Rough up the surface using a fork. (This will create lots of crispy bits when the pie bakes.) Scatter the remaining Cheddar and Parmesan cheeses over the top.

6. **Bake the pie.** Bake for 40 minutes or until the top is gold brown and the roughed-up edges are crispy. Remove from the oven and rest for 10 to 15 minutes.

7. **Serve.** Serve with a crisp mixed green salad, if desired.

VARIATIONS

Try changing up the cheese. Replacing the Cheddar with a mix of low-moisture mozzarella and smoked mozzarella is delicious.

For a crunchy topping, scatter 3 tablespoons of breadcrumbs over the top of the pie before baking.

Add 3 to 5 ounces (100–150g) diced cooked ham to the potato/cheese mixture.

Add additional flavorings when you're mashing the potatoes. For example, whole grain mustard, horseradish cream, and wasabi all work well in this pie. Start by adding 1 teaspoon, mix, and taste to see if you want to add more.

Breads & Pastries

Whether you're a novice baker or you've been making doughs for years, you'll find something in this chapter for you. These recipes feature pastry chef secrets and shortcuts to simplify making bakery-quality breads and pastries at home without sacrificing flavor or texture. You'll also find some authentic regional variations on Italian classics you might not have seen before.

Melt-In-Your-Mouth Glazed Donuts

PREP: 20 minutes, plus 3 hours to rise // **COOK:** 3 minutes, plus 5 minutes to cool // **YIELD:** 12 to 15 donuts

INGREDIENTS

FOR THE DONUTS

½ cup (120g) whole milk

1 medium egg, at room temperature

2 tsp (7g) active dry yeast

2 cups (280g) all-purpose flour

3 tbsp (45g) granulated white sugar

½ tsp salt

¼ tsp ground nutmeg

3 tbsp (40g) unsalted butter, melted

Neutral cooking oil, for greasing and frying

FOR THE GLAZE

5 tbsp (75g) unsalted butter, melted

3 tbsp whole milk

1 tsp vanilla extract

2 cups (240g) powdered sugar

SPECIAL EQUIPMENT

Stand mixer with dough hook attachment (recommended but not required)

Ring donut cutter or 2 round cookie cutters (one smaller to make the holes)

Dutch oven or heavy-bottomed pot

Instant-read thermometer

There's something so comforting about a classic, glazed yeast-raised donut. Before making any other donut, everyone should master this classic version. It's the mother of all the others, and it's the most popular—and to me, one of the most delicious!

1. **Warm the milk.** In a small, microwave-safe bowl or glass measuring cup, microwave the milk until lukewarm, about 30 seconds (don't let it get hot). Incorporate the egg into the milk and add the yeast. Allow this mixture to sit for 5 minutes (see page 18).

2. **Mix the dry ingredients.** In the bowl of a stand mixer or a large bowl, whisk together the flour, sugar, salt, and nutmeg.

3. **Combine and knead the dough.** Add the milk/yeast mixture and melted butter to the dry ingredients. Using a spatula or wooden spoon, roughly combine the dry ingredients with the melted butter and milk, then using the dough hook attachment of your stand mixer knead the dough on a low to medium speed until it comes together, then increase the speed to high and continue kneading the dough for another 3 minutes. After 3 minutes the dough should feel tacky to the touch and look smooth. (To knead by hand, see page 19.)

4. **Let the dough rise.** Remove the dough from the bowl, and using wet hands shape the dough into a ball. Lightly grease the bowl with ½ tablespoon of oil and place the dough back in the bowl. Cover with a damp kitchen towel or with plastic wrap and allow the dough to rise for 2 to 3 hours at room temperature.

5. **Prepare the donuts.** When the dough has doubled in size, turn it out onto a lightly floured work board. Gently press the dough down using your hands (do not knead the dough) and using a rolling pin, roll the dough out until it is ½ inch (1.25cm) thick. Using a donut cutter or round cookie cutters, cut out the donut rings. Place the donuts onto a lightly floured tray. (A good tip is to put each donut on a square of parchment paper—see page 19.) You can re-roll the scraps and cut out more donuts. (See re-rolling doughs, page 19.) If the dough pulls back, wrap the dough in plastic wrap and allow to rest for 30 minutes before rolling and cutting more donuts.

6. **Let the donuts rise.** Cover the donuts with a clean kitchen towel and allow to rise for 45 minutes to 1 hour at room temperature.

7. **Fry the donuts.** In a large Dutch oven or heavy-bottomed pot over medium heat, heat about 3 inches (7.5cm) of oil to 350°F (180°C). Once this temperature has been reached, reduce the heat slightly to maintain the temperature (see deep frying, page 25). Working in batches, fry the donuts until golden brown, about 1 to 2 minutes on each side. Transfer the donuts onto some paper towels and set aside.

>> Recipe continues on next page.

VARIATION

These are amazing in the air fryer! For air-fried donuts, follow the method through step 5. Before the second rise, brush the donuts with melted butter. After the second 45-minute rise, preheat the air fryer to 350°F (180°C). Grease the basket and gently place the donuts into the basket. Air fry for exactly 3 minutes. Dip the donuts in the glaze immediately.

8. **Make the glaze and glaze the donuts.** In a large bowl, whisk together the melted butter, milk, vanilla, and powdered sugar. The glaze should be smooth and loose. If it seems too thick, mix in an additional tablespoon of milk. While the donuts are still warm, dip them in the glaze. Place on a cooling rack or even better enjoy the donuts while they're still warm! As the donuts cool, the glaze will set.

MAKE AHEAD

The dough can be made ahead. See page 18 for instructions.

Donuts are best eaten fresh! However, you can store the donuts in an airtight container for up to 1 day. Reheat in the microwave for 20 seconds.

Bagels

ONE RECIPE, ENDLESS FLAVORS

PREP: 20 minutes, plus 2 hours 45 minutes to rise // **COOK:** 18 minutes // **YIELD:** 12 bagels

INGREDIENTS

1¾ cups (420g) warm water

2 tsp (7g) active dry yeast

5¼ cups (750g) all-purpose flour

¼ cup (50g) granulated white sugar

2 tsp salt

2 tbsp olive oil, plus more for greasing

1 large egg white, beaten (for egg wash)

SPECIAL EQUIPMENT

Stand mixer with dough hook attachment (recommended but not required)

Bagels are dear to my heart. When I was a kid, my dad would go out every Sunday to buy his newspaper and have breakfast, and he'd bring back half of his bagel for me. I want to dedicate this recipe to him. To this day when we're together, we still bond over a bagel—he has one half, I have the other. Everyone has their favorite kind of bagel. I'll show you how, from one simple dough, you can quickly make your favorite variety or even your very own assorted bagel box to share with your family and friends!

1. **Activate the yeast.** In a small bowl, combine the warm water and yeast. Let the mixture sit for 5 minutes or until foamy. (See page 18 for more on yeast.)

2. **Mix the dry ingredients.** In the bowl of a stand mixer, whisk together the flour, sugar, and salt.

3. **Combine and knead the dough.** Add the yeast mixture to the flour mixture. Using a dough hook attachment, mix on medium-low speed for about 3 minutes until the dough comes together. If the dough seems too dry, you can add 1 to 2 tablespoons of water. Add the oil, then increase the speed to high and continue kneading the dough for 5 minutes more. The dough should feel tacky to the touch and look smooth. Alternatively, you can make the dough by hand, but it requires arm muscle (see page 19). If kneading by hand, knead for about 15 minutes until it becomes elastic. After 15 minutes, add the oil and continue kneading the dough until the oil is fully incorporated. You'll know when the dough is ready because you'll be able to stretch it without it breaking and it will look smooth.

4. **Let the dough rise.** Remove the dough from the bowl, and using wet hands, shape the dough into a ball. Lightly grease the bowl with oil and place the dough back into the bowl. Cover with a damp kitchen towel or with plastic wrap and allow the dough to rise for about 2 hours at room temperature or until it has doubled in size.

5. **Shape the bagels.** Divide the dough into 12 equal portions; each portion should be roughly 3½ ounces (100g). Roll each portion of dough into a ball, then punch a hole through the middle with a finger. Using your hands, gently work the dough to make the hole bigger, and form a bagel shape. (Make the hole a little larger than you want for your finished bagel; it will close up during the second rise.) Place each bagel on a square of parchment paper. This will make it easy to move around later (see page 19).

6. **Let the bagels rise.** Cover the bagels and allow them to rise at room temperature for around 45 minutes.

7. **Preheat the oven and prepare the baking sheets.** Preheat the oven to 430°F (220°C) and line two baking sheets with parchment paper.

>> *Recipe continues on next page.*

Everything bagel. Everything bagels are topped with a mix of poppy seeds, sesame seeds, black sesame seeds, minced dried garlic, and salt. You can make your own or buy a ready-made seasoning mix. Sprinkle on after you've brushed the bagels with the beaten egg white.

Poppy seed. Sprinkle the poppy seeds onto the tops of your bagels just after you've brushed them with the beaten egg white.

Onion flakes topping. Rehydrate the dried onion flakes in water until soft (about 15 minutes) and sprinkle on top of your bagels 2 minutes before they finish baking. It's important to add them near the end, otherwise they'll burn.

Onion bagel dough. Before shaping your bagels, for every 3½ ounces (100g) of bagel dough, add ¼ teaspoon of onion powder, and knead into the dough to incorporate it evenly.

Egg bagel dough. Before shaping your bagels, for every 7 ounces (200g) of bagel dough, add 1 egg yolk and 2 teaspoons of flour. Knead the egg yolk and extra flour into the dough to incorporate evenly. The dough will get messy, so add a little extra flour if you need it.

Raisin bagels. Rehydrate the raisins in warm water for 30 minutes, then drain off the water and add the raisins to the dough just before you've finished mixing. Add as many raisins as you like.

8. **Dip the bagels.** Bring a large saucepan of water to a simmer. Turn off the heat and lower each bagel with its parchment paper into the water bath for about 20 seconds. Using tongs, remove the parchment paper. The bagels will float, so spoon water over the top of each bagel. This step is what gives bagels their characteristic chewy texture. Using a large, slotted spoon, remove the bagels and place on your prepared baking sheets, leaving space in between. Brush each bagel with the beaten egg white.

9. **Bake the bagels.** Bake the bagels in the preheated oven for 16 to 18 minutes or until they're golden brown. If you've added toppings (see variations), keep an eye on them to make sure the toppings don't burn.

10. **Serve.** Allow to cool for 10 minutes. At that point, they'll be cool enough to handle, and you will be able to pull them away from the parchment paper easily. Freshly baked bagels are delicious as is, but they're amazing toasted too.

MAKE AHEAD & FREEZE

Once cool, transfer the bagels to a zip-top bag and store at room temperature for up to 5 days or freeze for up to 1 month.

Irresistible Italian Donuts

PREP: 1 hour, plus 2 hours to rise // **COOK:** 15 minutes // **YIELD:** 8 to 12 donuts

INGREDIENTS

FOR THE DONUTS

1 medium high-starch potato like Yukon Gold, peeled and halved, about 4½oz (125g) when peeled

1 large egg, at room temperature

¾ cup (180g) whole milk

2 tsp (7g) active dry yeast

3 cups (420g) all-purpose flour, plus more for dusting

3 tbsp (35g) granulated white sugar

1 tsp salt

Zest of 1 lemon

4 tbsp (½ stick / 60g) unsalted butter, melted

Neutral cooking oil, for frying (about 1 quart / 1 liter)

FOR THE FILLING AND COATING

½ cup (100g) granulated white sugar

2 cups filling of choice (optional), such as Silky Pastry Cream (page 214) or Nutella

There's a secret ingredient in Italian donuts that makes them even fluffier than the classic American version: mashed potatoes. Yes, you read that right! You don't taste the potatoes—they're there for texture, bringing lightness and softness. If you're a donut connoisseur, you must try these. There are two versions: sugar ring donuts (graffe) and custard-filled donuts (bomboloni).

1. **Make the mashed potatoes.** Place the halved potato in a saucepan over high heat, add cold water to cover, and bring to a boil. Once the water is boiling, reduce the heat to medium and cook for 20 to 25 minutes or until tender. Drain and allow the steam to escape from the potato halves for 10 minutes until dry. Mash until smooth. (Use a potato ricer if you have one—it's important there are no lumps.) Cool for at least 20 minutes. You should have about ½ cup of mashed potatoes.

2. **Activate the yeast.** In a small, microwave-safe bowl or glass measuring cup, microwave the milk until lukewarm, about 30 to 40 seconds. (Don't let it get hot.) Whisk the egg into the milk and add the yeast. Allow to sit for 5 minutes.

3. **Mix the dry ingredients.** In the bowl of a stand mixer fitted with the whisk attachment, whisk together the flour, sugar, and salt. Zest the lemon directly into the mixture.

4. **Combine and knead the dough.** To the dry ingredients, add the melted butter, mashed potatoes, and the milk/egg mixture. Mix on medium-low speed until the dough comes together. Increase the speed to high and continue kneading the dough for 1 minute more. This dough doesn't need much mixing. (Alternatively, you can make the dough by hand; see the kneading section on page 19.)

5. **Let the dough rest.** Remove the dough from the bowl, and with wet hands, shape the dough into a ball. Cover with plastic wrap and allow to rest at room temperature for 1 to 1½ hours.

6. **Shape the donuts.** Turn out the dough onto a lightly dusted work surface. Using a rolling pin, roll out the dough to about ½ inch (1.25cm) thick. Using a round cookie or biscuit cutter, cut the dough into circles. For ring donuts, use a smaller cutter to cut out the center of each circle of dough, making a ring. (Don't cut a center hole if making bomboloni.) Place the circles on lightly floured baking sheets. (A good tip is to put each donut on a square of parchment paper; see page 19.) You can re-roll the scraps and cut out more donuts (page 19). If the dough pulls back, wrap the dough in plastic wrap and allow to rest for 30 minutes. Then roll the dough out and make more donuts.

7. **Allow the donuts to rise.** Cover the donuts and allow to rise for 1 to 1½ hours.

>> Recipe continues on next page.

Potato ricer (recommended but not required)

Stand mixer with dough hook attachment (recommended but not required)

3½-inch (9cm) round cookie or biscuit cutter

1-inch (2.5cm) round cookie cutter (optional, for ring donuts)

Instant-read thermometer

Chopstick (optional, for filled donuts)

Piping bag with ¼-inch (1cm) tip (optional, for filled donuts)

8. **Fry the donuts.** In a large Dutch oven or heavy-bottomed pot over medium heat, heat about 3 inches (7.5cm) of oil to 350°F (180°C). When this temperature is reached, reduce the heat slightly to maintain the temperature of the oil (see deep frying, page 25). Working in batches, fry the donuts until golden brown, about 1 to 2 minutes on each side. Transfer the donuts onto paper towels, and then while still hot, toss the donuts in the granulated sugar. Set aside to cool for 10 minutes and serve warm.

9. **Fill the bomboloni.** If you're making bomboloni, while the donuts are still warm, use a chopstick (or a similar utensil) to make a hole in the side of each donut, inserting the chopstick just over halfway into the donut. Use a piping bag to fill them with the filling(s) of your choice. You'll know when you've put enough filling into a donut because it will feel heavy in your hand.

10. **Serve.** Italian donuts are best eaten fresh—as soon as possible after making them. You really need to eat them on the same day you make them.

Cheater's Artisan Croissants

PREP: 1 hour, plus 3 hours to rise // **COOK:** 18 minutes // **YIELD:** 12 croissants

INGREDIENTS

FOR THE DOUGH

1 cup (240g) whole milk

1 medium egg, at room temperature

2 tsp active dry yeast

3 cups (420g) all-purpose flour

3 tbsp (35g) granulated white sugar

1 tsp salt

2 tbsp (30g) unsalted butter, at room temperature

FOR THE LAYERS

16 tbsp (2 sticks / 230g) unsalted butter, at room temperature

FOR THE EGG WASH

1 medium egg, beaten

SPECIAL EQUIPMENT

Stand mixer with dough hook attachment

In pastry chef circles, there's much debate about how many layers croissant dough should have. I'm going to let you in on a secret—the best artisan croissants have fewer layers than people think. Croissants made the traditional way take over a day to make because of the painstaking process of laminating the dough. This recipe is much easier and faster—it borrows ideas for quickly laminating doughs from the Indian subcontinent and the southern United States. We use the "French" quantity of butter and a little French pastry technique to give you true artisan croissants with the most beautifully defined layers. These croissants are incredible—you must try them!

1. **Prepare all the ingredients.** It's important to have all your ingredients ready to work with. For example, you will need to take your butter out of the fridge well in advance of starting the recipe to allow it to come up to room temperature.

2. **Activate the yeast.** In a medium, microwave-safe bowl or glass measuring cup, microwave the milk until lukewarm, about 30 to 40 seconds (don't let it get hot). Whisk the egg into the milk and add the yeast (see page 18). Allow this mixture to sit for 5 minutes.

3. **Make the dough.** To a stand mixer with a dough hook attachment, add the flour, sugar, and salt. Add the milk/egg mixture and mix on a slow speed for 2 minutes, then on a medium speed for another 3 minutes. With the mixer running, add the 2 tablespoons of butter. Continue mixing for 5 minutes more.

4. **Allow the dough to rest**. Put the dough in a greased bowl and cover with a damp towel or plastic wrap. Allow to rest at room temperature for 30 minutes. (Don't leave it longer than this.)

>> Recipe continues on next page.

5. **Divide the dough.** Divide the dough into 12 equal portions and roll into balls. Lightly flour the dough balls and your work surface. Using a rolling pin, roll out the dough balls into circles about 7 inches (18cm) in diameter. (See photos, opposite page.)

6. **Layer the dough.** Divide the 2 sticks of room-temperature butter into 11 equal portions (about 20 grams per portion). The butter needs to be super soft and spreadable, so whip it if it's not soft enough. Smear the top surface of all but one of the dough circles with the portions of butter, and layer the buttered circles of dough on top of each other. It's best to assemble the layers on a baking tray or cutting board to make it easy to transfer the stack to the freezer later.

7. **Use the unbuttered circle as the top layer.** Do your best to keep the circles evenly sized, but don't worry if they're a bit uneven. Gently press the stack of disks together using a rolling pin. Cover the stack with plastic wrap and put in the freezer for 30 minutes—don't leave it longer than this.

8. **Prepare the baking sheet.** Line a baking sheet with parchment paper.

9. **Prepare the croissants.** On a lightly floured work surface, roll out the stack of dough thinly into a large circle 14 to 15 inches (35–40cm) in diameter. Keep moving the dough around so it doesn't stick to your work surface. If the dough starts to stick, dust with a little more flour. Try to make the circle as evenly shaped as possible. Using a sharp knife, cut the circle into quarters, and then cut each quarter into 3 equal "triangles," creating 12 equal triangles of dough in total. Each triangle of dough will form one croissant.

10. **Roll up the croissants.** Starting at the wide base of the triangle, roll each croissant up tightly, all the way until you get to the pointed end. Gently bend the croissant into a crescent shape. Place the rolled croissants on the prepared baking sheet, leaving a good amount of space between each one.

11. **Allow the croissants to rise.** Cover the croissants with plastic wrap and allow to rise at room temperature for 3 hours or until doubled in size.

12. **Preheat the oven.** Preheat the oven to 400°F (200°C).

13. **Bake the croissants.** Gently brush the top surface of each croissant with beaten egg. Put the croissants into the preheated oven and bake for 5 minutes. After 5 minutes, turn the oven down to 350°F (180°C). Continue baking for 8 to 10 minutes more until the croissants are golden brown in color.

14. **Serve.** Remove the croissants from the oven and allow to cool for 5 minutes. Serve while they're still warm.

Soft & Fluffy Milk Bread

PREP: 20 minutes, plus 3 hours to rise // **COOK:** 18 minutes // **YIELD:** 12 rolls

INGREDIENTS

¾ cup + 3 tbsp (215g) whole milk, warmed

2 tsp (7g) active dry yeast

2½ cups (350g) all-purpose flour

3 tbsp (40g) granulated white sugar

1 tsp salt

2 tbsp (30g) unsalted butter, at room temperature

1 tbsp vegetable oil

½ tbsp cornstarch, for dusting

SPECIAL EQUIPMENT

Stand mixer with dough hook attachment

8 × 12-inch (20 × 30cm) glass or ceramic baking dish

Japanese milk bread is one of the softest, fluffiest breads ever created. This version is much simpler than the traditional method, but it captures much of what makes this kind of bread so special. These amazing, soft rolls will quickly become a staple in your family!

1. **Activate the yeast.** In a small bowl, incorporate the yeast into the warm milk and allow this mixture to sit for 5 minutes (see page 18).

2. **Mix the dry ingredients.** In the bowl of a stand mixer, whisk together the flour, sugar, and salt.

3. **Combine and knead the dough.** Add the yeast mixture to the dry ingredients. Using a dough hook attachment, mix on low to medium speed until the dough comes together, then increase the speed to high and continue kneading the dough for another 3 minutes. After 3 minutes, the dough should feel tacky to the touch and look smooth. If it seems dry, add an extra tablespoon of milk. Add the softened butter and continue kneading for 3 minutes more until the butter is fully incorporated and the dough is smooth.

4. **Let the dough rise.** Using wet hands, shape the dough into a ball. Lightly grease your bowl with oil and place the dough back into the bowl. Cover with a damp kitchen towel or with plastic wrap and allow the dough to rise for 2 to 3 hours at room temperature.

5. **Prepare the baking dish.** Line the baking dish with parchment paper.

6. **Shape the rolls.** Turn out the dough onto a lightly oiled work surface and divide it into 12 equal portions. Shape each portion into a ball and place into the prepared baking dish.

7. **Allow the rolls to rise again and preheat the oven.** Cover the rolls and allow to rise again at room temperature for 45 minutes to 1 hour. At the end of the rise time, preheat the oven to 320°F (160°C).

8. **Bake the rolls.** Dust the rolls with the cornstarch. Bake for 18 to 20 minutes. They will maintain a pale color when baked—they shouldn't brown too much.

9. **Serve.** Allow to cool for 5 minutes before serving. Serve warm.

> **MAKE AHEAD & FREEZE**
> Cooled rolls can be stored in a zip-top bag at room temperature for 1 to 2 days or in the freezer for up to 1 month. You can warm them up in the microwave or oven.

Soft Dinner Rolls

PREP: 20 minutes, plus 2 hours to rise // **COOK:** 20 minutes // **YIELD:** 8 to 12 dinner rolls

INGREDIENTS

FOR THE ROLLS

⅓ cup (80g) whole milk

⅓ cup (80g) water

1 large egg, at room temperature

2 tsp (7g) active dry yeast

2½ cups (350g) all-purpose flour

2 tbsp (30g) granulated white sugar

1½ tsp salt

2½ tbsp (40g) unsalted butter, melted, plus more for brushing the rolls

Oil, for greasing

FOR THE EGG WASH

1 medium egg, beaten

2 tbsp whole milk

SPECIAL EQUIPMENT

Stand mixer with dough hook attachment (recommended but not required)

8 × 6-inch (20 × 15cm) baking dish

VARIATIONS

Cheese bombs. When forming the rolls, before the second rise, place a cube of cheese in the middle of each roll. This will melt when the rolls bake, creating a gooey, cheesy center.

Bacon rolls. Before baking the rolls, sprinkle crispy bacon bits on top.

Garlic rolls. Crush a garlic clove into some melted butter. When the rolls come out of the oven, brush them with the garlic butter.

Nothing beats fresh homemade dinner rolls! These soft, fluffy rolls make a great side for any dish or are great eaten alone—yes, that's how I eat mine; and after making these, I bet you will too! I've also given you a few variations to liven them up when you want something a bit extra.

1. **Activate the yeast.** In a microwave-safe bowl, microwave the milk and water until lukewarm—about 30 to 40 seconds (don't let it get hot). Incorporate the egg and yeast and allow this mixture to sit for 5 minutes (see page 18).

2. **Mix the dry ingredients.** In the bowl of a stand mixer or large mixing bowl, whisk together the flour, sugar, and salt.

3. **Combine and knead the dough.** Using the dough hook attachment, mix the dry ingredients with the wet ingredients and the melted butter on low to medium speed until the dough comes together, then increase the speed to high and continue kneading the dough for another 3 minutes. After 3 minutes the dough should feel tacky to the touch and look smooth. (To make by hand, see page 19.)

4. **Let the dough rise.** Using wet hands, shape the dough into a ball. Lightly grease your bowl with ½ tablespoon of oil and place the dough back into the bowl. Cover with a damp kitchen towel or with plastic wrap and allow the dough to rise for 1 to 2 hours at room temperature or until doubled in size.

5. **Prepare the baking dish.** Generously butter the baking dish.

6. **Shape the rolls.** Turn the dough out onto a lightly floured work surface and divide it into 8 to 12 equal portions, depending on how large you want your rolls to be. Remove any excess flour and shape the dough portions into balls and place into the prepared baking dish, leaving some space between each roll.

7. **Allow the rolls to rise for a second time.** Cover the rolls and allow to rise again at room temperature for 45 minutes to 1 hour.

8. **Preheat the oven.** Preheat the oven to 350°F (180°C).

9. **Make the egg wash.** In a small bowl, whisk together the beaten egg and milk. Make sure to whisk well, so the egg is completely broken down into the milk.

10. **Bake the rolls.** Brush the rolls with the egg wash and bake for 18 to 20 minutes, until lightly golden in color

11. **Serve.** As soon as the rolls come out of the oven, brush with melted butter. Serve warm.

> **MAKE AHEAD & FREEZE**
> When cool, the rolls can be stored at room temperature in a zip-top bag for up to 2 days or frozen for up to 1 month. Warm them up in the microwave for 20 seconds or a low oven for 3 minutes.

MAKE AHEAD
Cinnamon rolls are best eaten fresh but can be stored in an airtight container at room temperature for a day or two. Reheat in the microwave.

The Fluffiest Cinnamon Rolls

PREP: 30 minutes, plus 2 hours to rise // **COOK:** 20 minutes, plus 5 minutes to cool // **YIELD:** 9 to 12 cinnamon rolls

INGREDIENTS

FOR THE DOUGH

¾ cup (180g) whole milk, warmed but not hot

1 medium egg, at room temperature

2 tsp (7g) active dry yeast

2¾ cups (380g) all-purpose flour

¼ cup (50g) granulated white sugar

½ tsp salt

4 tbsp (60g) unsalted butter, melted but not hot

½ tbsp vegetable oil, for greasing

FOR THE FILLING

4 tbsp (60g) unsalted butter, at room temperature

½ cup (100g) brown sugar (light or dark)

1 tbsp ground cinnamon

½ tbsp cornstarch

¼ tsp salt

FOR THE GLAZE

4oz (100g) Philadelphia cream cheese

⅓ cup (40g) powdered sugar

1 tsp vanilla extract

2 tbsp whole milk (optional)

SPECIAL EQUIPMENT

Stand mixer with dough hook attachment (recommended but not required)

The first time my mom and I had cinnamon rolls, we were at the mall. I was six years old, and we'd just arrived in the United States from a small town in Italy. The minute we walked in, I could smell the cinnamon and cream cheese. Not knowing what a mall was, I thought we were in a bakery! We immediately fell in love with the sweet, soft buns. Eventually, we figured out how to make these wonderful pastries ourselves—and this is our original recipe. Fluffy, sweet, and oh-so-comforting—nothing is better than homemade cinnamon rolls!

1. **Activate the yeast.** In a small bowl, whisk together the lukewarm milk and egg. Stir in the yeast and let sit for 5 minutes (see page 18).

2. **Mix the dry ingredients.** In the bowl of a stand mixer, whisk together the flour, sugar, and salt. Set aside.

3. **Combine and knead the dough.** To the dry ingredients, add the milk mixture and the melted butter. Use a rubber spatula or wooden spoon to roughly combine. Then, using the dough hook attachment, knead the dough on medium-low speed until it comes together. Increase the speed to high and continue kneading for another 3 minutes. After 3 minutes, the dough should feel tacky to the touch and look smooth. (To knead by hand, see page 19).

4. **Let dough rise.** Remove the dough from the bowl, and using wet hands shape the dough into a ball. Lightly grease the bowl with oil and place the dough back into the bowl. Cover with a damp kitchen towel or plastic wrap and allow the dough to rise at room temperature for 1 to 2 hours or until doubled in size.

5. **Prepare the filling.** In a medium bowl, combine the room-temperature butter, brown sugar, cinnamon, cornstarch, and salt.

6. **Make the rolls.** Turn out the dough onto a floured work surface and roll it into a rectangle. The dough should be about ¼ inch (6mm) thick. Spread the filling over the dough. Tightly roll the dough into a jelly roll shape and slice into 9 to 12 chunky cinnamon rolls, each about 2 to 3 inches (5–7.5cm) thick.

7. **Let the dough rise for a second time.** Grease a baking sheet well, and transfer the cinnamon rolls on to it. Cover with plastic wrap and allow to rise for 45 minutes.

8. **Preheat the oven.** Preheat the oven to 350°F (180°C).

9. **Make the glaze.** In a medium bowl, combine the cream cheese, powdered sugar, vanilla, and milk. If you prefer a thinner glaze, add more milk.

10. **Bake the rolls.** Once the cinnamon rolls have risen, bake in the preheated oven for 20 to 22 minutes.

11. **Glaze the cinnamon rolls.** As soon as the cinnamon rolls come out of the oven, smother them in as much glaze you like.

12. **Serve.** Allow to cool for 5 minutes, then enjoy warm.

English Muffins

(NO OVEN REQUIRED)

PREP: 20 minutes, plus 3 hours to rise // **COOK:** 12 minutes // **YIELD:** 6 muffins

INGREDIENTS

½ cup (120g) water

½ cup (120g) whole milk

2 tsp (7g) active dry yeast

2½ cups (350g) all-purpose flour

1 tsp salt

½ tbsp vegetable oil, for greasing

2 tbsp fine cornmeal

Butter, for the pan

SPECIAL EQUIPMENT

Stand mixer with dough hook attachment (recommended but not required)

One of my favorite breakfasts as a kid in New York was an English muffin with gooey melted Cheddar cheese. When I returned to Italy, I couldn't find English muffins anywhere (and to this day, Italy still doesn't have them). After much trial and error, I'm happy to share what I believe is one of the easiest and most delicious English muffin recipes—it doesn't even require an oven!

1. **Activate the yeast.** In a small, microwave-safe bowl or measuring cup, combine the milk and water. Microwave until lukewarm, about 30 to 40 seconds (don't let it get hot). Stir in the yeast and allow to sit for 5 minutes (see page 18).

2. **Mix the dry ingredients.** In the bowl of a stand mixer, whisk together the flour and salt.

3. **Combine and knead the dough.** Using the dough hook attachment on medium-low speed, combine the dry ingredients with the yeast mixture until the dough comes together. Increase the speed to high and continue kneading for another 3 minutes. After 3 minutes, the dough should feel tacky to the touch and look smooth. (To make the dough by hand, see the kneading section on page 19.)

4. **Let the dough rise.** Remove the dough from the bowl, and using wet hands, shape the dough into a ball. Lightly grease the bowl with oil and place the dough back into the bowl. Cover with a damp kitchen towel or plastic wrap and allow the dough to rise for 2 to 3 hours at room temperature.

5. **Prepare the baking sheets.** Dust two baking sheets with cornmeal.

6. **Shape the muffins.** Turn the dough out onto a lightly floured work surface and divide it into 6 equal portions. Shape the dough portions into balls and press them down. Each muffin should be about 3 to 3½ inches (8–9cm) across, and about 1¼ inches (3cm) thick. Place the muffins onto the prepared baking sheets.

7. **Allow the muffins to rise again.** Cover the muffins and allow to rise again for about 45 minutes.

8. **Cook the muffins.** Preheat a large skillet on a low heat for a few minutes. Add a tablespoon of butter, allow it to melt, and cook the muffins in batches for 5 or 6 minutes on each side. Add a little more butter each time you add a new batch of muffins to the pan.

9. **Serve.** Allow to cool for 10 minutes before serving. They're great split open and toasted.

MAKE AHEAD & FREEZE
Store covered at room temperature. Baked English muffins can be split and frozen—toast the muffin halves right from the freezer.

Buttery Soft Pretzels

PREP: 20 minutes, plus 2 hours to rise // **COOK:** 10 minutes // **YIELD:** 6 large pretzels

INGREDIENTS

FOR THE PRETZELS

½ cup (120g) warm water

¼ cup (60g) warm milk

2 tsp (7g) active dry yeast

2 cups (280g) all-purpose flour

2 tbsp (25g) granulated white sugar

1 tsp salt

2 tbsp (30g) unsalted butter, melted, plus more to coat

½ tbsp vegetable oil, to grease the bowl

1 egg white, beaten

FOR THE ALKALINE WATER BATH

6 cups (1.5 liters) water

⅓ cup (60g) baking soda

SPECIAL EQUIPMENT

Stand mixer with dough hook attachment (recommended but not required)

VARIATION

Cinnamon sugar pretzels. On a large plate, mix white granulated sugar and ground cinnamon to taste. After brushing each warm pretzel with melted butter, drop it into the cinnamon sugar and coat it all over.

MAKE AHEAD

Cooled pretzels can be stored at room temperature in a resealable zip-top bag for 1 to 2 days. Warm them up in the microwave or oven before eating.

Pretzels aren't a thing in Italy, so the first time I tried them was at Penn Station before boarding the train—every New Yorker knows the ones I mean. I've been hooked on soft pretzels ever since. You'll be amazed at how buttery and fragrant these pretzels are, and how easy they are to make at home.

1. **Activate the yeast.** In a small bowl, combine the warm water, milk, and yeast. Allow this mixture to sit for 5 minutes (see page 18).

2. **Mix the dry ingredients.** In the bowl of a stand mixer, whisk together the flour, sugar, and salt.

3. **Combine and knead the dough.** Add the yeast mixture and melted butter to the dry ingredients. Using the dough hook attachment, mix on low to medium speed until the dough comes together. Increase the speed to high and continue kneading the dough for another 3 minutes. After 3 minutes, the dough should feel tacky to the touch and look smooth. (To make the dough by hand, see page 19.)

4. **Let the dough rise.** Remove the dough from the bowl, and using wet hands, shape the dough into a ball. Lightly grease the bowl with oil and return the dough to the bowl. Cover with a damp kitchen towel or with plastic wrap and allow the dough to rise for 1 to 2 hours at room temperature, or until doubled in size.

5. **Prepare the baking sheets.** Line two baking sheets with parchment paper.

6. **Shape the pretzels.** Turn out the dough onto a lightly floured work surface and divide it into 6 equal portions. Shake off any excess flour. Using your hands, roll each portion of dough into a long, thin rope about 16 inches (40cm) long and ½ inch (1.3cm) thick. If the dough pulls back, cover and let it relax for 20 minutes. Shape the dough into a classic pretzel shape or another shape of your choosing.

7. **Allow the pretzels to rise again.** Place each pretzel on a square of parchment paper. This will make it easy to move around later (see page 19). Cover with a clean kitchen towel and allow to rise again for about 40 minutes.

8. **Preheat the oven.** Preheat the oven to 400°F (200°C).

9. **Dip the pretzels.** In a large, deep saucepan, combine the water and baking soda and bring to a boil. Turn off the heat, and lower each pretzel with its parchment paper into the water bath for about 15 seconds (see page 19). Using tongs, remove the parchment paper. The pretzels will float, so spoon water over the top of each pretzel. Using a large, slotted spoon, remove the pretzels and place on the prepared baking sheets, leaving space in between. Brush each pretzel with the beaten egg white.

10. **Bake the pretzels.** Bake for 8 to 10 minutes or until golden brown. While they're baking, melt another 2 to 3 tablespoons of butter in a small bowl. Remove the pretzels from the oven, and while still hot, brush with the melted butter.

11. **Serve.** Allow to cool for about 5 minutes removing the parchment paper. Serve warm.

Mom's Focaccia

PREP: 1 hour, plus 2 hours 30 minutes to rise // **COOK:** 20 minutes // **YIELD:** 1 focaccia; serves 8 to 10

INGREDIENTS

FOR THE DOUGH

1 medium high-starch potato like Yukon Gold, peeled and halved, about 4½oz (125g) when peeled

1 cup (240g) lukewarm water

2 tsp (7g) active dry yeast

2 tbsp olive oil, plus more for greasing

3 cups (420g) all-purpose flour

2 tsp salt

FOR THE TOPPINGS

3 tbsp tomato sauce (passata)

1 clove garlic, minced

½ cup cherry tomatoes, halved

¼ cup pitted olives, halved

Handful of roughly chopped fresh herbs (basil, thyme, oregano)

1 tsp flaked sea salt

2 tbsp olive oil, for drizzling.

SPECIAL EQUIPMENT

Potato ricer

Stand mixer with dough hook attachment (recommended but not required)

13 × 9-inch (33 × 22cm) pan at least 2 inches (5cm) deep

VARIATION

Potato and rosemary focaccia. For the toppings, add thinly sliced raw potato (the slices should be thin enough to almost see through), lots of rosemary, and drizzle generously with olive oil.

The iconic Italian bread, focaccia, has endless variations across Italy. I wanted to share my mom's version with you because it's truly my favorite version of this amazing bread.

1. **Make the mashed potatoes.** Place the halved potato in a saucepan, add cold water to cover, and bring to a boil over high heat. When boiling, reduce heat to medium and cook for 20 to 25 minutes until tender. Drain, and allow the steam to escape from the potatoes for 10 minutes until dry. Then mash until smooth (use a potato ricer if you have one—it's important there are no lumps). Cool for at least 20 minutes. You should have about ½ cup of mashed potato.

2. **Activate the yeast.** In a small bowl, combine the warm water and yeast. Add the olive oil, and allow the mixture to sit for 5 minutes (see page 18).

3. **Mix the dry ingredients.** In a stand mixer (or in large mixing bowl), whisk together the flour and salt. Add the mashed potato, and gently fork it through the flour.

4. **Combine and knead the dough.** Add the yeast mixture. Using the dough hook attachment, mix on medium-low speed until the dough comes together. Then increase the speed to high and continue kneading the dough for another 3 minutes. After 3 minutes the dough should feel tacky to the touch and look smooth. (To knead the dough by hand, see page 19.)

5. **Let the dough rise.** Remove the dough from the bowl and, using wet hands, shape the dough into a ball. Lightly grease the bowl with ½ tablespoon of oil and place the dough back into the bowl. Cover with a damp kitchen towel or with plastic wrap and allow the dough to rise for 1 to 1½ hours at room temperature.

6. **Prepare the baking tray.** Grease a 13 × 9-inch (33 × 23cm) baking pan generously with olive oil (about 3 tablespoons of oil).

7. **Shape the focaccia.** Turn out the dough directly into the baking tray and push it out into all the corners to fill the tray completely.

8. **Allow the dough to rise again.** Cover the tray with plastic wrap and allow the dough to rise again for 1½ hours.

9. **Preheat the oven.** Preheat the oven to 400°F (200°C).

10. **Prepare the focaccia for baking.** Wet your hands, then gently make indentations in the surface of the dough using your fingers. Mix the minced garlic into the tomato sauce. Spread in a thin layer over the top of the dough, all the way to the edges. Sprinkle over the tomatoes, olives, herbs, and flaked salt. Push the tomatoes and olives gently into the indentations in the dough. Drizzle the olive oil over the dough.

11. **Bake the focaccia.** Bake the focaccia for 20 to 25 minutes or until light golden brown.

12. **Serve.** Allow to cool for 5 minutes before serving warm.

MAKE AHEAD
When cool, store
covered at room
temperature for up
to 2 days. You can
rewarm the focaccia
in the oven.

Rustic No-Knead Bread

PREP: 10 minutes, plus 3 hours to rise // **COOK:** 45 minutes, plus 2 hours to cool // **YIELD:** 1 small loaf

INGREDIENTS

1¼ cups (300g) lukewarm water

2 tsp (7g) active dry yeast

3 cups (420g) all-purpose flour, plus more for dusting

2½ tsp salt

SPECIAL EQUIPMENT

Dutch oven

The area surrounding Rome in Italy is famous for its crunchy, open-textured bread. Every family has their own version, and every family thinks theirs is the best! This is my family's version. It's one of the easiest, most delicious breads you'll ever make—and there's no kneading required.

1. **Activate the yeast.** In a small bowl, incorporate the yeast into the water and allow this mixture to sit for 5 minutes (see page 18).

2. **Mix the dry ingredients.** In a large bowl, whisk together the flour and salt.

3. **Combine and mix the dough.** Add the yeast mixture to the flour and mix until there are no more dry patches of flour. The dough should be soft and sticky—just a bit too wet to knead. If your dough seems too dry, add more water 1 tablespoon at a time.

4. **Let the dough rise.** Cover the bowl with plastic wrap and leave at room temperature to rise for 3 hours or until doubled in volume. Every half hour, wet your hands with water, and gently lift the dough and stretch it out, then fold it over on itself. (See page 259 for photos of this folding process.) Do this two or three times in each "folding session," stretching the dough from different sides. This process creates the beginning of air pockets that will expand when the bread bakes to give an open texture with big holes. If you want, you can put the bowl in the fridge for up to 48 hours. The longer you leave the dough, the more flavor will develop, but it will make a great loaf even after the initial 3-hour rise.

5. **Preheat the oven and the Dutch oven.** Put the Dutch oven in the oven and preheat the oven to 450°F (230°C). Once the oven has reached temperature, continue preheating the Dutch oven for 5 to 10 minutes.

6. **Bake the bread.** Carefully (it's hot!) sprinkle the inside of the preheated Dutch oven with flour. Then, using wet hands, give the dough a final three folds. Moving quickly, pick up the dough and gently drop it into your preheated Dutch oven. Using a sharp knife, cut a slash into the top of the dough and sprinkle with a teaspoon of flour. Bake in the oven with the lid on for 30 to 35 minutes. Then remove the lid, lower the oven temperature to 400°F (200°C), and continue baking for another 10 to 20 minutes until the top of the loaf is a golden brown and looks crispy and crunchy.

7. **Allow the bread to cool.** Remove the bread from the Dutch oven and allow to cool upside down on a wire rack. Allow the bread to cool completely; this might take a couple of hours.

8. **Serve.** Slice the bread when it's completely cool. Even though it's tempting, don't cut into the loaf while it's still warm.

MAKE AHEAD & FREEZE

Dough can be made 1 day in advance (see page 18). Bread can be stored loosely wrapped in paper for 1 or 2 days at room temperature. To freeze, cover tightly in plastic wrap. Bread can be kept frozen for up to 1 month.

Two-Ingredient Flatbreads

PREP: 10 minutes, plus 15 minutes to rest dough // **COOK:** 8 minutes // **YIELD:** 4 flatbreads

INGREDIENTS

1 cup (140g) all-purpose flour, plus more for dusting

⅓ cup (85g) water

Salt, for sprinkling

Chopped fresh herbs (optional), for sprinkling

SPECIAL EQUIPMENT

Electric griddle (recommended but not required)

VARIATIONS

Garlic and herb flatbreads.
Melt 1 tablespoon of butter in a small pan and add a crushed garlic clove and 1 tablespoon of roughly chopped fresh soft herbs of your choice. Brush the flatbreads with the garlicky, herby butter mixture as soon as they're cooked.

Whole wheat flatbreads.
Use a mixture of half all-purpose flour and half whole wheat flour. You might need to add an extra tablespoon of water to the dough.

I make these flatbreads for lunch almost every day—no exaggeration! If you've never made bread before, this is the perfect way to get started. These flatbreads are so quick and easy to make. Fill them however you like or use them to dip in sauce. If you're a real carb lover, they're great on their own with a little salt.

1. **Mix the ingredients.** In a large bowl, combine the flour and water. Mix with a spoon to form a rough dough.

2. **Knead the dough.** Turn out the dough onto a lightly dusted work surface and knead for 3 to 5 minutes or until the dough becomes elastic.

3. **Divide the dough.** Divide the dough into 4 equal parts and roll into balls. Dust each ball with flour.

4. **Allow the dough to rest.** Place the balls on a plate, cover with a damp kitchen towel or plastic wrap, and allow to rest for about 15 minutes.

5. **Roll out the flatbreads.** On a lightly dusted work surface, roll out the balls into 6- to 7-inch (15–18cm) rounds. If the dough starts to stick, dust with a little more flour.

6. **Cook the flatbreads.** Heat the dry electric griddle or a large skillet to medium-high heat. Shake off any excess flour from the dough. Working with one at a time, add a flatbread to the griddle and cook for about 30 seconds. Flip and cook for 1 minute. When brown spots appear on the underside, it's cooked through. Flip again and cook for 30 seconds more.

7. **Serve.** Sprinkle with a little salt and serve immediately or wrap them in a clean kitchen towel to keep warm

> **MAKE AHEAD**
> When cool, the flatbreads can be stored at room temperature in a zip-top bag. Reheat in the microwave for 10 to 15 seconds.

Easy Churros

PREP: 20 minutes // **COOK:** 5 minutes // **YIELD:** 15 churros

INGREDIENTS

1 cup (240g) whole milk

1 tbsp (15g) unsalted butter

1 cup (140g) all-purpose flour

½ tsp salt

2 large eggs, at room temperature

Neutral cooking oil, for frying (about 1 quart / 1 liter)

Granulated white sugar, for coating

Ground cinnamon, for coating

SPECIAL EQUIPMENT

Dutch oven or heavy-bottomed pot

Piping bag with a star tip

Instant-read thermometer

If there's one recipe that's worth deep frying, it's this! Coated in cinnamon and sugar, crispy on the outside, and soft and tender on the inside, these pastries will quickly become one of your favorite treats. They're just like the ones you might have had at state fairs!

1. **Make the dough**. In a saucepan over medium heat, bring the milk and butter to a gentle boil. Once the mixture begins to boil, turn off the heat and stir in the flour and salt. Mix until a smooth dough forms. It should pull away from the sides of the pan. Allow the dough to cool for 10 minutes and then add the eggs one at a time, mixing thoroughly after each addition. Be patient at this stage—the mixture will separate at first, but keep mixing until each egg is fully incorporated. Transfer the dough to a piping bag with a star tip.

2. **Heat the oil.** In a large Dutch oven or heavy-bottomed pot, heat about 3 inches (7.5cm) of oil to 350°F (180°C).

3. **Fry the churros.** Working in batches, carefully pipe the churros into the hot oil, cutting them off the end of the piping tip with a pair of kitchen scissors to lower them gently in the oil. I make my churros about 4 inches (10cm) long, and I fry them in batches of 4 to 6 at a time. Fry each batch for 2 to 4 minutes or until golden brown. (For more tips on deep frying, see page 25.)

4. **Toss in cinnamon sugar.** In a large, shallow plate, combine the sugar and cinnamon. Remove the churros from the oil with a slotted spoon, drain on paper towels, and then toss them in the cinnamon sugar. Use as much or as little cinnamon as you like—it's entirely up to your personal taste.

5. **Serve.** Serve immediately while the churros are still hot.

Flour Tortillas

PREP: 15 minutes, plus 1 hour to rest // **COOK:** 25 minutes // **YIELD:** 12 small or 6 large tortillas

INGREDIENTS

2½ cups (360g) all-purpose flour, plus extra for dusting

¾ tsp salt

3 tbsp (40g) refined coconut oil

¾ cup (180g) warm water

SPECIAL EQUIPMENT

Electric griddle (recommended but not required)

Homemade flour tortillas taste a million times better than store-bought—they're an entirely different product with an amazing flavor and soft, pillowy texture. You'll be surprised how quickly and easily these come together, and they freeze beautifully. Traditionally, they're made using lard, but unfortunately store-bought lard isn't the right product, and in my opinion not worth using. Here, I'm using my preferred substitute—coconut oil.

1. **Mix the ingredients.** To a large bowl, add the flour and salt. Mix with a spoon to distribute the salt. Add the coconut oil and rub into the flour using your fingers. Add the warm water and mix well with a spoon until the dough begins to come together.

2. **Knead and rest the dough.** Turn the mixture out onto a work surface and knead until the dough has come together to form a smooth ball, about 10 minutes. Place the dough back in the bowl, cover, and let it rest for 30 minutes.

3. **Divide the dough and let it rest again.** Divide the dough into 12 equal parts if you're making small tortillas or 6 equal parts for large tortillas. Roll into balls. Dust each dough ball with flour. Cover the dough balls and allow to rest for another 30 minutes. (All this resting time is important because it will make it much easier to roll out the tortillas thinly, and it will help your tortillas "puff" when you cook them.)

4. **Roll out the tortillas.** On a lightly floured surface, roll out the dough balls into rounds. If the tortillas start to stick, dust with a little more flour. Roll out the tortillas as thinly as you can. Small tortillas should be about 6 inches (15cm) in diameter. Large tortillas should be about 10 inches (25cm) in diameter. Ideally, they should be rolled thinly enough to almost see through them if you hold them up to the light.

5. **Cook the tortillas.** Preheat the griddle or skillet to a medium-high heat. Cook the tortillas one at a time. Add a tortilla to the griddle and cook for about 15 seconds on one side, then flip and cook for 15 seconds on the second side. Then flip again and cook 45 seconds to 1 minute. The dough should bubble up a bit, and ideally, will really puff up. If it doesn't, increase the heat. Flip the tortilla one final time and cook for another 45 seconds to 1 minute. Repeat for all the tortillas.

6. **Serve.** Serve immediately or keep them warm wrapped in a clean dish towel.

MAKE AHEAD & FREEZE
Once cool, tortillas can be frozen in a zip-top bag and kept for up to 2 months.

Snacking Cakes

Cakes aren't just for celebrating. Sometimes you just crave a delicious cake that doesn't involve multiple layers and perfect frosting! These cakes are for those days when you want something sweet without too much fuss. You'll find blender recipes, one-bowl recipes, and simple ingredient lists to get you from no cake to cake as quickly as possible.

Blender Chocolate Snacking Cake

PREP: 5 minutes // **COOK:** 25 minutes, plus 1 hour to cool // **YIELD:** 1 cake; serves 8 to 10

INGREDIENTS

FOR THE CAKE

4 tbsp (½ stick / 60g) unsalted butter, melted

½ cup + 2 tbsp whole milk (150g), at room temperature

1 large egg

¾ cup (150g) white granulated sugar

½ cup (50g) unsweetened cocoa powder

½ cup + 2 tbsp (80g) all-purpose flour

½ tsp baking soda

1 tsp lemon juice or vinegar

¼ tsp salt

FOR THE GLAZE

7 tbsp (50g) unsweetened cocoa powder, sifted

7 tbsp (50g) powdered sugar

7 tbsp (100g) whole milk

¼ tsp salt

SPECIAL EQUIPMENT

7-inch (18cm) round cake pan

Blender

VARIATION

To make cupcakes, line a 12-cup muffin tin with paper liners. Divide the batter evenly among the paper liners. Bake for 18 to 22 minutes (do the toothpick test to check when they're ready). Allow to cool completely before glazing. The recipe makes 9 to 10 cupcakes.

When you want to whip up a cake quickly, my blender recipes are a great way to go. You simply add the ingredients to a blender, whizz them up for 10 seconds, and that's the batter made! This recipe includes instructions for an easy chocolate glaze, but you can decorate this cake however you want.

1. **Preheat the oven and prepare the pan.** Preheat the oven to 320°F (160°C). Grease and flour a 7-inch (18cm) round cake pan and line the bottom with parchment paper.

2. **Make the cake batter.** Add the ingredients to the blender in this exact order: milk, butter, egg, sugar, cocoa powder, flour, baking soda, lemon juice (add directly on top of the baking soda), and salt. Pulse the blender on and off at medium-high speed for 8 to 10 seconds (no more than this). At this point, you'll most likely have some unmixed ingredients on the sides or bottom of the blender, but don't continue to blend. Instead, using a rubber spatula, scrape the sides and bottom of the blender to finish combining all the ingredients.

3. **Bake the cake.** Transfer the batter to the prepared cake pan and bake for 25 to 30 minutes. Do the toothpick test (see page 15). When the toothpick comes out clean, the cake is ready.

4. **Cool the cake.** Allow the cake to sit in the pan for 5 minutes, then gently turn it over onto a cooling rack, remove the parchment paper, and allow to cool completely.

5. **Make the glaze.** In a medium bowl, whisk together the cocoa powder, powdered sugar, milk, and salt until the mixture is well combined and has a smooth, runny texture. Taste the glaze and add more sugar if you prefer it sweeter. If the glaze is a bit gritty, microwave for 45 seconds, and whisk again. Allow to cool before glazing the cake.

6. **Glaze the cake.** Put the cake on a wire rack and place the rack on a piece of parchment paper (the parchment paper will catch excess glaze and make cleanup easy). Pour the glaze over the top of the cake. Using a rubber spatula, gently push the glaze over the top surface of the cake and allow it to run down the sizes. Pick up the wire rack and gently tap it down onto the parchment paper. Repeat until the glaze has leveled out and the sides of the cake are covered.

7. **Serve**. Using two spatulas, carefully transfer to a serving plate. You need to be careful with this step because the cake is very soft and moist.

MAKE AHEAD & FREEZE
The cake will keep covered at room temperature for 2 to 3 days. To freeze, wrap tightly in plastic wrap and store in the freezer for up to 4 weeks (see page 14).

VARIATION

For a more traditional presentation, you can serve this cake in the cake pan, a bit like tiramisu. Clean the cake pan after you've removed the cake. Then, once the cake has cooled, put it back in the clean pan and drench with the milk bath. Decorate with the whipped cream.

Vanilla Tres Leches Cake

PREP: 15 minutes // **COOK:** 20 minutes, plus 1 hour to chill // **YIELD:** 1 cake, serves 6

INGREDIENTS

FOR THE CAKE

4 egg whites,
  at room temperature

½ tsp lemon juice or
  ¼ tsp cream of tartar

½ cup (100g) granulated
  white sugar

2 egg yolks

½ cup (120g) whole milk,
  at room temperature

1 tsp vanilla extract

¾ cup (100g) all-purpose
  flour

1 tsp baking powder

¼ tsp salt

FOR THE MILK BATH

¼ cup (80g) sweetened
  condensed milk

½ cup (120g) heavy cream

½ cup (120g) whole milk

1 tsp vanilla extract

¼ tsp salt

FOR THE TOPPING

1 cup (250g) heavy cream,
  cold

2 tbsp granulated white sugar

1 tsp vanilla extract

Fresh fruit (optional)

SPECIAL EQUIPMENT

7-inch (18cm) square
  cake pan

Handheld or stand mixer

MAKE AHEAD & FREEZE

The assembled cake can
be refrigerated for up to
2 days. Before soaking
the cake in the milk bath,
you can wrap it tightly in
plastic wrap and freeze
for up to 1 month.

Tres leches cake is so delicious, I couldn't help but include my recipe for it. For me, it's the perfect summer cake. It has an incredible milky, melt-in-your-mouth texture—and just like a glass of milk, it's best served right from the fridge. It's hard to be sure exactly when and where this cake originated, but the version we know today is loved throughout Latin America.

1. **Preheat the oven and prepare the pan.** Preheat the oven to 320°F (160°C). Grease and flour a 7-inch (18cm) square cake pan and line with parchment paper.

2. **Whip the egg whites.** In a stand mixer fitted with a whisk attachment (or in a large clean glass or metal bowl, using a handheld mixer), add the egg whites and either the lemon juice or the cream of tartar. Whip the egg whites until frothy. Then, with the mixer running, add the sugar 1 tablespoon at a time. When the egg whites have reached the stiff peak stage, stop whipping. (See Whipping Egg Whites, page 23.) Set aside.

3. **Make the cake batter.** In a large bowl, combine the egg yolks, milk, and vanilla. Sift in the flour, baking powder, and salt, and stir to combine. Stop mixing when no more spots of flour are visible. Gently fold in the whipped egg whites, making sure to retain as much air as you can. (See Folding, page 25.) Pour the cake batter into the prepared cake pan.

4. **Bake the cake.** Bake for 20 to 25 minutes. Do the toothpick test (see page 15). If the toothpick comes out clean, it's ready.

5. **Cool the cake.** Allow the cake to sit in the pan for 5 minutes. It will pull away from the sides and slightly deflate as the egg whites settle. Then gently turn it out onto a cooling rack, remove the parchment paper, and allow to cool completely.

6. **Make the milk bath.** To a large liquid measuring cup, add the sweetened condensed milk, heavy cream, milk, vanilla, and salt. Whisk to combine all the ingredients.

7. **Soak the cake.** Clean the cake pan you used to bake the cake and line with a piece of parchment paper, leaving an overhang. (This will make it easy to lift the soaked cake later.) Put the cake back in the pan on top of the parchment paper. Using a fork, poke holes all over the surface of the cake. Pour the milk bath mixture over the cake and refrigerate for 1 hour.

8. **Make the topping.** In a medium bowl, add the heavy cream, sugar, and vanilla. Whip the mixture until it reaches the medium peak stage and just holds its shape. (See Whipping Cream, page 23.) Be careful not to overwhip.

9. **Assemble the cake.** Gently lift the cake out of the cake pan and onto a serving plate. Spread the whipped cream over the top of the cake as evenly as you can.

10. **Serve.** Optionally, trim the edges of the cake. Cut into 6 equal rectangular pieces and serve. Top with any fresh fruit of your choice, if using.

Chocolate Tres Leches Cake

PREP: 15 minutes // **COOK:** 20 minutes, plus 1 hour to chill // **YIELD:** 1 cake; serves 6

INGREDIENTS

FOR THE CAKE

3 egg whites, at room temperature

½ tsp lemon juice or ¼ tsp cream of tartar

¾ cup (150g) granulated white sugar

5 tbsp (35g) unsweetened cocoa powder

½ cup (120g) whole milk

5 tbsp (70g) unsalted butter, melted and cooled slightly

3 egg yolks, at room temperature

¾ cup (100g) all-purpose flour

1½ tsp baking powder

¼ tsp salt

FOR THE MILK BATH

1 tbsp dark chocolate chips

2 tbsp unsweetened cocoa powder

½ cup (120g) whole milk

¼ cup (60g) heavy cream, cold

½ cup (120g) sweetened condensed milk, cold

¼ tsp salt

FOR THE TOPPING

6 tbsp dark chocolate chips

1 cup (250g) heavy cream

1 tbsp granulated white sugar

SPECIAL EQUIPMENT

7-inch (18cm) square cake pan

Handheld or stand mixer

After discovering tres leches cake, I couldn't resist making a chocolate version. The idea of drenching a cake in chocolate milk sounded very nostalgic to me, as well as amazing.

1. **Preheat the oven and prepare the pan.** Preheat the oven to 320°F (160°C). Grease and flour a 7-inch (18cm) cake pan and line with parchment paper.

2. **Whip the egg whites.** To a stand mixer fitted with a whisk attachment (or in a large clean glass or metal bowl, using a handheld mixer), add the egg whites and either the lemon juice or the cream of tartar. Whip the egg whites until frothy. Then, with the mixer running, add the sugar 1 tablespoon at a time. When the egg whites have reached the stiff peak stage, stop whipping.

3. **Make the cake batter.** To a large bowl, add the cocoa powder and milk. Heat in the microwave for 40 seconds, and then mix well. Add the melted butter and stir. Now add the egg yolks and mix quickly. Sift in the flour, baking powder, and salt and stir to combine. Stop mixing when no more spots of flour are visible. Gently fold in the whipped egg whites (see page 23), trying to retain as much air as possible. Pour the cake batter into the prepared cake pan.

4. **Bake the cake.** Bake the cake for 20 to 25 minutes. Do the toothpick test (see page 15). If the toothpick comes out clean, it's ready.

5. **Cool the cake.** Allow the cake to sit in the pan for 5 minutes. It might pull away from the sides and slightly deflate as the egg whites settle. Then gently turn it out onto a cooling rack, remove the parchment paper, and allow to cool completely.

6. **Make the milk bath.** To a large glass measuring cup, add the chocolate chips, cocoa powder, and milk. Heat in the microwave until the chocolate has melted, stirring every 30 seconds. Add the cold heavy cream, sweetened condensed milk, and salt, and whisk to combine.

7. **Soak the cake.** Line the cake pan you used to bake the sponge cake with a piece of parchment paper, leaving an overhang. Put the sponge cake on top of the parchment paper. Use a fork to gently poke holes all over the surface of the cake. Pour the chocolate milk mixture over the cake and refrigerate for 1 hour.

8. **Make the topping.** In a medium, microwave-safe bowl, microwave the chocolate chips and half of the heavy cream, stirring every 30 seconds, until the chocolate chips have melted. Add the sugar and stir to dissolve. Add the remaining heavy cream and stir to combine. Refrigerate until cold. Once completely cold, use a mixer to whip the mixture until it reaches the medium peak stage (see page 23) and just holds its shape. Be careful not to overwhip.

9. **Assemble the cake.** Gently lift the cake out of the cake pan and onto a serving plate. Spread the chocolate whipped cream over the top of the cake as evenly as you can.

10. **Serve.** Trim the edges if desired and cut into 6 equal pieces.

MAKE AHEAD & FREEZE

The assembled cake can be stored in the refrigerator for up to 2 days.

The unsoaked cake can be made ahead, wrapped tightly and plastic wrap, and frozen for up to 1 month (see page 14).

Incredibly Moist Blender Carrot Cake

PREP: 5 minutes // **COOK:** 22 minutes, plus 1 hour to cool // **YIELD:** 1 cake; serves 6 to 9

INGREDIENTS

FOR THE CAKE

1½ medium carrots (115g), peeled and cut into large chunks

½ cup (100g) neutral oil, such as canola or vegetable

1 large egg

½ cup (120g) whole milk, at room temperature

½ cup (100g) brown sugar (light or dark)

1 cup (150g) all-purpose flour

¼ tsp salt

1 tsp ground cinnamon

1 tsp vanilla extract

¾ tsp baking powder

¼ tsp baking soda

½ tsp white wine vinegar or apple cider vinegar

FOR THE FROSTING

6oz (150g) Philadelphia cream cheese, cold

½ cup (60g) powdered sugar

1 tsp vanilla extract

SPECIAL EQUIPMENT

7-inch (18cm) square cake pan

Blender

Handheld mixer or stand mixer

This might be the easiest ever carrot cake recipe! It's so easy and delicious, you'll want to make it every day. The cake batter comes together in less than one minute—no grating of carrot required.

1. **Preheat the oven and prepare the pan.** Preheat the oven to 320°F (160°C). Grease and flour the cake pan and line the bottom with parchment paper.

2. **Make the cake batter.** In a high-speed blender, pulse the carrots until finely shredded. Add the remaining ingredients into the blender in this order: oil, egg, milk, sugar, flour, salt, cinnamon, vanilla, baking powder, baking soda, and vinegar (add the vinegar directly onto the baking soda). Pulse the blender on and off at medium-high speed for 8 to 10 seconds (no more than this). At this point, you'll most likely have some unmixed ingredients on the sides or bottom of the blender, but don't continue to blend. Instead, using a rubber spatula, scrape the sides and bottom of the blender to finish combining all the ingredients.

3. **Bake the cake.** Transfer the batter to the prepared cake pan and bake for 22 to 25 minutes. Do the toothpick test (see page 15). When the toothpick comes out clean, the cake is ready.

4. **Cool the cake.** Allow the cake to sit in the pan for 5 minutes, then gently turn it over onto a cooling rack, remove the parchment paper, and allow to cool completely.

5. **Make the frosting.** In a stand mixer with a whisk attachment (or in a medium bowl, if using a handheld mixer), beat the cream cheese, powdered sugar, and vanilla extract until everything is well combined and the frosting has a loose, creamy texture.

6. **Frost the cake.** Spread the frosting over the top of the cooled cake.

VARIATION

To make cupcakes, line a 12-cup muffin tin with paper liners. Divide the batter evenly among the paper liners. Bake for 18 to 20 minutes (do the toothpick test to check when they're ready). Allow to cool completely before frosting. The recipe makes 10 to 12 cupcakes.

MAKE AHEAD & FREEZE

This cake can be kept in the refrigerator, covered, for up to 3 days. Take it out of the fridge 20 minutes before serving. To freeze, wrap tightly in plastic wrap and store in the freezer for up to 4 weeks (see page 14).

Banana Custard Cake

PREP: 15 minutes // **COOK:** 20 minutes, plus 1 hour to cool // **YIELD:** 1 cake; serves 9

INGREDIENTS

FOR THE CUSTARD

¼ cup + 2 tbsp (80g) granulated white sugar

2½ tbsp cornstarch

¼ tsp salt

1⅓ cup (330g) whole milk

2 medium eggs

1 tsp vanilla extract

FOR THE CAKE

4 egg whites, at room temperature

½ tsp lemon juice or ¼ tsp cream of tartar

⅓ cup + 1 tbsp (85g) granulated white sugar

1 medium ripe banana (4oz / 115g), plus optional extra slices of banana for topping

2 egg yolks

½ cup whole milk (120g), at room temperature

1 tsp vanilla extract

¾ cup + 1 tbsp (120g) all-purpose flour

1 tsp baking powder

¼ tsp salt

SPECIAL EQUIPMENT

7-inch (18cm) square cake pan

Handheld mixer or stand mixer

MAKE AHEAD

This cake can be stored in the fridge covered, for up to 2 days (see page 14). If topping with fresh banana, add this just before serving.

If you love banana bread like I do, you'll really love this banana cake! Think of it as the angel food cake version of banana bread. It has a super-soft texture and is topped with a delicious layer of vanilla custard. It's so good, I would say—ditch the banana bread and make this instead! Except why choose when you can have both? (See Moist Blender Banana Bread, page 72.)

1. **Prepare the cake pan.** Grease and flour a 7-inch (18cm) square cake pan and line with parchment paper.

2. **Make the custard.** In a large saucepan, off the heat, whisk together the sugar, cornstarch, and salt. Add the milk and eggs and whisk to combine. Gently bring the mixture to a simmer over medium-low heat, stirring continuously to make sure nothing burns on the bottom or sides of the pan. Stir until the mixture thickens (less than a minute from the moment it starts to simmer). Turn off the heat, add the vanilla, and whisk to combine. Transfer the custard to a medium bowl and cover the surface with plastic wrap to prevent a skin forming. Refrigerate for at least 1 hour.

3. **Preheat the oven.** Preheat the oven to 320°F (160°C).

4. **Whip the egg whites.** To a stand mixer with a whisk attachment (or a large clean glass or metal bowl if using a handheld mixer), add the egg whites and either the lemon juice or the cream of tartar. Beat the egg whites until foamy/frothy, then with the mixer running, add the sugar 1 tablespoon at a time. When the egg whites have reached the stiff peak stage (see page 23), stop whisking and set aside.

5. **Mash the banana.** In a medium bowl, mash the banana using a fork until it has a smooth, creamy texture with no lumps. (Or pulse it in a food processor.)

6. **Make the cake batter.** In a large bowl, combine the egg yolks, milk, and vanilla. Add the mashed banana and sift in the flour, baking powder, and salt. Stir to combine. Stop mixing when there are no more spots of flour visible. Gently fold in the whipped egg whites (see page 25), making sure to retain as much air as you can. Pour the cake batter into the prepared cake pan.

7. **Bake the cake.** Bake the cake for 20 to 25 minutes. Do the toothpick test (see page 15). If the toothpick comes out clean, it's ready.

8. **Cool the cake.** Allow the cake to sit in the pan for 5 minutes. Gently turn it over onto a cooling rack, remove the parchment paper, and allow to cool completely.

9. **Add the custard topping.** Take the custard out of the fridge. It will be quite solid at this point, so give it a good whisk to loosen it up. Transfer the cake to a serving plate, and pour the custard on top of the cake, letting it run down the sides. Use enough custard to cover the cake (you might have some left over). Tap the plate on the countertop to level the custard. Use a spatula to smooth out the custard if required.

10. **Serve.** Trim the edges if desired and cut into 9 equal square pieces to serve. Top with slices of fresh banana, if desired.

One-Bowl Lemon Pound Cake

PREP: 10 minutes // **COOK:** 1 hour, plus 2 hours to cool // **YIELD:** 1 cake; serves 10

INGREDIENTS

8 tbsp (1 stick / 115g) unsalted butter, at room temperature

¾ cup (150g) granulated white sugar

Zest of 2 large lemons

1 tsp vanilla extract

2 large eggs, at room temperature

¼ cup (60g) plain Greek yogurt, at room temperature

1½ cups (210g) all-purpose flour

1 tsp baking powder

¼ tsp salt

¾ cup (180g) whole milk

SPECIAL EQUIPMENT

8 × 4-inch (20 × 10cm) loaf pan

Handheld mixer or stand mixer

VARIATION

Lemon drizzle cake. Make the cake as directed and allow to cool for 30 minutes. In a small bowl, whisk together 1 cup (120g) powdered sugar, the grated zest of 1 lemon, and 3 tablespoons (45g) freshly squeezed lemon juice. Mix well to make a glaze. Drizzle the glaze over the still-warm (but not hot) pound cake.

This lemon pound cake is soft, fluffy, and super moist. Traditionally, pound cake is made with equal quantities of butter, sugar, eggs, and flour, but I've made a few adjustments to the usual recipe so that it literally melts in your mouth. Did I mention how easy it is to make, and uses only one bowl for the prep? Oh yes, I did—it's in the title!

1. **Preheat the oven and prepare the pan.** Preheat the oven to 320°F (160°C). Grease and flour an 8 × 4-inch (20 × 10cm) loaf pan and line the bottom with parchment paper, leaving some overhang to make it easy to lift the cake out of the tin.

2. **Make the batter.** To a stand mixer with a paddle attachment (or a large bowl, if using a handheld mixer), add the butter, sugar, lemon zest, and vanilla. (Make sure to zest the lemons directly over the bowl to capture as much lemon oil as possible.) Mix for about 1 minute. Add the eggs one a time, continuing to mix until each egg is just incorporated. Add the yogurt and mix to incorporate. Don't worry if the mixture curdles at this point—it will come back together. Using a fine mesh sieve, sift in the flour, baking powder, and salt. Add the milk and mix on medium low until there are no spots of flour remaining (about 1 minute). The batter should look smooth.

3. **Bake the cake.** Transfer the cake batter to the prepared loaf tin and bake for 1 hour. Do the toothpick test (see page 15). If the toothpick comes out clean, the cake is ready; if it's not ready, allow the cake to bake for longer. Keep checking every 5 minutes until it's done.

4. **Cool the cake.** Allow the cake to sit in the pan for 10 minutes, then lift it out and transfer to a cooling rack to allow it to cool completely. (It's important you don't leave the cake to cool completely in the pan—it will become soggy if you do.)

MAKE AHEAD & FREEZE
Once cool, store in an airtight container for 4 or 5 days. You can also freeze the cake for a month, wrapped tightly in plastic wrap (see page 14). Defrost at room temperature before serving.

Classic New York Cheesecake

PREP: 30 minutes // **COOK:** 1½ hours, plus 8 hours to chill // **YIELD:** 1 cheesecake; serves 10 to 12

INGREDIENTS

FOR THE CRUST

5½ tablespoons (80g) unsalted butter, melted

5oz (150g) graham crackers (about 10 graham crackers)

FOR THE FILLING

27oz (750g) Philadelphia cream cheese, at room temperature

¾ cup (150g) sour cream, room temperature

1 tbsp vanilla extract

1 cup (200g) granulated white sugar

3 medium eggs, at room temperature

3 tbsp (30g) all-purpose flour

¼ tsp salt

Fresh strawberries and strawberry sauce (optional), to serve

SPECIAL EQUIPMENT

8-inch (20cm) springform pan

Handheld mixer or stand mixer

Offset spatula (not required, but recommended)

> **MAKE AHEAD**
> The cheesecake will keep covered in the fridge for 3 days.

I grew up in New York, so of course I had to include a fantastic New York-style cheesecake recipe. This simple recipe is designed to give you a creamy, zero-crack cheesecake, and it doesn't even require a water bath.

1. **Preheat the oven and prepare the pan.** Preheat the oven to 300°F (150°C). Lightly grease the interior of an 8-inch (20cm) springform pan with butter, coating the bottom and sides. Line the base of the pan with a circle of parchment paper and place the pan on a baking sheet.

2. **Prepare the crust.** In a medium, microwave-safe bowl, microwave the butter until melted. Put the graham crackers in a zip-top bag and crush them to a fine texture with a rolling pin. Add the crushed graham crackers to the butter and stir to combine.

3. **Form the crust.** Transfer the butter/crumb mixture into the prepared springform pan. Using the back of a tablespoon, distribute and press the crumb mixture to form an even layer on the bottom of the pan.

4. **Make the filling.** In a stand mixer fitted with a paddle attachment (or a large bowl, if using a hand mixer), beat the cream cheese, sour cream, and vanilla on medium speed until smooth, about 30 seconds. With the mixer running at low speed, add the sugar in a stream. Increase the speed to medium and continue beating the mixture for about 1 minute until it looks uniform. Add the eggs one at a time, beating the mixture to incorporate each egg before adding the next. As soon as the eggs are incorporated, stop mixing. Add the flour 1 tablespoon at a time and then the salt, continuing to beat on medium-low speed until incorporated.

5. **Scrape the bowl and mix again.** Using a rubber spatula, scrape the bottom and sides of the bowl. The cream cheese will settle at the bottom of the mixer, so it's important to scrape the bottom well to avoid streaks in your cheesecake. Give one last mix on low speed for about 20 seconds.

6. **Assemble the cheesecake.** Transfer the cheesecake filling onto the prepared crust. Smooth the surface of the filling using an offset spatula. Gently tap the pan on the countertop a few times to release any air bubbles that might have formed.

7. **Bake and cool the cheesecake.** Bake for 1 hour. The edge of the cheesecake should be set, but the center should wobble when you give the pan a nudge. Turn the oven off and leave the cheesecake in the oven with the door closed for 20 minutes. Then, open the oven door and allow the cheesecake to sit for another 10 minutes. Finally, carefully remove the cheesecake from the oven and allow to cool completely in the pan at room temperature. When cool, cover with a plate, and refrigerate for at least 8 hours or ideally overnight.

8. **Serve.** Gently run a knife around the edge of cheesecake to release it from the sides of the pan. Remove the cheesecake from the pan and place on a serving plate. Cut into slices and serve with fresh strawberries and a little strawberry sauce, if desired.

No-Bake Mini Cheesecakes

PREP: 5 minutes, plus 15 minutes to chill // **COOK:** None // **YIELD:** 6 mini cheesecakes

INGREDIENTS

2½ tbsp (30g) unsalted butter, melted

3oz (80g) graham crackers or digestive biscuits

14oz (400g) Philadelphia cream cheese, cold

¾ cup (200g) heavy cream, cold

½ cup (100g) granulated white sugar

1 tsp vanilla extract

6 strawberries (optional), to garnish

SPECIAL EQUIPMENT

Handheld mixer or stand mixer

6-cup muffin tin (or 6 ramekins, if preferred)

Paper liners

Piping bag (optional)

These quick and easy no-bake cheesecakes are perfect for satisfying cheesecake cravings, and they're great for parties too!

1. **Prepare the muffin tin.** Line the muffin tin with 6 paper liners.

2. **Crush the graham crackers.** Put the graham crackers in a zip-top bag and crush them to a fine texture using a rolling pin.

3. **Make the crust.** In a bowl, mix the crushed graham crackers and the melted butter until well combined. Using a teaspoon, divide the mixture evenly among the paper liners. Press down firmly to form the cheesecake crust. (I like to use the base of a small drinking glass to do this, but the back of a spoon also works.)

4. **Make the cheesecake filling.** To a large bowl, add the cream cheese, heavy cream, sugar, and vanilla. Using electric beaters, beat the mixture until it's smooth and creamy. The mixture should be quite stiff. The ingredients must be cold for them to whip up—this will take a couple of minutes.

5. **Add the filling to the crust.** Using a piping bag (or a spoon), top each crust with the cheesecake filling, minimizing gaps and making sure to fill the paper liners completely. Smooth them with the back of a knife.

6. **Chill the cheesecakes.** Put the cheesecakes in the freezer for about 15 minutes to set before serving and top each cheesecake with a strawberry, if desired.

MAKE AHEAD & FREEZE
Mini cheesecakes can be stored covered in the refrigerator for up to 3 days. Before serving, put them in the freezer for 15 minutes to set up and to make the liners easier to peel back. They also freeze beautifully and will keep for about 1 month. Defrost in the fridge before serving.

Coffee Crumb Cake

PREP: 10 minutes // COOK: 30 minutes, plus 1 hour to cool // YIELD: 1 cake; serves 6 to 9

INGREDIENTS

FOR THE CRUMB TOPPING

¾ cup (115g) all-purpose flour

½ cup (100g) brown sugar (light or dark)

1 tsp ground cinnamon

½ tsp salt

6 tbsp (¾ stick / 85g) unsalted butter, cold, cut into small cubes

FOR THE CAKE

¾ cup (115g) all-purpose flour

1 tsp baking powder

½ tsp ground cinnamon

¼ tsp baking soda

¼ tsp salt

4 tbsp (½ stick / 60g) unsalted butter, melted

1 tsp vanilla extract

½ cup (100g) granulated white sugar

1 large egg, at room temperature

½ cup (120g) plain Greek yogurt, at room temperature

FOR THE ICING (OPTIONAL)

3 tbsp whole milk

½ cup (60g) powdered sugar

1 tsp vanilla extract

SPECIAL EQUIPMENT

7-inch (18cm) square cake pan

Coffee crumb cake is the original snacking cake. It's so good, there's no need to wait until you're having coffee to eat this!

1. **Preheat the oven and prepare the cake pan.** Preheat the oven to 340°F (170°C). Grease and flour an 7-inch (18cm) square cake pan and line the bottom with parchment paper, leaving some overhang so you can lift the cake out of the pan.

2. **Make the crumb topping.** To a medium bowl, add the flour, brown sugar, cinnamon, salt, and the cubes of cold butter. Using your fingertips, rub the butter into the dry ingredients to form large crumbs, fine crumbs, or a mixture of sizes. (I like a mixture of sizes.) Set aside.

3. **Mix the dry ingredients.** In another medium bowl, whisk together the flour, baking powder, cinnamon, baking soda, and salt.

4. **Make the cake batter.** In a large bowl, whisk the melted butter, vanilla, and sugar until well combined. Add the egg and whisk until fully incorporated. Using a rubber spatula, scrape the bottom and sides of the bowl. Add the flour mixture and the yogurt and mix until there are no more visible spots of flour. The batter should look smooth and quite thick. Scrape the bottom and sides of the bowl and transfer the batter to the prepared cake pan. Sprinkle the crumb topping over the batter, spreading it evenly on the surface of the cake.

5. **Bake the cake.** Bake for 30 to 35 minutes. Do the toothpick test (see page 15). If the toothpick comes out clean, the cake is ready.

6. **Cool the cake.** Allow the cake to sit in the pan for 5 minutes, then lift it out and transfer to a cooling rack and allow to cool completely.

7. **Add the icing drizzle, if desired.** In a small bowl, whisk together the milk, powdered sugar, and vanilla. Drizzle over the cooled cake.

MAKE AHEAD & FREEZE

When cool, store in an airtight container for up to 4 days or wrap tightly in plastic wrap and freeze for up to 1 month (see page 14). Defrost at room temperature.

Vanilla Custard Overload Cake

PREP: 15 minutes // **COOK:** 25 minutes, plus 30 minutes to cool // **YIELD:** 1 large cake or 2 small cakes; serves 8 to 10

INGREDIENTS

FOR THE CAKE(S)

1⅓ cups (180g) all-purpose flour

2 tsp baking powder

¼ tsp salt

⅛ tsp grated nutmeg

¼ tsp ground cinnamon

5 tbsp (75g) unsalted butter, at room temperature

½ cup (100g) granulated white sugar

2 tbsp coconut oil, melted, or vegetable oil

1 tsp vanilla extract

2 large eggs, at room temperature

⅓ cup (80g) plain yogurt, at room temperature

3 tbsp (40g) whole milk, at room temperature

FOR THE CUSTARD

6 tbsp (80g) granulated white sugar

4 tsp cornstarch

¼ tsp salt

1⅓ cups (320g) whole milk

4 large egg yolks

1 tsp vanilla extract

White chocolate chips (optional), for sprinkling

SPECIAL EQUIPMENT

One deep 7- to 8-inch (18–20cm) baking dish or two deep 5-inch (13cm) baking dishes
The dish(es) should be ceramic or glass and about 3 inches (7.5cm) deep.

Soft vanilla cake, creamy custard—what more do you need? In fall or winter, when you want a cozy, comforting treat, this will hit the spot. It's a hug in a dish!

1. **Preheat the oven and prepare the baking dish(es).** Grease and flour the baking dish(es). Preheat the oven to 320°F (160°C).

2. **Mix the dry ingredients.** In a large bowl, whisk together the flour, baking powder, salt, nutmeg, and cinnamon. Set aside.

3. **Make the batter.** In another large bowl, cream together the butter, sugar, oil, and vanilla extract. Mix until well combined, about 1 minute. Add the eggs one at a time, whisking until each egg is fully incorporated before adding the next. Using a rubber spatula, scrape the bottom and sides of your bowl. Add the flour mixture, yogurt, and milk and mix until there are no more visible spots of flour. The batter should look smooth. Scrape the bottom and sides of the bowl and transfer to the prepared baking dish(es).

4. **Bake the cake(s).** Bake the cake(s) for 25 to 30 minutes. Do the toothpick test (see page 15). If the toothpick comes out clean, it's ready. Allow the cakes to cool completely.

5. **Make the custard.** To a large saucepan, add the sugar, cornstarch, and salt. Whisk to distribute the cornstarch through the sugar. Add the milk and egg yolks and whisk to combine. Place over medium-low heat and gently bring the mixture to a simmer, stirring continuously to avoid burning. Stir until the mixture thickens. Turn off the heat, add the vanilla, and whisk vigorously until smooth. If your custard isn't smooth, you can pass it through a sieve.

6. **Assemble the cake.** Allow the custard to cool for 10 minutes, whisking from time to time to stop a skin forming, then pour over the cake(s) while the custard is still warm. If using, sprinkle the white chocolate chips on top of the custard.

7. **Serve.** Take the baking dish(s) to the table and serve immediately.

> **MAKE AHEAD & FREEZE**
> You can make the cake (without the custard) ahead of time, wrap tightly in plastic wrap, and freeze until ready to use (see page 14).

Birthday Cakes

Birthdays are universal. Everyone has one, and there's no birthday party without cake! Whether you're a classic vanilla or chocolate cake person or you feel like switching things up, this chapter has you covered. Enjoying cake is one of the great simple pleasures in life, so I recommend you don't wait for a birthday to make one of these!

Classic Vanilla Birthday Cake

PREP: 15 minutes // **COOK:** 22 minutes, plus 1 hour to cool // **YIELD:** One 2-layer cake; serves 8 to 10

INGREDIENTS

FOR THE CAKE LAYERS

1¾ cups (240g) all-purpose flour

3 tsp baking powder

¼ tsp salt

8 tbsp (1 stick / 115g) unsalted butter, at room temperature

3 tbsp (45g) vegetable oil

¾ cup (150g) granulated white sugar

1 tbsp vanilla extract

3 large eggs, at room temperature

½ cup (120g) plain yogurt, at room temperature

½ cup (120g) whole milk, at room temperature

FOR THE FROSTING AND DECORATION

1 batch American Buttercream Frosting (page 208)

Sprinkles

SPECIAL EQUIPMENT

Two 7-inch (18cm) round cake pans

Handheld mixer or stand mixer

This is my version of the timeless classic vanilla birthday cake with sprinkles—it's soft and delicious and will stay moist for days. One bite and you'll be taken back to your childhood. This recipe can be easily adapted to make cupcakes or a sheet cake.

1. **Preheat the oven and prepare the pans.** Preheat the oven to 320°F (160°C). Grease and flour two 7-inch (18cm) cake pans and line the bottom of each pan with parchment paper.

2. **Mix the dry ingredients.** In a large bowl, whisk together the flour, baking powder, and salt.

3. **Make the batter.** In a stand mixer with a paddle attachment (or in another large bowl, if using a handheld mixer), cream together the softened butter, oil, sugar, and vanilla. Mix until well combined, about 1 minute. Add the eggs one at a time, mixing until each egg is fully incorporated before adding the next. Using a rubber spatula, scrape the bottom and sides of the bowl. Add the flour mixture, yogurt, and milk, and mix until there are no more visible spots of flour. The batter should look smooth. Scrape the bottom and sides of your bowl and divide the batter evenly between the two prepared cake pans.

4. **Bake the cakes.** Bake the cakes for 22 to 25 minutes. Do the toothpick test (see page 15). If the toothpick comes out clean, the cakes are ready.

5. **Cool the cakes.** Allow the cakes to sit in the pans for 5 minutes, then gently turn them out onto a cooling rack upside down, remove the parchment paper, and allow the cakes to cool completely.

6. **Assemble and frost the cake.** When the cake layers have cooled completely, assemble and frost the cake as desired. (See page 17 for guidance on frosting.)

VARIATIONS

To make cupcakes, spoon the cake batter into cupcake liners and bake at 320°F (160°C) for 16 to 20 minutes (do the toothpick test to check for doneness). Allow to cool completely before decorating with frosting. The recipe makes 16 to 18 cupcakes.

To make a vanilla sheet cake, prepare a 9 × 13-inch (23 × 33cm) cake pan. Bake at 320°F (160°C) for about 20 minutes. Do the toothpick test to check for doneness.

MAKE AHEAD & FREEZE

Unfrosted cake layers can be wrapped tightly in plastic wrap and frozen for up to 1 month. You can also freeze the entire frosted cake, covered. Defrost the cake slowly in the fridge overnight on the day before you want to serve it. (See page 14 for guidance on freezing cakes.)

Rich & Moist Chocolate Cake

PREP: 15 minutes // **COOK:** 22 minutes, plus 1 hour to cool // **YIELD:** One 2-layer cake; serves 8 to 10

INGREDIENTS

FOR THE CAKE LAYERS

1½ cups (210g) all-purpose flour

½ cup (60g) unsweetened cocoa powder

3 tsp baking powder

¼ tsp salt

1½ sticks (165g) unsalted butter, at room temperature

1⅓ cups (270g) white granulated sugar

3 large eggs, at room temperature

1 cup (240g) whole milk

2 tbsp brewed espresso coffee (optional)

FOR THE FROSTING

1 batch Whipped Ganache Frosting (page 210)

SPECIAL EQUIPMENT

Two 7-inch (18cm) round cake pans

Handheld mixer or stand mixer

VARIATION

To make cupcakes, spoon the cake batter into cupcake liners and bake for 16 to 20 minutes (do the toothpick test to check for doneness). Allow to cool completely before frosting. The recipe makes about 18 cupcakes.

This easy-to-make chocolate cake is just plain delicious. The cake is rich and moist, and the whipped ganache frosting is incredible! It makes a great celebration cake.

1. **Preheat the oven and prepare the cake pans.** Preheat the oven to 320°F (160°C). Grease and flour two 7-inch (18cm) cake pans and line the bottom of each pan with parchment paper.

2. **Mix the dry ingredients.** In a large bowl, whisk together the flour, cocoa powder, baking powder, and salt. Set aside.

3. **Mix the wet ingredients.** In the bowl of a stand mixer (or in a large bowl, if using a handheld mixer), cream together the softened butter and sugar. Mix until well combined, about 1 minute. Add the eggs one at a time, mixing until each egg is fully incorporated before adding the next. Using a rubber spatula, scrape the bottom and sides of the bowl.

4. **Heat the milk and coffee.** To a small microwave-safe bowl, add the milk and the coffee, if using, and warm in the microwave for 1 minute or until hot.

5. **Combine the wet and dry ingredients.** To the bowl with the butter mixture, add the flour mixture and milk and espresso, and mix until there are no more visible spots of flour. The batter should look smooth. Scrape the bottom and sides of the bowl and divide the batter evenly between the two prepared cake pans.

6. **Bake the cakes.** Bake the cakes for 22 to 25 minutes. Do the toothpick test (see page 15). If the toothpick comes out clean, the cakes are ready.

7. **Cool the cake layers.** Allow the cakes to sit in the pans for 5 minutes, then gently invert them onto a cooling rack, remove the parchment paper, and allow the cakes to cool completely.

8. **Assemble and frost the cake.** When the cake layers have cooled completely, assemble and frost the cake as desired. (See page 17 for guidance on frosting.)

MAKE AHEAD & FREEZE
Unfrosted cake layers can be wrapped tightly in plastic wrap and frozen for up to 1 month. You can also freeze the entire frosted cake, covered. Defrost the cake slowly in the fridge overnight on the day before you want to serve it. (See page 14 for guidance on freezing cakes.)

Classic Yellow Cake

PREP: 15 minutes // COOK: 22 minutes, plus 1 hour to cool // YIELD: One 2-layer cake; serves 8 to 10

INGREDIENTS

FOR THE CAKE

1¾ cups (240g) all-purpose flour

3 tsp baking powder

½ tsp salt

1 stick (115g) unsalted butter, room temperature

¾ cup (150g) granulated white sugar

3 tbsp (45g) refined coconut oil or vegetable oil

1 tbsp vanilla extract

Zest of ¼ large lemon

6 large egg yolks, at room temperature

¾ cup (180g) whole milk, at room temperature

FOR THE FROSTING AND DECORATION

1 batch Instant Fudge Frosting (page 216)

Sprinkles (optional)

SPECIAL EQUIPMENT

Two 7-inch (18cm) round cake pans

Handheld mixer or stand mixer

VARIATION

To make cupcakes, spoon the cake batter into cupcake liners and bake for 16 to 20 minutes (do the toothpick test to check when they're ready). Allow to cool completely before frosting. This recipe makes about 16 cupcakes.

If you're in the mood for a classic American dessert, this take on yellow cake with fudge frosting is for you. It will take you straight back to childhood. It has the the iconic yellow cake made with egg yolks that everyone wants and an incredible fudge frosting that comes together in seconds. After you've tried it, you won't make fudge frosting any other way.

1. **Preheat the oven and prepare the pans.** Preheat the oven to 320°F (160°C). Grease and flour two 7-inch (18cm) cake pans and line the bottom of each pan with parchment paper.

2. **Mix the dry ingredients.** In a large bowl, whisk together the flour, baking powder, and salt.

3. **Make the batter.** In a stand mixer with a paddle attachment (or in a large bowl, if using a handheld mixer), cream together the softened butter, sugar, oil, vanilla, and lemon zest. (You don't need much, just two or three "gratings" from the lemon.) Mix until well combined, about 1 minute. Add the egg yolks three at a time, whisking until fully incorporated before adding the next batch of egg yolks. Using a spatula, scrape the bottom and sides of the bowl. Add the flour mixture and milk and mix until there are no more visible spots of flour. The batter should look smooth. Scrape the bottom and sides of the bowl and divide the batter evenly between the two prepared cake pans.

4. **Bake the cakes.** Bake the cakes for 22 to 25 minutes. Do the toothpick test (see page 15). If the toothpick comes out clean, the cakes are ready.

5. **Cool the cake layers.** Allow the cakes to sit in the pans for 5 minutes, then gently invert onto a cooling rack, remove the parchment paper, and allow the cakes to cool completely.

6. **Assemble and frost the cake.** When the cake layers have cooled completely, assemble and frost the cake as desired. (See page 17 for guidance on frosting.) Decorate with sprinkles, if desired.

MAKE AHEAD & FREEZE

Unfrosted cake layers can be wrapped tightly in plastic wrap and frozen for up to 1 month. You can also freeze the entire frosted cake, covered. Defrost the cake slowly in the fridge overnight on the day before you want to serve it. (See page 14 for guidance on freezing cakes.)

The Most Incredible Strawberry Cake

PREP: 40 minutes // COOK: 18 minutes, plus 1 hour to cool // YIELD: One 3-layer cake; serves 10

INGREDIENTS

FOR THE FILLING

18oz (500g) fresh
strawberries, plus a few
extra berries

2 tbsp water

1 cup (200g) granulated
white sugar

Zest of 1 large lemon

1 tbsp lemon juice

¼ tsp salt

1 tsp vanilla extract

FOR THE CAKE

1¾ cups (240g) all-purpose
flour

3 tsp baking powder

½ tsp salt

8 tbsp (1 stick / 115g)
unsalted butter, at
room temperature

¾ cup (150g) granulated
white sugar

3 tbsp (45g) vegetable oil

2 tsp vanilla extract

3 medium eggs, at
room temperature

½ cup (120g) plain yogurt,
at room temperature

½ cup (120g) whole milk,
at room temperature

FOR THE FROSTING

1½ batches Cream Cheese
Frosting (page 209)

This strawberry cake packs a powerful strawberry punch! The secret is the filling made from fresh strawberries along with a homemade strawberry caramel, which will ooze out of the cake deliciously when you cut a slice—imagine a caramel sauce, but fruity instead of buttery.

1. **Make the filling.** In a food processor, blend the strawberries and water into a smooth purée. Pass the purée through a sieve into a medium tall-sided saucepan. (Take your time with this and then discard the seeds and pulp. You should end up with about 1½ cups of seedless product.) Add the sugar, lemon zest, lemon juice, and salt. Stirring continuously, heat the mixture over medium heat until it starts to boil gently. Lower the heat and allow the mixture to boil gently for 10 to 15 minutes (the timing will depend on the water content of your strawberries), stirring every few minutes to make sure it doesn't burn or boil over. It's ready when it lightly coats the back of a spatula. Turn off the heat and stir in the vanilla. Transfer to a medium, heat-proof bowl, allow to cool, and then chill in the fridge.

2. **Preheat the oven and prepare the pans.** Preheat the oven to 320°F (160°C). Grease and flour three 7-inch (18cm) cake pans and line the bottom of each pan with parchment paper.

3. **Mix the dry ingredients.** In a large bowl, whisk together the flour, baking powder, and salt.

4. **Make the batter.** In a stand mixer with a paddle attachment (or in a large bowl, if using a handheld mixer), cream together the softened butter, sugar, oil, and vanilla. Mix until well combined, about 1 minute. Add the eggs one at a time, mixing until each egg is fully incorporated before adding the next. Using a rubber spatula, scrape the bottom and sides of the bowl. Add the flour mixture, yogurt, and milk, and mix until there are no more visible spots of flour. The batter should look smooth. Scrape the bottom and sides of the bowl and divide the batter evenly among the three prepared cake pans. Don't worry if it looks like there's not much batter in each cake pan—these cake layers are designed to be a little thinner than for a two-layer cake.

5. **Bake the cakes.** Bake the cakes for 18 to 22 minutes. Do the toothpick test (see page 15). If the toothpick comes out clean, the cakes are ready. (If your oven isn't large enough to bake three cake pans at once, bake in batches).

6. **Cool the cake layers.** Allow the cakes to sit in the pans for 5 minutes, then gently turn them out upside down onto a cooling rack. Remove the parchment paper, and allow the cakes to cool completely.

>> *Recipe continues on next page.*

Food processor

Three 7-inch (18cm) round
cake pans

Handheld mixer or
stand mixer

Piping bag with a ½-inch
(1cm) round tip

VARIATION

As a shortcut, instead of
making a strawberry caramel,
you can use a store-bought
strawberry jam or jelly.

7. **Assemble and frost the cake.** Place a small dollop of frosting onto a serving plate and place one cake layer upside down on the plate. The small dollop of frosting will help "glue" the cake onto the serving plate, making sure it won't move around as you assemble your cake. Add a small amount of frosting on top of the cake layer and spread it out evenly into a thin layer, about a ¼ inch (5mm) thick. Using a piping bag, pipe a ½-inch (1cm) border of frosting around the outer edge to contain the strawberry caramel filling. Add a generous amount of the filling, spreading it evenly up to the piped border. Add a few pieces of chopped fresh strawberry, if desired.

8. Spread a thin layer of frosting onto the underside of the next cake layer, which will form a frosting sandwich on top of the filling on the first layer. Add the second cake layer and repeat the process of adding frosting and strawberry caramel filling. Follow the same process for the third layer. Apply a thin crumb coat of frosting to the entire cake, starting with the sides of the cake, so it doesn't move around too much (see page 17). Chill the cake in the freezer for 30 minutes (don't forget it!), then apply a final layer of frosting.

9. **Decorate and serve.** To decorate, just before serving, cut some fresh strawberries in half, and pat the cut sides dry with kitchen paper. Apply a small amount of frosting to the cut sides, and "glue" the strawberry halves onto the sides and the top of the cake.

MAKE AHEAD & FREEZE
Unfrosted cake layers can be wrapped tightly in plastic wrap and frozen for up to 1 month (see page 14). The strawberry caramel filling can be made in advance and refrigerated in an airtight container for up to 2 weeks.

MAKE AHEAD & FREEZE
Unfrosted cake layers can be made ahead of time, wrapped tightly in plastic wrap, and frozen. You can also freeze the entire frosted cake, covered. (See page 14.) To defrost, transfer the cake to the fridge the day before you want to serve it.

One-Pan Rainbow Cake

PREP: 15 minutes // **COOK:** 22 minutes, plus 1 hour to cool // **YIELD:** One 2-layer cake; serves 8 to 10

INGREDIENTS

FOR THE CAKE LAYERS

1¾ cups (240g) all-purpose flour

3 tsp baking powder

½ tsp salt

8 tbsp (1 stick / 115g) unsalted butter, at room temperature

3 tbsp (45g) vegetable oil

¾ cup (150g) granulated white sugar

2 tsp vanilla extract

3 large eggs, at room temperature

½ cup (120g) plain yogurt, at room temperature

⅓ cup (80g) whole milk, at room temperature

Gel-based food coloring in red, orange, yellow, green, blue, and purple

FOR THE FROSTING AND DECORATION

1 batch Cream Cheese Frosting (page 209; color as desired)

Sprinkles (optional)

SPECIAL EQUIPMENT

Two 7-inch (18cm) round cake pans

6 small disposable paper bowls

Handheld mixer or stand mixer

Lots of rainbow cakes recipes require a separate cake pan for each color. That's just too many cake pans and too much washing up for my liking! This method lets you bake the entire rainbow in one pan. For this recipe, I've doubled it up to make a two-layer birthday cake, but you can just bake one layer if you prefer.

1. **Preheat the oven and prepare the cake pans.** Preheat the oven to 320°F (160°C). Grease and flour two 7-inch (18cm) cake pans and line the bottom of each pan with parchment paper.

2. **Mix the dry ingredients.** In a large bowl, whisk together the flour, baking powder, and salt.

3. **Make the base batter.** In a stand mixer with a paddle attachment (or in a large bowl, if using a handheld mixer), cream together the softened butter, oil, sugar, and vanilla. Mix until well combined, about 1 minute. Add the eggs one at a time, mixing until each egg is fully incorporated before adding the next. Using a spatula, scrape the bottom and sides of the bowl. Add the flour mixture, yogurt, and milk. Mix until there are no more visible spots of flour. The batter should look smooth.

4. **Make the rainbow batters.** Divide the base batter evenly among the six disposable bowls. Add a different color of food coloring to each bowl—red, orange, yellow, green, blue, and purple—and mix well until the colors are even.

5. **Prepare the rainbow cakes.** Divide the purple batter between the two prepared cake pans. Tap the cake pans gently on the countertop to release any air bubbles and to gently spread out the cake batter. (It's okay if it doesn't spread to the edges of the pans.) Following the rainbow, take the blue batter, and similarly divide it between the cake pans, pouring it in the center of the previous cake batter. Again, gently tap the pan. Repeat this process with the green, yellow, orange, and red batters. You should end up with a rainbow effect, with rough concentric circles. Don't worry about being too precise—the cakes will look great if you take care not to let the different colors bleed into each other too much.

6. **Bake the cakes.** Bake the cakes for 22 to 25 minutes. Do the toothpick test (see page 15). If the toothpick comes out clean, the cakes are ready.

7. **Cool the cake layers.** Allow the cakes to sit in the pans for 5 minutes, then gently turn them out upside down onto a cooling rack, remove the parchment paper, and allow the cakes to cool completely.

8. **Assemble and frost the cake.** When the cake layers have cooled completely, assemble and frost the cake as desired. (See page 17 for guidance on frosting.) Decorate with sprinkles, if desired.

Chocolate Chip Cookie Cake

PREP: 15 minutes // **COOK:** 22 minutes, plus 1 hour to cool // **YIELD:** One 2-layer cake; serves 8 to 10

INGREDIENTS

FOR THE CAKE

8 tbsp (1 stick / 115g) unsalted butter

1¾ cups (240g) all-purpose flour

3 tsp baking powder

½ tsp salt

½ cup (100g) granulated white sugar

¼ cup (50g) packed brown sugar (light or dark)

3 tbsp (45g) refined coconut oil or vegetable oil

2 tsp vanilla extract

3 medium eggs, at room temperature

½ cup (120g) plain yogurt, at room temperature

½ cup (120g) whole milk, at room temperature

⅔ cup (100g) chocolate chips

FOR THE FROSTING AND DECORATION

1 batch American Buttercream Frosting (page 208)

20 or more Mini Chocolate Chip Cookies (page 226)

SPECIAL EQUIPMENT

Two 7-inch (18cm) round cake pans

VARIATION

To make cupcakes, spoon the cake batter into cupcake liners and bake for 16 to 20 minutes (do the toothpick test to check for doneness). Allow to cool completely before decorating with frosting and mini chocolate chip cookies. The recipe makes about 18 cupcakes.

When you can't decide between cookies and cake, this is the best of both worlds! This super moist cake captures everything you love about chocolate chip cookies in cake form.

1. **Make the brown butter.** Add the butter to a small saucepan and brown over medium heat. (See page 25 for how to make brown butter.) Transfer the brown butter to a large heat-safe bowl and set aside to cool for 30 to 40 minutes at room temperature.

2. **Preheat the oven and prepare the pans.** Preheat the oven to 320°F (160°C). Grease and flour two 7-inch (18cm) cake pans and line the bottom of each pan with parchment paper.

3. **Mix the dry ingredients.** In a large bowl, whisk together the flour, baking powder, and salt.

4. **Make the batter.** To the bowl with the brown butter, add the white sugar, brown sugar, oil, and vanilla extract. Mix until well combined (about 1 minute). Add the eggs one at a time, whisking until each egg is fully incorporated before adding the next. Using a rubber spatula, scrape the bottom and sides of the bowl. Add the flour mixture along with the yogurt and milk. Mix until there are no more visible spots of flour. The batter should look smooth.

5. **Add the chocolate chips.** In a small bowl, toss the chocolate chips with 1 teaspoon flour. (This will prevent the chocolate chips from sinking to the bottom of the batter.) Add the chocolate chips to the cake batter and stir to combine, scraping the bottom and sides of the bowl. Divide the batter evenly between the two prepared cake pans.

6. **Bake the cakes.** Bake the cakes for 22 to 25 minutes. Do the toothpick test (see page 15). If the toothpick comes out clean, the cakes are ready.

7. **Cool the cake layers.** Allow the cakes to sit in the pans for 5 minutes, then gently invert onto a cooling rack, remove the parchment paper, and allow the cakes to cool completely.

8. **Assemble and frost the cake.** When the cake layers have cooled completely, assemble and frost the cake as desired. (See page 17 for guidance on frosting.) If desired, decorate the cake with mini chocolate chip cookies. Attach the cookies to the cake using a small dollop of frosting. Alternatively, you can simply decorate the cake with chocolate chips.

MAKE AHEAD & FREEZE

Unfrosted cake layers can be wrapped tightly in plastic wrap and frozen for up to 1 month. You can also freeze the entire frosted cake, covered. Defrost the cake slowly in the fridge overnight on the day before you want to serve it. (See page 14 for guidance on freezing cakes.)

Moist Lemon Cake

PREP: 15 minutes // **COOK:** 22 minutes, plus 1 hour to cool // **YIELD:** One 2-layer cake; serves 8 to 10

INGREDIENTS

FOR THE CAKE LAYERS

1¾ cups (240g) all-purpose flour

3 tsp baking powder

½ tsp salt

8 tbsp (1 stick / 115g) unsalted butter, at room temperature

¾ cup (150g) granulated white sugar

3 tbsp refined coconut oil, melted, or vegetable oil

Zest of 3 large lemons

3 large eggs, at room temperature

½ cup (120g) plain yogurt, at room temperature

½ cup (120g) whole milk, at room temperature

Yellow gel-based food coloring (optional)

FOR THE FROSTING

1 batch Cream Cheese Frosting (page 209)

Zest of 2 large lemons (stir into the frosting)

SPECIAL EQUIPMENT

Two 7-inch (18cm) round cake pans

Handheld mixer or stand mixer

VARIATION

For extra lemony frosting, add 2 tablespoons of Silky Lemon Curd (page 212) to the frosting.

This soft lemon cake with a tangy cream cheese frosting is amazing. If you like your cake extra lemony like I do, be sure to try the variation for kicking the frosting up a notch!

1. **Preheat the oven and prepare the pans.** Preheat the oven to 320°F (160°C). Grease and flour two 7-inch (18cm) cake pans and line the bottom of each pan with parchment paper.

2. **Mix the dry ingredients.** In a large bowl, whisk together the flour, baking powder, and salt. Set aside.

3. **Make the batter.** In a stand mixer with a paddle attachment (or another large bowl, if using a hand mixer), cream together the butter, sugar, oil, and lemon zest. (Make sure to grate the lemon zest directly over the bowl, to catch all the flavorful lemon oil in the skin. Zest only the outer yellow skin, not the inner white pith.) Mix until well combined, about 1 minute. Add the eggs one at a time, whisking until each egg is fully incorporated before adding the next. Using a rubber spatula, scrape the bottom and sides of your bowl. Add the flour mixture, yogurt, and milk, and mix until there are no more visible spots of flour. The batter should look smooth. Quickly mix in a few drops of food coloring, if desired, until the batter reaches a uniform shade. Scrape the bottom and sides of your bowl and divide the batter evenly between the two prepared cake pans.

4. **Bake the cakes.** Bake the cakes for 22 to 25 minutes. Do the toothpick test (see page 15). If the toothpick comes out clean, the cakes are ready.

5. **Cool the cake layers.** Allow the cakes to sit in the pans for 5 minutes, then gently turn them out onto a cooling rack, remove the parchment paper, and allow the cakes to cool completely. The cakes should have little or no doming.

6. **Assemble and frost the cake.** When the cake layers have cooled completely, assemble and frost the cake as desired. (See page 17 for guidance on frosting.) Decorate as you prefer—I decorated mine with piped cream cheese frosting.

MAKE AHEAD & FREEZE
Unfrosted cake layers can be wrapped tightly in plastic wrap and frozen for up to 1 month. You can also freeze the entire frosted cake, covered. Defrost the cake slowly in the fridge overnight on the day before you want to serve it. (See page 14 for guidance on freezing cakes.)

Easy Ice Cream Cake

PREP: 20 minutes // **COOK:** 12 minutes, plus 6 hours to freeze // **YIELD:** 1 ice cream cake; serves 12

INGREDIENTS

FOR THE CAKE

⅓ cup + 1 tbsp (60g) all-purpose flour

1 tsp baking powder

¼ tsp salt

3 medium or large eggs, at room temperature

1 tsp vanilla extract

½ cup (100g) white granulated sugar

4 tbsp (60g) whole milk

¼ cup (35g) unsweetened cocoa powder

Sprinkles (optional), for decorating

FOR THE ICE CREAM

2 cups (500g) heavy cream, cold

1 tbsp vanilla extract

1½ cups (300g) sweetened condensed milk, cold

Mix-ins of choice (optional; see Variations)

SPECIAL EQUIPMENT

16 × 12-inch (40.5 × 30.5cm) baking pan with shallow edges

Handheld mixer or stand mixer

Piping bag

VARIATIONS

I like to add additional toppings to this cake, such as chocolate sauce, chocolate chips, caramel sauce, or Oreo cookie crumbs.

MAKE AHEAD & FREEZE

This cake can be tightly wrapped in plastic wrap and stored in the freezer for up to 2 weeks.

There's only one thing better than birthday cake—ice cream birthday cake! You'll need less than 30 minutes to put this amazing cake together, including making an easy homemade ice cream, but plan to prepare it at least six hours in advance to allow the ice cream to freeze.

1. **Preheat the oven and prepare the baking sheet.** Preheat the oven to 320°F (160°C). Grease a 16 × 12-inch (40.5 × 30.5cm) baking pan, line with parchment paper, and grease the parchment paper as well.

2. **Mix the dry ingredients.** In a large bowl, whisk together the flour, baking powder, and salt. Set aside.

3. **Make the cake batter.** In a stand mixer with a whisk attachment (or a large glass or metal bowl, if using a handheld mixer) whip the eggs and vanilla until the eggs start to become foamy. With the mixer running, gradually add the sugar. Whip until the mixture triples in volume, becomes pale in color, and forms ribbons.

4. **Bloom the cocoa powder.** To a small microwave-safe bowl, add the milk and microwave for 30 seconds. Stir in the cocoa powder until it forms a smooth paste.

5. **Finish the cake batter.** Add the cocoa powder and milk mixture to the whipped egg mixture and incorporate it quickly (about 15 seconds). Don't worry if the mixture deflates slightly. Gently fold in the dry ingredients, making sure to scrape the bottom of the bowl to ensure the flour is fully incorporated. Stop mixing as soon as everything is incorporated to keep as much air in the batter as possible.

6. **Bake the cake.** Spread the batter onto the prepared baking pan. Using an offset spatula, spread the batter to the edges of the pan to form a thin layer. Bake for 10 to 12 minutes. Do the toothpick test (page 15) to check for doneness.

7. **Cool and cut the cake.** Allow the cake to cool completely. Flip the pan upside down on a cutting board. Remove the pan and the parchment paper. Cut the cake in half to form two 12 × 8-inch (30.5 × 20cm) rectangles.

8. **Prepare the ice cream base.** Chill the mixer bowl in the freezer for 15 minutes before making the ice cream base. In a stand mixer with a whisk attachment (or a large bowl, if using a handheld mixer), whip the heavy cream and vanilla until soft peaks form (see page 23). Add the sweetened condensed milk and whip the mixture until it forms stiff peaks. Transfer the mixture to a piping bag.

9. **Assemble and freeze the cake.** Gently place one cake layer on a piece of parchment paper on a freezer-safe tray. (Be careful not to break the thin cake). Working quickly, pipe a tall layer of ice cream mix onto the cake and smooth it out. Gently place the second cake layer on top of the ice cream, being careful not to push down too hard. Pipe another layer of ice cream base onto the top of the cake, and smooth out. Decorate with sprinkles. Freeze for at least 6 hours or ideally overnight.

10. **Serve.** Remove the cake from the freezer about 20 minutes before serving.

VARIATION

To make cupcakes, spoon the cake batter into cupcake liners and bake at 320°F (160°C) for 16 to 20 minutes (do the toothpick test to check for doneness). Allow to cool completely before decorating with frosting. The recipe makes 16 to 18 cupcakes.

Red Velvet Cake

PREP: 20 minutes // COOK: 22 minutes, plus 1 hour 40 minutes to cool // YIELD: One 2-layer cake; serves 8 to 10

INGREDIENTS

FOR THE CAKE

1½ cups (215g) all-purpose flour

1½ tbsp (12g) unsweetened cocoa powder

1½ tsp baking powder

¾ tsp baking soda

½ tsp salt

10 tbsp (1¼ sticks / 150g) unsalted butter, at room temperature

1 cup (200g) granulated white sugar

2 tsp vanilla extract

3 medium eggs, at room temperature

Red gel-based food coloring

¾ cup (180g) whole milk, at room temperature

1 tsp apple cider vinegar (or white wine vinegar or lemon juice)

FOR THE FROSTING

1 batch Cream Cheese Frosting (page 209)

FOR THE DRIP

¾ cup (4½oz / 125g) white chocolate, cut into small pieces

¼ cup (1½oz / 40g) milk chocolate, cut into small pieces

⅓ cup (80g) heavy cream

Red gel-based food coloring

SPECIAL EQUIPMENT

Two 7-inch (18cm) round cake pans

Handheld mixer or stand mixer

This was the first of my cakes to go viral on YouTube, so it's dear to my heart. The cake is delicious and moist, and while the decoration might look daunting, it's one of the easiest cakes to decorate.

1. **Preheat the oven and prepare the cake pans.** Preheat the oven to 320°F (160°C). Grease and flour two 7-inch (18cm) round cake pans and line the bottom of each pan with parchment paper.

2. **Mix the dry ingredients.** In a large bowl, whisk together the flour, cocoa powder, baking powder, baking soda, and salt.

3. **Make the batter.** In a stand mixer with a paddle attachment (or in a large bowl, if using handheld mixer), cream together the softened butter, sugar, and vanilla. Mix until well combined, about 1 minute. Add the eggs one at a time, mixing until each egg is fully incorporated before adding the next. Add red gel-based food coloring a few drops at a time and mix until the red color is evenly distributed and deep enough for your liking. Using a rubber spatula, scrape the bottom and sides of the bowl. Add the flour mixture, milk, and vinegar, and mix until there are no more visible spots of flour. The batter should look smooth. Scrape the bottom and sides of your bowl and divide the batter evenly between the two prepared cake pans.

4. **Bake the cakes.** Bake the cakes for 22 to 25 minutes. Do the toothpick test (see page 15). If the toothpick comes out clean, the cakes are ready.

5. **Cool the cakes.** Allow the cakes to sit in the pans for 5 minutes, then gently turn them out upside down onto a cooling rack, remove the parchment paper, and allow the cakes to cool completely.

6. **Assemble and frost the cake.** When the cake layers have cooled completely, assemble and frost the cake. Use a bench scraper to achieve a smooth, even surface for applying the drip. (See page 17 for guidance on frosting.)

7. **Add the chocolate drip.** In a small microwave-safe bowl, microwave the white chocolate, milk chocolate, and cream, stirring every 30 seconds until the chocolate is melted. Add the red food coloring and mix until the ganache has an even red color. Let cool at room temperature for 15 to 20 minutes. Meanwhile, put the cake back in the freezer for 20 minutes. When the ganache is slightly above room temperature (it should still be runny), take the cake out of the freezer, pour the ganache over the top of the cake. Spread it out evenly over the top surface, allowing some parts to drip down over the edge of the cake.

MAKE AHEAD & FREEZE

Unfrosted cake layers can be wrapped tightly in plastic wrap and frozen for up to 1 month. You can also freeze the entire frosted cake, covered. Defrost the cake slowly in the fridge overnight on the day before you want to serve it. (See page 14 for guidance on freezing cakes.)

Five-Minute Tiramisu

PREP: 5 minutes, plus 3 hours to chill // **COOK:** None // **YIELD:** 1 tiramisu; serves 10

INGREDIENTS

1 cup (250g) heavy cream, cold

6 medium pasteurized egg yolks, at room temperature

½ cup (100g) granulated white sugar

16oz (450–500g) mascarpone cheese, at room temperature

2 cups (500g) brewed espresso coffee, cooled

10oz (300g) ladyfinger cookies, such as Savoiardi

2–3 tbsp unsweetened cocoa powder, for dusting

SPECIAL EQUIPMENT

Handheld mixer or stand mixer

12 × 8-inch (30 × 20cm) glass or ceramic serving dish, a few inches deep

Piping bag (optional)

I know, I know. Tiramisu isn't exactly your typical birthday cake, but for me and most Italians, it is an iconic dessert for birthdays. Once you try this, you'll understand why it's such a crowd pleaser—everyone loves it, from kids to grandparents. It's so easy, it comes together in a few minutes. This is the version I was brought up with, but you can change it up with different flavors, such as the strawberry variation.

1. **Whip the heavy cream.** Using a mixer with a whisk attachment, whip the cold heavy cream until it forms soft peaks (see page 23). Refrigerate until ready to use.

2. **Make the mascarpone cream.** To a large bowl, add the room-temperature egg yolks and sugar. Using a mixer with a whisk attachment, beat for 3 to 5 minutes until the sugar has dissolved and the mixture is thick and pale in color. Add half of the mascarpone and mix until fully incorporated. Add the second half of the mascarpone, and stop mixing as soon as the mascarpone/egg mixture becomes whipped and fluffy. Using a rubber spatula, gently fold in the whipped cream, scraping to the bottom of the bowl to make sure all the ingredients are evenly distributed.

3. **Assemble the tiramisu.** Pour the cooled coffee into a medium bowl. Dip the ladyfingers in the coffee (about 3 seconds) and arrange in a layer in the bottom of the serving dish. Using a spoon, spread a layer of the mascarpone cream over the ladyfingers. Repeat the process alternating the dipped cookies and cream for another layer or two, until the cookies are used up. Cover the top layer with mascarpone cream, and smooth out with a knife or offset spatula. (Alternatively, you can apply the final layer of mascarpone cream using a piping bag to create fancy dollops.) Dust the top of the tiramisu with cocoa powder.

4. **Chill the tiramisu.** Cover well and refrigerate for at least 3 hours, and ideally overnight.

5. **Serve.** Serve the tiramisu cold, straight from the fridge.

VARIATION

Strawberry tiramisu. Replace the coffee with 1 pound (450g) fresh strawberries. Pulse the strawberries in a food processor with 3 tablespoons granulated white sugar, 2 tablespoons water, and ½ tablespoon fresh lemon juice until puréed. Allow to sit for 1 hour. Then, dip the lady fingers in the strawberry mixture as you would with the coffee. Top with additional fresh strawberries instead of dusting with cocoa powder.

Cookies & Cream Cake

PREP: 15 minutes // **COOK:** 22 minutes, plus 1 hour to cool // **YIELD:** One 2-layer cake; serves 8 to 10

INGREDIENTS

FOR THE CAKE LAYERS

1½ cups (210g) all-purpose flour

3 tsp baking powder

¼ tsp salt

12 Oreo cookies or other similar cookies, crushed into small pieces

3 egg whites, at room temperature

1 stick (115g) unsalted butter, at room temperature

¾ cup (150g) granulated white sugar

3 tbsp (45g) refined coconut oil or vegetable oil

2 tsp vanilla extract

½ cup (120g) plain yogurt, at room temperature

½ cup (120g) whole milk, at room temperature

FOR THE FROSTING AND DECORATION

1 batch American Buttercream Frosting (page 208) or Cream Cheese Frosting (page 209)

6 Oreo cookies or other similar cookies, crushed into small pieces

Chocolate sauce (optional), for drizzling

SPECIAL EQUIPMENT

Two 7-inch (18cm) round cake pans

Handheld mixer or stand mixer

Everybody loves cookies and cream, and this cake delivers everything people love about the classic combination of rich chocolate sandwich cookies and sweet vanilla cream. If you're looking for a crowd-pleaser birthday cake, this is it!

1. **Preheat the oven and prepare the cake pans.** Preheat the oven to 320°F (160°C). Grease and flour two 7-inch (18cm) cake pans and line the bottom of each pan with parchment paper.

2. **Mix the dry ingredients.** In a large bowl, whisk together the flour, baking powder, and salt. Set aside.

3. **Crush the cookies.** Put the cookies in a plastic bag and smash with a rolling pin until crushed into small pieces. (Don't make fine crumbs—you want some chunks of cookie that you can taste in the final cake.) Set aside.

4. **Whip the egg whites.** In a stand mixer with a whisk attachment (or a large, clean glass or metal bowl, if using a handheld mixer), whip the egg whites until they form stiff peaks (see page 23). Set aside.

5. **Make the batter.** In a clean mixer bowl (or in another large bowl, if using a handheld mixer), cream together the softened butter, sugar, oil, and vanilla. Mix until well combined, about 1 minute. Using a rubber spatula, scrape the bottom and sides of the bowl. Add the flour mixture along with the yogurt and milk and mix until there are no visible spots of flour. Add the whipped egg whites and fold in (see page 25) until the batter is uniform with no clouds of egg white. The batter should look light and airy. Add the crushed cookies, and gently fold in. Scrape the bottom and sides of the bowl and divide the batter evenly between the two prepared cake pans.

6. **Bake the cakes.** Bake for 22 to 25 minutes. Do the toothpick test (see page 15). If the toothpick comes out clean, the cakes are ready.

7. **Cool the cake layers.** Allow the cakes to sit in the pans for 5 minutes, then gently invert them onto a cooling rack, remove the parchment paper, and allow the cakes to cool completely.

8. **Assemble and frost the cake.** When the cake layers have cooled completely, assemble and frost the cake as desired. (See page 17 for guidance on frosting.) Decorate the top and sides of the cake with more crushed cookies. Drizzle with chocolate sauce, if desired.

MAKE AHEAD & FREEZE
Unfrosted cake layers can be wrapped tightly in plastic wrap and frozen for up to 1 month. You can also freeze the entire frosted cake, covered. Defrost the cake slowly in the fridge overnight on the day before you want to serve it. (See page 14 for guidance on freezing cakes.)

Quick Microwave Birthday Cake

PREP: 10 minutes // **COOK:** 10 minutes, plus 30 minutes to cool // **YIELD:** 1 cake; serves 8 to 10

INGREDIENTS

FOR THE CAKE

1 cup + 2 tbsp (160g) all-purpose flour

2 tsp baking powder

¼ tsp salt

6 tbsp (85g) unsalted butter, at room temperature

½ cup (100g) granulated white sugar

1 tsp vanilla extract

¾ cup (180g) whole milk, at room temperature

¼ cup (65g) plain yogurt, at room temperature

FOR THE FROSTING AND DECORATION

⅓ batch American Buttercream Frosting (page 208)

Sprinkles

SPECIAL EQUIPMENT

8-inch (20cm) round microwave-safe dish or silicone cake pan

VARIATIONS

You can change up this cake by using different frostings. Try Instant Fudge Frosting (page 216) for a chocolate variation.

This birthday cake is quick to put together, making it an ideal snacking cake. It's also perfect if you've forgotten someone's birthday and need something last minute!

1. **Prepare the baking dish.** Grease and flour the baking dish, and line the bottom with parchment paper.

2. **Mix the dry ingredients.** In a medium bowl, whisk together the flour, baking powder, and salt. Set aside.

3. **Mix the wet ingredients.** In a large bowl, using a rubber spatula, cream together the soft, room-temperature butter, sugar, and vanilla.

4. **Combine the wet and dry ingredients.** To the butter mixture, add the dry ingredients, the milk, and the yogurt. Using the spatula, mix until all the ingredients are well combined. Stop mixing as soon as there are no more visible spots of flour. Make sure to scrape the bottom and sides of the bowl.

5. **Microwave the cake.** Pour the mixture into the prepared baking dish and microwave on high for 5 minutes. Do the toothpick test (see page 15). If the toothpick comes out clean, the cake is ready. Because of the way the cake cooks in the microwave, test the center and the bottom of the cake. If it's still wet, continue to microwave in 1-minute intervals, checking for doneness after each minute. The cooking time will depend on your microwave, but it shouldn't take more than 8 to 10 minutes in total.

6. **Frost the cake.** Allow the cake to cool for 10 minutes in the dish. After 10 minutes, unmold the cake, remove the parchment paper, and allow to cool completely before frosting it. Frost with buttercream according to the style you want (see page 17) and decorate with sprinkles.

// NOTE

The difficulty level for this recipe is "moderate" because every microwave and container is different, so it may take some trial and error to arrive at the precise cooking time. Once you've got that sorted for your setup, the recipe itself is easy.

MAKE AHEAD
Store covered at room temperature for up to 1 day.

Shortcut Fancy Birthday Cake

PREP: 10 minutes, plus 4 hours to chill // **COOK:** None // **YIELD:** 1 cake; serves 10 to 12

INGREDIENTS

FOR THE FROSTING

11oz (300g) Philadelphia
  cream cheese, cold

1¼ cups (300g) heavy
  cream, cold

¾ cup (100g) powdered
  sugar

2 tsp vanilla extract

Sprinkles (optional),
  for decoration

FOR THE CAKE LAYERS

36 store-bought cookies
  (any crispy cookie, ideally
  rectangular)

1 cup (240g) whole milk,
  for dipping cookies

SPECIAL EQUIPMENT

Handheld mixer or
  stand mixer

Piping bag

I'm going to share with you a trick for making a super-fancy four-layer cake in just a few minutes. It's completely no-bake, and if you love milk and cookies, you'll love this take on icebox cake. You will need to make it at least a few hours before you want to serve it.

1. **Make the frosting.** In a stand mixer (or a large bowl, if using a hand mixer), beat the cream cheese, heavy cream, powdered sugar, and vanilla extract until the mixture forms stiff peaks (see page 23). Don't overmix or the mixture will become loose. Transfer to a piping bag.

2. **Assemble the cake.** Pour the milk into a medium bowl (you will be dipping the cookies in this). Dip a cookie into the milk for 3 or 4 seconds, and place on a serving plate or a parchment-lined tray. Repeat 8 times to form the first layer of the cake in a 3-by-3 grid of cookies. For this first layer, you can secure the cookies to the serving plate using a little frosting. Pipe frosting on to the first layer of cookies to a thickness of about ½ inch (1.5cm). Smooth out the frosting using a knife or an offset spatula.

3. Repeat this process using the remaining cookies until you have made four layers. Cover the sides and top of the cake with the remaining frosting and smooth it out.

4. **Chill the cake.** Refrigerate the cake, covered, for at least 4 hours—or ideally overnight—to allow the cookies to soften.

5. **Serve.** Take the cake out of the fridge 30 minutes before serving, and decorate the top of the cake with sprinkles.

Frostings, Fillings, & Creams

From cream cheese frosting and pastry cream to silky lemon curd and chocolate ganache, these flavorful fillings will inspire you to get creative and elevate your bakes to a whole new level.

American Buttercream Frosting

PREP: 5 minutes // **COOK:** None // **YIELD:** Enough to frost a 7- or 8-inch (18–20cm) 2-layer cake

This smooth and silky vanilla buttercream comes together in minutes. If you're familiar with traditional buttercream recipes, you'll notice that this recipe uses about half the typical amount of sugar. It's still sweet, but it's much more enjoyable for the way we eat today. A pastry chef secret is to age the buttercream for 48 hours to 72 hours in advance of when you want to use it. This really allows the vanilla flavor to develop.

1. **Beat the butter.** In a stand mixer with a paddle attachment (or in a large bowl, if using a handheld mixer), beat the butter for 30 seconds or until smooth.

2. **Add the other ingredients.** Add the powdered sugar, vanilla, and salt, and mix on low speed just until combined. Increase to medium speed and continue mixing for 2 minutes or until well combined. Scrape the bottom and sides of the bowl. Buttercream can be used immediately or stored until ready for use. (The vanilla flavor will continue to develop for 48 to 72 hours in the fridge.)

INGREDIENTS

3 sticks (350g) unsalted butter, at room temperature

3 cups (350g) powdered sugar

1 tbsp vanilla extract

¼ tsp salt

SPECIAL EQUIPMENT

Handheld mixer or stand mixer

// BEST USES

Use for frosting cakes and cookies such as the Classic Vanilla Birthday Cake (page 178), Chocolate Chip Cookie Cake (page 190), or Lofthouse Sugar Cookies (page 240).

VARIATION

For chocolate buttercream, follow the method as directed and add ½ cup (60g) of unsweetened cocoa powder and 2 tablespoons of freshly brewed coffee at the end of step 2. Continue mixing until incorporated.

MAKE AHEAD & FREEZE

Buttercream can be made up to 7 days in advance and stored in an airtight container in the fridge. Once ready to use, remove the buttercream from the refrigerator and bring to room temperature for 45 minutes to 1 hour (it will be solid when it comes out of the fridge). Once softened, mix well before frosting a cake or cupcakes.

This frosting freezes beautifully in an airtight container for up to 1 month. Thaw overnight in the refrigerator, then bring to room temperature and mix well before frosting cakes.

Cream Cheese Frosting

PREP: 5 minutes // **COOK:** None // **YIELD:** Enough to frost a 7- or 8-inch (18–20cm) 2-layer cake

I hear many stories of people having trouble making cream cheese frosting that's stiff enough for frosting a cake. Don't be daunted! It's super easy, as well as super quick, if you follow my technique. I developed this method when running a hotel kitchen. Sometimes, we'd run out of cream cheese frosting unexpectedly and the chefs needed a way to make new batches, fast. You will spend a total of just one minute mixing this frosting—it doesn't get much quicker than that!

1. **Prepare the butter.** In a medium bowl, using a handheld mixer, cream the room-temperature butter (and a few drops of food coloring, if using) until smooth. Set aside.

2. **Mix the cream cheese and sugar.** In a stand mixer with paddle attachment (or in a large bowl, if using a handheld mixer), whip the powdered sugar and cold cream cheese for 30 seconds. Do not whip for more time than this, otherwise the cream cheese will start to warm up. Be careful the powdered sugar doesn't fly everywhere! At this stage, the mixture might seem loose.

3. **Add the butter.** Immediately add the soft butter and continue whipping on high speed until just incorporated. Don't whip for longer than 30 seconds, or you risk the frosting going runny. When the room temperature butter hits the cold cream cheese, a stiff frosting will form. If your frosting goes runny, it is most likely because your cream cheese is not cold enough. Don't worry. Just put the frosting in the fridge to firm up. Keep in mind, you must whip this frosting on high speed, or the room-temperature butter will seize up when it hits the cold cream cheese.

INGREDIENTS

8 tbsp (1 stick / 115g) unsalted butter,
  at room temperature

Gel-based food coloring (optional)

2 cups (250g) powdered sugar

16oz (450–500g) full-fat Philadelphia cream
  cheese, very cold

SPECIAL EQUIPMENT

Handheld mixer or stand mixer

// BEST USES

Use for frosting cakes such as Red Velvet Cake (page 196), Moist Lemon Cake (page 192), or The Most Incredible Strawberry Cake (page 184).

// NOTES

You must use Philadelphia brand cream cheese for this recipe—the original, full-fat version. Supermarket own-brand cream cheese might not work—some brands contain too much water.

The cream cheese must be cold. Work quickly and take out of the fridge at the very last minute before using. If you've just got home from the supermarket with the cream cheese and it's warmed up a bit, put it in the freezer for 15 minutes and then transfer to the fridge.

You will need to take the butter out of the fridge as early as possible, well before you start baking. The butter must be super soft so it can be incorporated into the cold cream cheese almost immediately.

MAKE AHEAD

Frosting can be refrigerated in an airtight container for up to 2 days. When you're ready to use it, remove from the fridge and let it sit for 5 to 10 minutes. Give it a quick stir with a whisk, and you're ready to frost your cake!

Whipped Ganache Frosting

PREP: 5 minutes // **COOK:** 2 minutes, plus 45 minutes to chill // **YIELD:** Enough to frost a 7- to 8-inch (18–20cm) 2-layer cake

INGREDIENTS

5½oz (150g) 70% cocoa dark chocolate, such as Lindt, chopped into small pieces

3½oz (100g) good-quality milk chocolate, such as Lindt, chopped into small pieces

1½ cups (360g) heavy cream (36% fat or higher)

13oz (350g) Nutella, at room temperature

SPECIAL EQUIPMENT

Handheld mixer or stand mixer

// BEST USES

Use as a frosting for the Rich & Moist Chocolate Cake (page 180) or as a filling for holiday cookies (page 246) or French Macarons (page 76).

This whipped ganache frosting is truly incredible. It's rich and decadent with a smooth, silky texture. The addition of everyone's favorite chocolate-hazelnut spread gives it a subtle, delicious hazelnut flavor. You will want to mix the ingredients for this ahead of time because it needs to chill in the fridge before you can whip it up into an amazing frosting.

1. **Prepare the chocolate.** Place the chopped dark and milk chocolate in the bowl of a stand mixer (or in a large heat-safe bowl, if using a hand mixer). Set aside. The smaller the pieces, the more easily the chocolate will melt.

2. **Heat the cream.** In a medium saucepan, warm the cream over medium heat until it begins to simmer. Do not let it boil.

3. **Mix the cream and chocolate.** Quickly pour the hot cream over the chocolate, and let it stand for 2 minutes to allow the chocolate to begin to melt. Using a rubber spatula or the whisk attachment of a stand mixer, mix until all the chocolate has melted and a smooth ganache has formed. At first, it might seem like the ingredients aren't mixing properly, but keep going—the ganache will come together.

4. **Add the Nutella.** Stir in the Nutella until well combined.

5. **Chill the ganache.** Cover and refrigerate for 45 minutes, stirring every 10 minutes to help chill the ganache evenly. It needs to be fully chilled before whipping.

6. **Whip the ganache.** Using a whisk attachment, whip the mixture until it lightens in color and becomes spreadable, about 2 minutes. You may think the mixture can't possibly form a frosting, but if it's cold, it will whip up beautifully! Do not overwhip, otherwise the frosting will split.

7. **Use immediately.** Spread the frosting on your cake immediately after whipping. In cool weather, the frosted cake can be kept at room temperature. In warm weather, refrigerate the cake. Take the cake out of the fridge 40 minutes before serving to allow the cake and frosting to soften up.

Dark Chocolate Ganache

PREP: 5 minutes // **COOK:** 2 minutes, plus 20 minutes to cool // **YIELD:** About 2 cups

INGREDIENTS

8oz (240g) 70% cocoa dark chocolate, such as Lindt, chopped into small pieces

1 cup (240g) heavy cream (36% milkfat or higher)

SPECIAL EQUIPMENT

Handheld mixer (for whipped ganache)

VARIATION

Add 1 to 2 tablespoons of your preferred spirit or liqueur. Dark rum, Cognac, and bourbon all work well, as do Cointreau, Baileys, and crème de menthe. These variations are perfect for the holidays.

Classic chocolate ganache has only two ingredients—dark chocolate and cream—but it has many applications. I'm giving you the classic version, which has a 1:1 ratio of chocolate to cream.

1. **Prepare the chocolate.** To a large heat-safe bowl, add the chopped-up chocolate. Set aside. (The smaller the pieces of chocolate, the more easily they will melt.)

2. **Heat the cream.** In a medium saucepan, heat the cream over medium heat, until it begins to simmer. Do not let it boil.

3. **Mix the cream and chocolate.** Quickly pour the hot cream over the chopped-up chocolate, and let it stand for 2 minutes to allow the chocolate to begin to melt. Then, using a rubber spatula, mix until all the chocolate has melted and a smooth ganache has formed. At first, it might seem like the ingredients aren't mixing properly, but keep going—it will come together.

4. **Cool the ganache.** Allow to cool to room temperature. The ganache will thicken as it cools.

5. **Use as desired.** Ganache can be used for any of the following:

   - **Runny ganache.** Allow the ganache to cool at room temperature for 20 to 30 minutes, then use as a glaze for pastries or for cake drips.

   - **Soft creamy frosting.** Allow the ganache to sit at room temperature for at least 1 hour or until it thickens to a soft consistency. Use to fill cookies.

   - **Whipped ganache.** Refrigerate the ganache for about 45 minutes, stirring every 10 minutes. (This allows the ganache to cool more evenly and remain soft.) Once cool, add an additional ½ cup (120g) cold heavy cream and, using a handheld mixer, whip until the ganache is whipped and lightened in color. Don't overwhip. Use to frost cupcakes or cakes. (For a super delicious version of whipped ganache, try the version on page 210).

   - **Firm ganache.** Refrigerate the ganache for at least 6 hours. Then, using a small ice cream scoop, create truffles. Place the truffles onto some parchment paper. Quickly roll the truffles between your hands and coat in cocoa powder, powdered sugar, or shredded coconut.

> **MAKE AHEAD**
> Refrigerate in an airtight container for up to 5 days. Before using, allow to sit at room temperature for 45 minutes. Mix well before using.
>
> Store in an airtight container in the freezer for up to 1 month. Defrost overnight in the fridge before using. Then, allow to sit at room temperature for 45 minutes. Mix well before using.

Silky Lemon Curd

PREP: 5 minutes // COOK: 5 minutes // YIELD: Enough to fill a 2- or 3-layer cake

INGREDIENTS

3–4 lemons

3 medium eggs

2 egg yolks

1 cup (200g) granulated white sugar

1½ tbsp (15g) cornstarch

5½ tbsp (80g) unsalted butter, chopped into
  small pieces

SPECIAL EQUIPMENT

Handheld mixer or stand mixer

// BEST USES

Use as a tangy filling for the Moist Lemon
Cake (page 192), French Macarons (page 76),
or holiday cookies (page 246).

Lemon curd is a delicious filling for cakes, tarts, and pastries. For me, lemon curd is all about tangy lemon flavor and a silky-smooth texture. I find store-bought versions disappointing, and many recipes don't give me the texture I'm looking for. The secret to the texture in this recipe is the ratio of egg white to egg yolk.

1. **Zest and juice the lemons.** Into a medium bowl, zest 3 lemons. Juice the lemons, and add exactly ½ cup plus 2 tablespoons (140g) of lemon juice to the bowl with the lemon zest. (You may need to juice the fourth lemon.) Set aside.

2. **Mix the eggs, sugar, and cornstarch.** In a large bowl, using a handheld mixer, beat the whole eggs, egg yolks, and sugar until well combined. Add the cornstarch and mix until combined.

3. **Make the lemon curd.** In a large saucepan, combine the lemon juice/ zest mixture and the egg/sugar mixture and place over low heat. Heat, stirring continuously, until the mixture has thickened (the mixture thickens as the eggs cook). Alternate between using a whisk and a rubber spatula, so you can scrape the bottom and edges of the pan. If you see steam coming off the top of the liquid, remove the pan from the heat for a few seconds, continuing to stir. Then put the pan back on the heat. As soon as the mixture has thickened (it will take about 5 minutes), turn off the heat.

4. **Add the butter.** Add the chopped-up butter a few pieces at a time and stir into the mixture until all the butter has melted.

5. **Strain the curd.** Strain the curd through a fine mesh sieve into a clean heat-safe bowl. Cover and allow to cool.

MAKE AHEAD
Lemon curd will keep in an airtight container in the fridge for about 1 week. Before using, give it a quick mix.

Stabilized Whipped Cream

PREP: 20 minutes // **COOK:** None // **YIELD:** Enough to fill a 2- or 3-layer cake

Whipped cream is delicious, but it doesn't hold for long before it collapses. This version, stabilized with mascarpone, is light and airy, and will hold its shape much better than regular whipped cream.

1. **Prepare the bowl.** Place the bowl of the stand mixer, or a large glass or metal bowl if using a handheld mixer, in the freezer for 10 minutes. This allows the cream to whip faster and hold its structure better.

2. **Mix the mascarpone and sugar.** Take the bowl out of the freezer and add the cold mascarpone cheese and sugar. Using a mixer, mix until smooth and combined.

3. **Whip the cream.** Add the cold cream and vanilla extract and mix on low speed until just combined. Increase the speed to high, and whip just until stiff peaks form (see page 23) then stop mixing.

4. **Use immediately.** Although this recipe is designed to be stable, it's at its best as soon as it's been made. Keep any cakes you make with this frosting refrigerated. Take out of the fridge 30 minutes before serving.

INGREDIENTS

½ cup (100g) mascarpone cheese, cold

¼ cup (50g) granulated white sugar

1½ cups (350g) heavy cream, cold

2 tsp vanilla extract

SPECIAL EQUIPMENT

Handheld mixer or stand mixer

// BEST USES

Use as a filling and/or frosting for any vanilla or chocolate cake, or serve on the side with any slice of cake.

VARIATION

To make regular whipped cream, omit the mascarpone. It's so easy to make, there's no need to ever buy canned whipped cream again!

MAKE AHEAD

Store in an airtight container in the fridge for up to 3 days. If the cream has loosened, whip again.

Silky Pastry Cream

PREP: 3 minutes // **COOK:** 5 minutes, plus 1 hour to cool // **YIELD:** Enough to fill a 2- or 3-layer cake

INGREDIENTS

½ cup (100g) granulated white sugar, plus extra for dusting

2½ tbsp cornstarch

¼ tsp salt

1⅓ cups (320g) whole milk

2 medium eggs

2 tsp vanilla extract

// BEST USES

Use as a filling for the Classic Vanilla Birthday Cake (page 178), Irresistible Italian Donuts (page 126), or French Macarons (page 76)

VARIATIONS

You can add 1 to 2 tablespoons of any spirit or liqueur to flavor the pastry cream: dark rum, Cognac, bourbon, Cointreau, and Grand Marnier all work well. These variations are particularly good during the holidays.

Pastry cream is easier to make than you might think. It makes an amazing filling for cakes, donuts, and other pastries; a great lining for fruit tarts; and is the base for most soufflés. If you're familiar with traditional pastry cream recipes, you'll notice a few differences here. I designed the recipe to make it simpler, faster, more convenient, and, yes, better! My version has an amazing, silky texture. It uses whole eggs instead of the traditional egg yolks; cornstarch instead of the traditional mix of cornstarch and all-purpose flour; and, unlike with the traditional method, there's no need to temper the eggs. With my easy method, pastry cream takes only a few minutes to make.

1. **Combine the dry ingredients.** To a medium saucepan, add the sugar, cornstarch, and salt. Set aside.

2. **Combine the wet ingredients.** To a large liquid measuring cup, add the milk and eggs. Stir well until fully combined.

3. **Combine the dry and wet ingredients.** In a slow stream, add the wet ingredients to the dry ingredients in the saucepan. Whisk constantly as you're adding the liquid. Initially, this creates a slurry, which will ensure that the cornstarch disperses evenly into the milk.

4. **Cook the pastry cream.** Heat the mixture in the saucepan over medium-low heat, whisking constantly. Bring to a gentle boil and cook until it starts to thicken, about 1 minute. Switch to using a spatula so you can scrape the bottom, edges, and sides of the pan. The pastry cream will start to thicken only after the mixture has come to a gentle boil, and it will thicken a lot more as it cools.

5. **Add the vanilla.** Turn off the heat and stir in the vanilla.

6. **Finish the pastry cream.** Pour the pastry cream through a fine mesh sieve into a heat-safe bowl. Dust the surface of the pastry cream with sugar (this will stop a skin from forming). Allow to cool. Whisk before using.

MAKE AHEAD

Press a layer of plastic wrap onto the surface of pastry cream and refrigerate for up to 3 days. When ready to use, give it a good whisk before using (it will be too firm to use as is). If it's still too thick, whisk in a tablespoon of milk.

Royal Icing

PREP: 10 minutes // **COOK:** None // **YIELD:** About 2 cups (enough to decorate a large batch of cookies)

INGREDIENTS

2 large egg whites

1 tbsp lemon juice

1 tsp flavor extract of choice, such as vanilla or almond

4 cups (500g) powdered sugar

Gel-based food coloring (optional)

// BEST USES

Use for decorating cookies such as Quick Gingerbread Cookies (page 270), No-Spread Cutout Sugar Cookies (page 268), and the Custom Holiday Cookie Box (page 246).

Whether you're decorating holiday cookies or you're building your dream gingerbread house, royal icing is the perfect choice. It pipes easily, doesn't spread, and dries with a hard, shiny finish. Note that this icing contains raw egg whites, so use pasteurized egg whites if you have any concerns about consuming raw eggs.

1. **Whisk the egg whites.** In a large bowl, whisk the egg whites until foamy.

2. **Add the lemon juice and flavoring.** Add the lemon juice and the flavored extract and whisk to incorporate.

3. **Add the sugar.** Add the powdered sugar 1 tablespoon at a time, whisking continuously until all the sugar has been incorporated. The texture should be thick and spreadable. If you prefer the icing thicker, add extra powdered sugar. If you prefer it thinner, add extra lemon juice.

4. **Add color, if using.** To a batch of icing that you want to color, add the food coloring a few drops at a time, mixing well after each addition. Keep going until the icing has reached something close to your desired color. Keep in mind the color will continue to develop over a few hours, so it's hard to be precise.

5. **Use for decoration.** When using the icing, keep the batch you're using covered with plastic wrap because it dries quickly.

MAKE AHEAD

The icing can be made ahead and refrigerated in an airtight container for up to 1 week. Mix before using. If it becomes a bit stiff, add 1 teaspoon of lemon juice to restore its spreadable consistency.

Instant Fudge Frosting

PREP: 5 minutes // **COOK:** 5 minutes, plus 30 minutes to chill // **YIELD:** Enough to frost a 7- to 8-inch (18–20cm) 2-layer cake

This fudge frosting comes together so quickly and easily, it's like magic.

1. **Melt the chocolate.** In a microwave-safe bowl, heat the chocolate in the microwave, stirring every 30 seconds, until the chocolate is melted. Set aside.

2. **Boil the water.** In a small saucepan, bring the water to a boil.

3. **Make the frosting.** To the bowl of a stand mixer (or in a large bowl, if using a hand mixer), add the sugar, butter, cocoa powder, and salt. Add the hot water. Mix until well combined. Add the melted chocolate and mix until combined. The frosting should look creamy but loose.

4. **Chill the frosting.** Refrigerate the frosting for at least 30 minutes or until thick enough to spread.

VARIATION

For a richer tasting frosting, replace the water with whole milk.

INGREDIENTS

2oz (60g) 75% cocoa dark chocolate, chopped

⅓ cup + 1½ tbsp (100g) water

3¼ cups (400g) powdered sugar

10½ tbsp (1⅓ stick / 150g) unsalted butter, at room temperature

⅔ cup (80g) unsweetened cocoa powder

½ tsp salt

SPECIAL EQUIPMENT

Handheld mixer or stand mixer

// BEST USES

Use as a frosting for the Classic Yellow Cake (page 182) or Classic Vanilla Birthday Cake (page 178) or as a filling for holiday cookies (page 246).

Italian Salted Caramel

PREP: 1 minute // **COOK:** 12 minutes, plus 3 hours to cool // **YIELD:** ¾ cup

INGREDIENTS

1¼ cups (250g) granulated white sugar

11 tbsp (165g) warm water, divided

¼ tsp salt

// BEST USES

Drizzle over chocolate cakes or ice cream, or add to whipped cream to serve with the Apple Cinnamon Snacking Cake (page 264).

This pure salted caramel contains no dairy. It's all delicious caramel. It's great drizzled over cake, or ice cream. If you've never tried pure caramel before, you need to give this a try! You always need to be careful when making caramel—it can get very hot and can burn you if it splashes.

1. **Partially dissolve the sugar.** To a large, tall saucepan (use a pan that's light color on the inside so you can see the color of the caramel as it forms), add the sugar and 5 tablespoons (75g) water. Place the pan over low heat and let the sugar begin to dissolve into the water, about 2 minutes. Do not stir the mixture, but you can gently swirl the pan to move the sugar around.

2. **Caramelize the sugar.** Once the sugar has partially dissolved, increase the heat to medium-high. Continue to swirl the mixture (do not stir it!), and heat until the sugar has melted and achieves a golden amber color. (The sugar will first start to brown around the sides of the pan.) As soon as the caramelized sugar reaches the desired color (timings will vary, but it will likely be around 10 minutes), remove the pan from the heat.

3. **Add the remaining water and salt.** Carefully stand back and add the remaining 6 tablespoons (90g) warm water and the salt. (Be careful the hot mixture doesn't splash you.) Stir to form a uniform caramel and ensure the salt dissolves. Don't taste the caramel while it's hot—it will burn you!

4. **Strain.** Strain the caramel through a fine mesh sieve into a clean, heat-safe bowl. Allow to cool. Refrigerate for at least 3 to 4 hours. The caramel with thicken as it cools.

> **MAKE AHEAD**
> The caramel will keep in an airtight container for several months.

Childhood Favorites

The foods of childhood can be so nostalgic; the smell of opening a fresh package of Oreo cookies or the excitement of waiting in line at McDonald's for a McFlurry. This chapter includes homemade recreations of classic American brands made with simple ingredients and clever techniques. I hope you'll find at least one of these delicious treats takes you back to your childhood.

DIY Peanut Butter Cups

PREP: 10 minutes, plus 30 minutes to cool // **COOK:** None // **YIELD:** 8 peanut butter cups

INGREDIENTS

FOR THE FILLING

2 tbsp (30g) unsalted butter, at room temperature

⅓ cup (90g) smooth peanut butter, at room temperature

¼ cup (40g) powdered sugar

FOR THE CHOCOLATE CASES

7oz (200g) milk chocolate

SPECIAL EQUIPMENT

Handheld mixer

3 small disposable piping bags

16 paper cupcake liners

These homemade peanut butter cups are so quick and easy to put together, it's hard to believe how delicious and close they are to the real thing. This is an ideal first baking project, and great for practicing piping skills. You can easily double or triple this recipe if you want to make a bigger batch to gift to friends.

1. **Make the filling.** In a medium bowl, using a handheld mixer, beat the soft, room-temperature butter until it's creamy. Add the room-temperature peanut butter and mix until well-incorporated. Add the powdered sugar and mix well. When everything is mixed, the filling should have a smooth, creamy texture. Transfer the filling to a piping bag and set aside.

2. **Melt and temper the chocolate.** Chop the chocolate into very small pieces. Set aside one third of the chopped chocolate and put the rest into a microwave-safe bowl. Microwave the bowl until the chocolate is melted, stirring every 30 seconds. Once melted, stir in the chopped chocolate you set aside. Stir until it's all melted and smooth.

3. **Make the bases.** Double up the paper cupcake liners to make sure the peanut butter cups hold their shape. Arrange the 8 doubled-up liners on a tray. Transfer one third of the melted chocolate to a piping bag and pipe a thin layer of chocolate into each doubled-up cupcake liner. Put the tray of cupcake liners in the freezer for a few minutes for the chocolate bases to set.

4. **Add the filling.** Take the cupcake liners out of the freezer and pipe a dollop of the filling onto the center of each base. Make sure to leave a little space between the edge of the filling and the edge of the cupcake liner. Wet your fingers with water, and gently dab down the filling so it forms a flat disk.

5. **Make the sides and tops.** It's important the remaining chocolate is fully melted. If it looks like it has thickened and begun to set, pop it back in the microwave for 30 seconds to loosen up before transfering to a piping bag. Pipe chocolate to form the tops of the peanut butter cups—use just enough to cover the filling. Gently tap each liner on the countertop to make sure there are no air bubbles and to level the chocolate out. Refrigerate for 15 minutes or until the chocolate is fully set.

6. **Serve.** When the chocolate is set, the peanut butter cups are ready to serve.

MAKE AHEAD
Peanut butter cups can be stored in an airtight container at room temperature for up to 1 week. In warm weather, store in the fridge.

Instant DIY McFlurry

PREP: 5 minutes, plus 3 hours to freeze // **COOK:** None // **YIELD:** 5 servings

INGREDIENTS

2 cups (500g) heavy cream

¾ cup (250g) sweetened condensed milk

2 tsp vanilla extract

1–2 tsp whole milk

Toppings of choice, such as M&M's minis or crushed Oreo cookies

SPECIAL EQUIPMENT

Ice cube trays, where each well holds about 1 ounce of liquid (about 2 tbsp)

Food processor

Piping bag with a star tip

// NOTE

Unless you have a powerful food processor, I recommend processing these in small batches of 8 cubes or fewer.

If you find that the ice cream machine at your local McDonald's is often broken, here's a method I developed to make something very similar to a McFlurry at home. It couldn't be easier. Ahead of time, you freeze a no-churn ice cream mix in ice cube trays. Then, whenever you're craving a creamy blended ice cream treat, you pop out a few of the premade cubes and whiz them up in a food processor. Add your favorite mix-ins to create your favorite flavor!

1. **Prepare the cubes.** In a large liquid measuring cup or medium bowl with a spout, combine the heavy cream, condensed milk, and vanilla. Do not whip; just mix until the ingredients are well combined. Pour the mixture into an ice cube tray or silicone mold and freeze for 3 to 4 hours until solid.

2. **Blend.** To a food processor, add 8 frozen cubes and 1 tablespoon of milk. Pulse until you reach a creamy soft-serve consistency. (Add a little more milk if you need to but don't add too much or you'll end up with a milkshake!)

3. **Serve.** Mix in your favorite toppings and serve immediately. Alternatively, working quickly (before your ice cream melts), transfer the plain ice cream to a piping bag fitted with a star tip, and pipe into a serving dish. Then top with M&M's, crushed Oreos, or any other toppings of your choice.

Instant Frozen Yogurt

PREP: 5 minutes, plus 3 hours to freeze // **COOK:** None // **YIELD:** 5 servings

INGREDIENTS

FOR THE BASE
1¾ cups (400g) heavy cream
¾ cup (170g) plain Greek yogurt
⅔ cup (130g) superfine sugar or
  granulated white sugar

FOR PLAIN
8 frozen cubes of base mixture
1–2 tbsp whole milk

FOR CHOCOLATE
8 frozen cubes of base mixture
1–2 tbsp whole milk
1 tbsp unsweetened cocoa powder

FOR STRAWBERRY
8 frozen cubes of base mixture
1–2 tbsp whole milk
1–2 tbsp strawberry jam or a few
  frozen strawberries

SUGGESTED TOPPINGS
Chopped nuts, chopped up fresh fruit,
  Salted Caramel Sauce (page 217),
  chocolate chips, smashed cookies,
  brownie bites, chopped-up candy bars

SPECIAL EQUIPMENT
Ice cube trays, where each well holds
  about 1 ounce of liquid (about 2 tbsp)
Food processor

If you've ever tried to make frozen yogurt by putting regular yogurt in the freezer, you know that doesn't work—you end up with a rock hard, frozen brick. This recipe is the secret to making amazing, soft-serve style frozen yogurt at home. The base mixture is frozen in ice cube trays, making it easy to whip up a serving of froyo in less than a minute. Try plain, chocolate, or strawberry to start—or get creative and make whatever flavors you like!

1. **Prepare the base.** In a large liquid measuring cup, combine the heavy cream, yogurt, and sugar. Do not whip; just mix until the ingredients are well combined and the sugar is dissolved. Pour the mixture into an ice cube tray or silicone mold and freeze until solid.

2. **Make the frozen yogurt.** Unless you have a powerful food processor, I recommend blending no more than 8 frozen cubes of base mixture at a time (about one serving).

   Plain: Transfer 8 frozen cubes of base mixture into a food processor along with 1 tablespoon of milk. Pulse until you reach a creamy, soft-serve consistency. Add a little more milk if you need to but don't add too much or you'll end up with a milkshake!

   Chocolate: Follow the process for the plain frozen yogurt but also add the cocoa powder into the food processor.

   Strawberry: Follow the process for the plain frozen yogurt but also add the strawberry jam or frozen strawberries into the food processor. (Do not add fresh strawberries, or the froyo will melt.)

3. **Serve.** Mix in your favorite toppings and serve immediately. Alternatively, working quickly, you can put the frozen yogurt in a piping bag without the toppings, and pipe it into serving dishes.

Mini Chocolate Chip Cookies

PREP: 15 minutes // **COOK:** 8 minutes, plus 30 minutes to cool // **YIELD:** 162 mini cookies

INGREDIENTS

2 cups (300g) all-purpose flour

½ tsp baking powder

½ tsp salt

1⅓ stick (160g) unsalted butter

½ cup (100g) white granulated sugar

½ cup (100g) brown sugar (light or dark)

1 tsp vanilla extract

1 large egg

1 tbsp whole milk, as needed

1½ cups (250g) mini semisweet chocolate chips, plus more for topping

SPECIAL EQUIPMENT

Sturdy piping bag (or two flimsier piping bags, doubled up)

This might become your new favorite way of eating cookies! This recipe makes a lot of cookies—more than 150—but they're teeny tiny. With this pastry chef method, it will take you only about 15 minutes to prepare these. The secret is a loose dough that you can pipe. These are amazing eaten as "cookie cereal" drenched in milk.

1. **Preheat the oven and prepare the baking sheets.** Preheat the oven to 320°F (160°C). Line three baking sheets with parchment paper.

2. **Mix the dry ingredients.** In a large bowl, whisk together the flour, baking powder, and salt. Set aside.

3. **Melt the butter.** In another large bowl, melt the butter in a microwave (see page 25).

4. **Mix the wet ingredients.** To the melted butter, add the white sugar, brown sugar, and vanilla. Stir with a whisk until the mixture is smooth and has cooled slightly. Add the egg and mix to incorporate.

5. **Combine the dry and wet ingredients.** Add the dry ingredients to the wet and, using a rubber spatula, mix. The dough should look like very soft cookie dough and have a pipeable texture. If the mixture seems too stiff, add 1 tablespoon of milk. Stir in the chocolate chips and transfer the mixture to a piping bag. If your piping bag isn't sturdy, double it up to make a stronger one. Cut a small opening at the tip to pipe the cookies. The opening should be small enough that you have good control when piping, but large enough so the chocolate chips come out easily.

6. **Pipe the cookies.** Pipe mini cookies, about 1 inch (2.5cm) in diameter, onto the baking sheets. Aim for piping 6 rows of 9 cookies on each baking sheet, leaving space between each cookie. Using lightly wet fingers, gently dab down the cookies to smooth out any pointy bits. Add a couple of extra chocolate chips onto the top of each cookie.

7. **Bake the cookies.** Bake for 5 to 8 minutes, until golden in color. Allow the cookies to cool completely on the baking sheets, where they will continue to cook and crisp up.

8. **Serve.** My favorite way to serve these cookies is to put a bunch into a bowl, pour over some milk, and eat them like cereal!

MAKE AHEAD
When cool, store the cookies in an airtight container at room temperature for up to a week.

Homemade Pop-Tarts

PREP: 40 minutes // **COOK:** 15 minutes, plus 20 minutes to cool // **YIELD:** 8 pastries

INGREDIENTS

1¾ cups (250g) all-purpose flour

½ cup (80g) powdered sugar

¼ tsp salt

10½ tbsp (1⅓ sticks / 150g) unsalted butter, cold, cut into small pieces

1 egg white

¾ cup strawberry jam, for the filling

½ batch Royal Icing (optional, page 215)

Sprinkles (optional), to taste

SPECIAL EQUIPMENT

Food processor

Pizza cutter wheel (not required but recommended)

Piping bag

VARIATIONS

You don't have to stick to strawberry jam. Use whatever fillings you like—different flavor jams, Nutella, or any type of spread you can think of!

MAKE AHEAD

Unbaked pastries can be frozen and baked off as needed. Once frozen, wrap them tightly in plastic wrap and place in a resealable zip-top bag. They'll keep for up to 3 months.

These toaster pastries have been around for decades, and there are many recipes out there for homemade versions. Most of them use piecrust, but that's not the right kind of pastry—if you've ever had Pop-Tarts, you know they aren't as buttery or flaky. My version is much more like "the real thing," although I think these are way more delicious than the store-bought version.

1. **Prepare the baking sheets.** Line two baking sheets with parchment paper.

2. **Make the pastry.** In a food processor, pulse the flour, sugar, salt, and cold butter until just combined, about 30 seconds. Add the egg white, and pulse again until a rough dough forms.

3. **Roll out the dough.** Transfer the dough onto a lightly floured work surface and, using your hands, bring the dough together. Using a rolling pin, roll out the pastry to about ¼ inch (6mm) thick. If you find the pastry is too soft to work with, put it in the fridge for 30 minutes to firm up.

4. **Cut the dough.** Using a pizza cutter wheel, trim the pastry into a large rectangle. Then cut out rectangles the size of Pop-Tarts, about 4½ x 3 inches (11.5 x 7.5cm). You want to prepare 16 rectangles. Re-roll the dough and the scraps to get the number of rectangles you need.

5. **Form the pastries.** Place 4 rectangles of pastry onto each prepared baking sheet. Then place 2 or 3 heaping teaspoons of strawberry jam onto each rectangle. Spread it out, leaving about a ½-inch (1.25cm) border all the way round. Using wet fingers, spread a little water over the border to help seal the pastries. Then place another rectangle of pastry on top, sandwiching the jam in the middle. (Don't worry about aligning them perfectly.) Press the edges down firmly with your fingers to seal the sandwiches. Using a pizza wheel cutter, trim a small amount from all the edges to neaten them up. Place in the freezer for about 10 minutes to firm up.

6. **Preheat the oven.** Preheat the oven to 350°F (180°C).

7. **Bake the pastries.** Bake for 15 to 20 minutes or until the pastry crusts are a light golden-brown color. Remove from the oven and allow to cool completely.

8. **Frost the pastries.** If desired, pipe a layer of icing on top of each pastry, leaving a rough ¾-inch (2cm) border. Don't be too neat with the icing; it's supposed to look a little uneven. You can smooth it out using a toothpick. Add a few sprinkles and leave the icing to set.

9. **Serve.** These are delicious as is, but once the icing has set completely and gone hard (leave them until the next day), they are absolutely designed to go in your toaster to warm up. (Once set, the icing won't melt or drip in the toaster). It's your choice—have them however you prefer.

Easy Microwave Cake Pops

PREP: 5 minutes // **COOK:** 3 minutes, plus 10 minutes to cool // **YIELD:** 10 to 12 cake pops

INGREDIENTS

4 tbsp (60g) unsalted butter

¼ cup (60g) granulated white sugar

½ cup (120g) + 3 tbsp whole milk, divided

½ tsp vanilla extract

⅔ cup (100g) all-purpose flour

1 tsp baking powder

¼ tsp salt

1½ tbsp unsweetened cocoa powder, sifted

2–3 tbsp marshmallow fluff

2–3 tbsp Nutella

7oz (200g) good-quality chocolate, chopped

1 tbsp coconut oil

Sprinkles (optional)

SPECIAL EQUIPMENT

10–12 cake pop sticks

Styrofoam block (optional), for holding the cake pops while the shells set

Every kid loves cake pops! In bakeries, cake pops are made with leftover cake scraps, but who has scraps of cake lying around at home? The good news is, there's no need to bake a whole cake just to create scraps when you want cake pops. Instead, you can quickly make some mug cakes in the microwave and use those to make just the amount of cake pops you need.

1. **Make the batter.** In a large microwave-safe bowl, melt the butter. Add the sugar, ½ cup (120g) milk, and vanilla and stir well using a fork. Add the flour, baking powder, and salt. Using a rubber spatula, mix to combine until a smooth batter forms.

2. **Divide the batter and add the cocoa powder.** Divide the batter evenly between two bowls. Into one bowl, sift the cocoa powder and add the remaining 3 tablespoons of milk. Mix to combine. You now have one bowl of vanilla cake batter and one bowl of chocolate cake batter.

3. **Make the mug cakes.** Divide the vanilla cake batter evenly between 2 mugs. Divide the chocolate cake batter evenly between another 2 mugs. Microwave two mugs at a time for 60 to 90 seconds. Scoop out the cooked mug cakes into 2 bowls—one for the vanilla, and one for the chocolate—and allow to cool for 5 to 10 minutes.

4. **Form the cake pops.** Using your hands, break up the mug cakes into small pieces. Add the marshmallow fluff to the vanilla cake pop crumbs and add the Nutella to the chocolate cake pop crumbs. Mix to combine. Then, using your hands, roll the mix into balls. You should get 5 to 6 cake pops of each flavor.

5. **Make the chocolate shell.** In a medium microwave-safe bowl, microwave the chocolate and coconut oil, stirring every 30 seconds until the chocolate is just melted.

6. **Add the sticks to cake pops.** Dip one end of a cake pop stick into the melted chocolate, then insert into a cake pop ball. Repeat for all the cake pops. Place the cake pops into the freezer for 10 minutes.

7. **Dip the cake pops.** If the chocolate in the bowl has started to set, pop it back in the microwave to melt again, stirring every 30 seconds. Take the cake pops out of the freezer one at a time and dip in the melted chocolate. Allow any excess chocolate to drip back into the bowl. Then, quickly coat in sprinkles and set aside on parchment paper. (Or, for a prettier presentation, insert the sticks in a Styrofoam block to hold them upright while the shell sets). The shell should set quickly, but if it's not setting as fast as you'd like, put the cake pops in the fridge for 5 minutes.

8. **Serve.** When the coating is set, the cake pops are ready to serve.

> **MAKE AHEAD**
> Cake pops can be stored in an airtight container at room temperature for 2 days.

Stuffed Sandwich Cookies

PREP: 20 minutes // **COOK:** 13 minutes, plus 15 minutes to cool // **YIELD:** 22 cookies (11 chocolate, 11 vanilla)

INGREDIENTS

FOR THE CHOCOLATE COOKIES

¾ cup (100g) all-purpose flour

½ cup (60g) powdered sugar

3½ tbsp (25g) Dutch-process cocoa powder

¼ tsp salt

5½ tbsp (75g) unsalted butter, cold, cut into ½-inch (1cm) cubes

1 egg yolk

1 tsp vanilla extract or strong coffee

Black gel-based food coloring (optional)

FOR THE VANILLA COOKIES

1 cup (140g) all-purpose flour

⅓ cup (40g) powdered sugar

¼ tsp salt

5½ tbsp (75g) unsalted butter, cold, cut into ½ inch (1cm) cubes

1 egg yolk

2 tsp vanilla extract

FOR THE FILLING

8 tbsp (1 stick / 115g) unsalted butter, at room temperature

2 tsp vanilla extract

1 cup (120g) powdered sugar

SPECIAL EQUIPMENT

1½-inch (4cm) round cookie cutter

Food processor

Handheld mixer or stand mixer

For many people, stuffed, sandwich-style cookies like Oreos have a special place in childhood memories. Not everyone agrees how they're best eaten—dunked in milk or twisted and separated—but I think we can all agree they're delicious! I'm giving you my two favorite versions of homemade Oreos here—classic chocolate and golden vanilla.

1. **Prepare the baking sheets.** Line two baking sheets with parchment paper.

2. **Make the chocolate dough.** To a food processor, add the flour, sugar, cocoa powder, salt, and butter. Pulse for 15 seconds. Add the egg yolk, vanilla or coffee, and food coloring, if using. Pulse until a dough comes together. Be patient—it will form a dough! Remove the dough from the food processor and place it on a clean work surface. Wash and dry the food processor bowl before making the vanilla dough.

3. **Make the vanilla dough.** To a food processor, add the flour, sugar, salt, and butter. Pulse for 15 seconds. Add the egg yolk and vanilla and pulse until a dough comes together.

4. **Roll out the cookie doughs.** Working with one batch of dough at a time, transfer the dough to an unfloured surface and work it using your hands until it's completely uniform. (Don't worry about overworking this dough.) Now very lightly flour the surface, and using a rolling pin, roll out the dough thinly to around ⅛ inch (3mm) thick. (This thickness will match the store-bought versions, but these are your cookies—if you like them a little thicker, roll the dough out thicker.)

5. **Cut out the cookies.** Using a 1½-inch (4cm) diameter cookie cutter, cut out the cookies. Transfer to the prepared cookie sheets leaving a little space between each cookie. Place the baking sheets in the freezer for 15 minutes.

6. **Preheat the oven.** Preheat the oven to 350°F (180°C).

7. **Bake the cookies.** Bake the cookies for 13 to 15 minutes or until the golden cookies are lightly colored. Remove from the oven. Leave on the baking sheet for 5 minutes, then transfer to a wire rack and allow to cool completely.

8. **Make the filling.** In a stand mixer (or a medium bowl, if using a handheld mixer), beat the butter and vanilla until soft, then add the powdered sugar a few tablespoons at a time. Continue beating until fully incorporated. Transfer to a piping bag.

9. **Assemble the cookies.** Pipe a dollop of the filling into the center of the cookie. Take a second cookie and gently press down onto the filling to make a sandwich. Press evenly, pushing out the filling to the edge of the sandwich. Repeat for all the cookies.

10. **Serve.** Serve with a glass of milk.

> **MAKE AHEAD**
> Store the cookies in an airtight container at room temperature for up to 5 days.

Homemade Marshmallows

PREP: 5 minutes // **COOK:** 15 minutes, plus 5 minutes to cool // **YIELD:** 40 to 100 marshmallows

INGREDIENTS

1½ cups (200g) cornstarch, for dusting

5 sheets unflavored gelatin or ½oz (12g) gelatin powder

½ cup (120g) + 3 tbsp water, divided

1 cup (200g) granulated white sugar

2oz (60g) light corn syrup or honey

¼ tsp salt

1 tsp vanilla extract

Gel-based food coloring (optional)

SPECIAL EQUIPMENT

Stand mixer

Candy thermometer

Piping bag with round tip

MAKE AHEAD
Store in an airtight container at room temperature for 2 weeks.

Believe it not, marshmallows are one of the easiest childhood favorites to recreate at home. Most home methods use a baking dish, but it can take up to 12 hours for them to be ready that way. Using this method, they're ready to enjoy just 5 minutes after you've made them. These are squishy and delicious and can be made in any size you want—from mini to giant.

1. **Heat-treat the cornstarch.** Spread the cornstarch on a baking sheet and place in a 350°F (180°C) oven for 5 minutes. When cool, pass through a fine mesh sieve to break up any clumps that form. Make sure cornstarch is fully cooled before using.

2. **Prepare the work surface.** Dust your work surface generously (and I mean generously!) with heat-treated cornstarch. (There should be enough cornstarch that you can't see your countertop.)

3. **Hydrate the gelatin.** To the bowl of a stand mixer, add the gelatin sheets and ½ cup of water. If you're using gelatin powder, sprinkle the gelatin over the water, mix, and allow to stand.

4. **Boil the sugar.** In a tall saucepan over medium heat, combine the sugar, corn syrup, and the remaining 3 tablespoons of water. Stir the mixture and bring to a boil. Then heat, without stirring, until the mixture reaches 240°F (115°C)—use a candy thermometer to measure the temperature.

5. **Add the sugar to the gelatin.** With the mixer off, quickly but carefully pour the hot sugar mixture over the gelatin and add the salt. Stand back and beat the mixture on high speed for 5 to 8 minutes or until it reaches medium/stiff peaks (see page 23). Do not touch the bowl or the mixture; it will be very hot. After beating the mixture, the bowl should be cooled to room temperature.

6. **Add vanilla and transfer to a piping bag.** Beat in the vanilla and a few drops of food coloring, if using. Quickly transfer the mixture to a piping bag with a round tip. The size of the tip will determine the diameter of the marshmallows.

7. **Pipe out the marshmallows.** Pipe out the marshmallows in long ropes onto your prepared work surface. Work fast, as the mixture sets up quickly. Dust the top and sides generously with more cornstarch and allow the marshmallows to sit for at least 5 minutes or until set. (They need to be completely covered). Once the marshmallows are properly set, dust your hands with cornstarch, and gently roll the marshmallow ropes in the cornstarch and cut them into pieces. Place the marshmallows in a fine mesh sieve and shake off the excess cornstarch.

8. **Serve**. These are delicious to eat after sitting for around 5 minutes. If you let them sit for a couple of hours, they'll become even more bouncy and squishy.

Grab-and-Go Snack Cakes

PREP: 15 minutes // **COOK:** 12 minutes, plus 30 minutes to cool // **YIELD:** 16 snack cakes (8 vanilla; 8 chocolate)

INGREDIENTS

FOR THE CAKE

1 cup + 1 tbsp (160g) all-purpose flour

2 tsp baking powder

¼ tsp salt

5 tbsp (75g) unsalted butter, at room temperature

½ cup (100g) granulated white sugar

1½ tbsp (25g) vegetable oil

1 tsp vanilla extract

2 medium eggs

½ cup (120g) + 3 tbsp whole milk, divided

3 tbsp (25g) unsweetened cocoa powder

FOR THE CHOCOLATE SHELL

14oz (400g) good-quality chocolate, chopped

2 tbsp refined coconut oil, plus more as needed

Sprinkles (optional)

SPECIAL EQUIPMENT

Two 7-inch (18cm) square cake pans

MAKE AHEAD

The snack cakes are best eaten fresh, but they'll keep in an airtight container at room temperature for 3 days. In warm weather, store them in the fridge.

Snack cakes are easy to make, and the homemade version is more delicious than any packaged snack. Take a few to school or work, serve them at a party, or just enjoy with a cold glass of milk.

1. **Preheat the oven and prepare the pans.** Preheat the oven to 350°F (180°C). Grease and flour the cake pans and line with parchment paper.

2. **Mix the dry ingredients.** In a large bowl, whisk together the flour, baking powder, and salt.

3. **Make the vanilla cake batter.** In another large bowl, add the butter, sugar, vegetable oil, and vanilla. Using a whisk, cream the ingredients together. Add the eggs one at a time, whisking to incorporate each one before adding the next. Add ½ cup milk (120g) and the dry ingredients. Using the whisk, mix until everything is combined and there are no lumps.

4. **Prepare the vanilla cake.** Pour half of the batter into one of the prepared cake pans, leaving the rest in the bowl (this will become the chocolate cake batter). Smooth out the batter in the cake pan using an offset spatula.

5. **Make the chocolate cake batter.** In a small bowl, warm the remaining 3 tablespoons of milk in a microwave. Add the cocoa powder and stir with a spoon until the mixture is smooth. Add the cocoa powder/milk mixture to the bowl with the remaining cake batter. Using the whisk, quickly mix until the batter is a uniform chocolate color. Stop as soon as everything is incorporated. This should take only a few seconds.

6. **Prepare the chocolate cake.** Pour the chocolate cake batter into the second prepared cake pan. Smooth out the batter using an offset spatula.

7. **Bake and cool the cakes.** Put both cake pans in the oven and bake for 12 to 15 minutes. Check after 12 minutes using the toothpick test (see page 15). Cool the cakes in their pans for about 5 minutes, and then take them out of the pans, remove the parchment paper, and allow them to cool completely.

8. **Prepare the cakes for dipping.** Cut each cake in half, and then each of those halves into four equal rectangular bars. Put the cakes in the freezer for 10 minutes.

9. **Make the chocolate shell.** In a large, shallow, microwave-safe bowl, microwave the chocolate and coconut oil, stirring every 30 seconds until the chocolate is just melted. The consistency should be loose and runny. If it seems thick, add an extra tablespoon of coconut oil. Allow to cool for 5 to 10 minutes before using.

10. **Dip the snack cakes.** Remove one cake bar at a time out of the freezer and dunk it in the melted chocolate. Using an offset spatula, cover the cake completely in chocolate. Remove the cake by balancing it on the offset spatula. Allow any excess chocolate to drip off. Add the sprinkles, if using, and place on some parchment paper. Repeat the process for all 16 snack cakes. To set more quickly, refrigerate for 10 minutes.

Pizza Rolls

PREP: 30 minutes // **COOK:** 10 minutes // **YIELD:** 16 to 20 pizza rolls

INGREDIENTS

3 cups (420g) all-purpose flour

4 tsp baking powder

1 cup + 1 tbsp (260g) whole milk

½ cup (100g) seasoned pizza sauce, plus more for dipping

3½oz (100g) shredded cheese, such as low-moisture mozzarella

1 large egg, beaten

1 cup (250g) breadcrumbs or cracker crumbs

Vegetable oil, for frying

SPECIAL EQUIPMENT

Dutch oven or heavy pot

Instant-read thermometer

VARIATIONS

Try different fillings, but remember a little goes a long way. Some ideas that work well are ham and cheese or pepperoni.

Who doesn't love pizza rolls—they're all your favorite pizza flavors in crunchy, bite-size pieces! These were a cafeteria lunch staple in the 1990s.

1. **Make the dough.** In a large bowl, mix the flour, baking powder, and milk until the mixture comes together to form a rough dough. Turn the dough out onto a work surface and knead for about 1 minute or until it comes together. If the dough seems dry, you can add an additional splash of milk. Divide the dough into two equal pieces and wrap well with plastic wrap. Set aside to rest at room temperature for 20 minutes.

2. **Assemble the pizza rolls.** Roll out the first portion of dough into a square shape about ⅛ inch (3mm) thick. (The dough needs to be thin—it will puff up during frying.) Using the back of a knife, gently trace an outline of the pizza rolls in the dough (draw a 4 × 4 or 4 × 5 grid). To the center of each rectangle on your grid, add about 1 teaspoon of pizza sauce and 1 teaspoon of shredded cheese, leaving a border of exposed dough. Lightly brush the borders of exposed dough with the beaten egg. Roll out the second piece of dough and place it on top of the fillings. Seal the edges, tightly pressing down with your hands. Using a pizza cutter, cut out the rolls. Seal the edges of the rolls with a fork.

3. **Coat the pizza rolls.** Toss the rolls in the beaten egg and then coat the rolls in breadcrumbs. Make sure the rolls are completely coated, including the edges; that way, they won't open during frying.

4. **Deep fry the pizza rolls.** To a large Dutch oven or heavy bottomed pot, add oil to a depth of at least 3 inches (2.5cm). Bring the oil to 350°F (180°C) and deep fry the pizza rolls in small batches for 3 to 4 minutes, or until golden.

5. **Serve.** Serve with extra pizza sauce on the side for dipping.

MAKE AHEAD & FREEZE

The uncooked pizza rolls can be stored in a zip-top bag in the freezer. Deep fry directly from frozen (they will take a little more time to cook when frozen).

DIY Lofthouse Sugar Cookies

PREP: 20 minutes // **COOK:** 9 minutes, plus 15 minutes to cool // **YIELD:** 10 to 12 cookies

INGREDIENTS

FOR THE COOKIES

1 cup (140g) all-purpose flour

¼ tsp baking powder

¼ tsp salt

5 tbsp (70g) unsalted butter, at room temperature

½ cup (100g) granulated white sugar

1 tsp vanilla extract

1 medium egg, at room temperature

1 tbsp whole milk

FOR THE FROSTING

4 tbsp (60g) unsalted butter, at room temperature

½ cup (60g) powdered sugar

1 tsp vanilla extract

2 drops of pink gel food coloring (optional, or use another color)

Sprinkles, to decorate

SPECIAL EQUIPMENT

Handheld mixer

These homemade sugar cookies are thick, super soft, and unapologetically sweet, just like the store-bought version. Make the classic pink frosting or change the color to suit your occasion!

1. **Prepare the baking sheet.** Line a baking sheet with parchment paper.

2. **Combine the dry ingredients.** In a medium bowl, whisk together the flour, baking powder, and salt. Set aside.

3. **Make the dough.** In a medium bowl, using a spatula, cream the butter, sugar, and vanilla until combined. Add the egg and mix until combined. Add the dry ingredients and milk, and mix using a spatula until the dough comes together. The dough will be sticky. Cover the bowl with plastic wrap and place in the freezer for 20 minutes. Don't forget it!

4. **Preheat the oven.** Preheat the oven to 350°F (180°C).

5. **Shape the cookies.** Using a small ice-cream scoop, scoop 12 cookies onto the prepared baking sheet leaving 2 to 3 inches (5–7.5cm) between each ball of dough. For signature smooth-top cookies, use lightly floured hands to gently roll each ball of dough until smooth. Keep the ball shapes—don't flatten the cookies.

6. **Bake the cookies.** Bake the cookies for about 9 minutes. The cookies will look soft and won't brown. Allow the cookies to cool on the baking sheet for 5 minutes to firm up, then transfer to wire rack to cool completely.

7. **Make the frosting.** To a medium bowl, add the butter, sugar, vanilla, and food coloring, if using. Using a handheld mixer, mix until combined.

8. **Frost the cookies.** Using an offset spatula, gently spread frosting across the top of each cookie. Top with sprinkles.

9. **Serve.** Serve the cookies immediately or put in an airtight container for about 2 hours to allow the frosting to set and for the cookies to soften further.

MAKE AHEAD
Store the cookies in an airtight container at room temperature for up to 5 days.

Ice Cream Bars

PREP: 10 minutes, plus overnight to freeze // **COOK:** None // **YIELD:** 8 to 10 bars

INGREDIENTS

FOR THE ICE CREAM

2 cups (500g) heavy cream

1 (14oz / 400g) can
  sweetened condensed milk

1 tbsp vanilla extract

½ tsp salt

FOR THE CHOCOLATE SHELL

11oz (300g) dark chocolate

2–3 tbsp refined coconut oil

Chopped salted peanuts
  or almonds (optional),
  to taste

SPECIAL EQUIPMENT

Ice cream bar molds or ice
  pop molds

Wooden treat sticks

VARIATIONS

No mold required bars. If you
don't have an ice cream bar
mold, you can still make these.
Freeze the ice cream base in
a square cake pan lined with
parchment paper. When
frozen, cut the block of ice
cream into bar shapes and
insert sticks. Put the bars back
into the freezer for 15 minutes
to firm up before dipping in the
chocolate shell.

Chocolate ice cream. If you
prefer chocolate ice cream
to vanilla, add ½ cup (50g)
of unsweetened cocoa powder
to the ice cream mix. Give it
a good stir to incorporate.
Then pour into the molds
as directed.

Ice cream bars are an iconic summer treat—who doesn't love creamy vanilla ice cream coated in rich chocolate? With my method, they're super easy and quick to make at home. Just remember to start the night before you want the bars, to allow the ice cream to freeze overnight. If you don't have molds for the ice cream bars, don't worry—you can still make these.

1. **Make the ice cream.** To a large liquid measuring cup or a large bowl with a spout, add the heavy cream, sweetened condensed milk, vanilla, and salt. Using a spoon, mix for 1 minute until everything is well combined. Don't whip the mixture to incorporate air, but make sure the condensed milk is evenly distributed through the cream. Pour the mixture into the ice cream bar molds, add the wooden sticks according to the instructions on your mold, and freeze the ice cream overnight.

2. **Unmold the ice cream bars.** Carefully run your ice cream mold under hot water and remove the ice cream bars from the mold. Place the bars on a plate or tray lined with parchment paper and return to the freezer for 15 minutes.

3. **Prepare the chocolate shell.** Melt the chocolate and the coconut oil in the microwave, stirring every 30 seconds until the chocolate is melted completely. Transfer the melted chocolate into a tall glass. (You'll dip the ice cream bars into the glass, so make sure the diameter is wide enough to accommodate the bars.)

4. **Dip the ice cream bars.** Allow the melted chocolate to come to room temperature before starting to dip the ice cream bars, otherwise the ice cream will melt on contact with the hot chocolate. Take the ice cream bars out of the freezer one at a time and dip each in the chocolate. Work quickly—you need to dip each bar immediately as it comes out of the freezer, otherwise the chocolate shell won't stick. Allow the excess chocolate to drip off back into the glass. The shell will harden in seconds.

5. **Make nut-covered bars (optional).** Spread the chopped nuts on a plate. Working quickly, dip an ice cream bar into the chocolate. Let the excess chocolate drip off, and immediately roll the bar in the chopped nuts before the shell has a chance to set. (This is my favorite version!)

MAKE AHEAD

Wrap the finished ice cream bars in parchment paper, place in a resealable zip-top bag, and store in the freezer until you want to eat them.

Leftover chocolate shell can be kept in the fridge, covered. When you're ready to use it, melt in the microwave and pour over any dessert—it works well poured over ice cream or fresh fruit.

Holiday Baking

The smell of cinnamon and sugar filling the house and the excitement of making and sharing homemade treats create memories that last a lifetime. Whether you want to cozy up with a mug of hot chocolate, enjoy some delicious cookies, or tackle something more advanced, there's something here for everyone. Grab your mixing bowls, turn up the holiday tunes, and let the baking begin!

Custom Holiday Cookie Box

ONE RECIPE, ENDLESS FLAVORS

PREP: 1 hour // **COOK:** 15 minutes per sheet of cookies // **COOL:** 15 minutes // **YIELD:** About 100 cookies

INGREDIENTS

FOR THE BASE DOUGH

6⅔ sticks (750g) unsalted butter, at room temperature

2½ cups (300g) powdered sugar

1 tbsp vanilla extract

½ tsp salt

3 large egg whites, at room temperature

6½ cups (900g) all-purpose flour

SPECIAL EQUIPMENT

Stand mixer

Cookie cutters

Piping bag with a medium star tip

Boxes for packaging cookies (optional)

This cookie selection box is sure to impress your family, friends, neighbors, and coworkers during the holidays. The trick to this recipe is the method of quickly turning one big batch of base dough into several different cookie varieties. Then, you change things up even more with different fillings and drizzles. So, it's time to get baking and put the collection of cookie cutters that's been hiding in your drawer to good use!

1. **Make the base dough.** In a stand mixer with a paddle attachment, combine the butter, sugar, vanilla extract, and salt. Mix until the ingredients are well combined, and the mixture looks fluffy. Add the egg whites and continue mixing until fully incorporated. Add the flour in three batches, mixing to fully incorporate each batch before adding the next. Don't worry about overmixing; the large amount of butter will inhibit gluten development as you incorporate the batches of flour.

2. **Divide the dough.** Divide the dough into five equal portions. The dough will be soft because you will pipe some of the cookies.

>> *Recipe continues on next page.*

⅕ batch of base dough

FOR THE LINZER COOKIES

⅕ batch of base dough

½ cup (60g) blanched almond flour

4 tbsp (40g) all-purpose flour

¼ tsp almond extract

Jam of choice, for the filling

FOR THE GINGERBREAD COOKIES

⅕ batch of base dough

4 tbsp (40g) all-purpose flour

3 tsp ground cinnamon

3 tsp unsweetened cocoa powder

3 tsp ground ginger

FOR THE VANILLA SUGAR COOKIES

⅕ batch of base dough

5 tbsp (50g) all-purpose flour

½ tsp vanilla extract

FOR THE CHOCOLATE SUGAR COOKIES

⅕ batch of base dough

5 tbsp whole milk

7½ tbsp (60g) sweetened cocoa powder

2 tbsp (20g) all-purpose flour

Dark Chocolate Ganache (page 211) or Nutella, for the filling

3. **Prepare the baking sheets.** Line several baking sheets with parchment paper.

4. **Prepare each cookie dough.**

Piped Butter Cookies: Transfer one portion of the dough to a piping bag fitted with a star tip. Onto a parchment-lined baking sheet, pipe out the cookies. You can pipe whatever shapes you like (I like to pipe them into *S*-shapes) but try to be as consistent as you can in terms of shape and size. If this is your first time piping cookies, don't worry if things go a bit wrong—you'll get better with practice, and whatever the shapes you pipe, the cookies will be delicious! Put the baking sheet in the fridge for at least 30 minutes to allow the cookies to set up.

Linzer Cookies: In a medium bowl, combine one portion of base dough with the almond flour, all-purpose flour, and almond extract. Using a rubber spatula, mix until the dough starts to form. Switch to use your hands to finish bringing the dough together. Put the dough between two pieces of parchment paper and, using a rolling pin, roll out the dough to about ¼ inch (6mm) thickness. Place the dough, still sandwiched in parchment paper, in the fridge for at least 30 minutes.

Gingerbread Cookies: Follow the same method as for the Linzer cookie dough but use the gingerbread cookie dough ingredients. When you've rolled it out, place the dough, still sandwiched in parchment paper, in the fridge for at least 30 minutes.

Vanilla Sugar Cookies: Follow the same method as for the Linzer cookie dough but use the vanilla sugar cookie dough ingredients. When you've rolled it out, place the dough, still sandwiched in parchment paper, in the fridge for at least 30 minutes.

Chocolate Sugar Cookies: In a small microwave-safe bowl, warm the milk. Add the cocoa powder and stir well to make a paste. Follow the same method as for the Linzer cookie dough but use the cocoa powder/milk paste and the flour. When you've rolled it out, place the dough, still sandwiched in parchment paper, in the fridge for at least 30 minutes.

5. **Preheat oven.** Preheat the oven to 350°F (180°C).

6. **Cut out the cookies.** Take a sheet of dough out of the fridge and place on a work surface. Remove the top piece of parchment paper. Cut out the cookies using cookie cutters of your choice. For the Linzer cookies and chocolate sugar cookies, you will need one base and one top for each cookie; into each top, cut out a small hole of your preferred shape (such as a circle, star, or heart). Place the cookies onto prepared baking sheets. If the dough gets too soft as you're working, put it back in the fridge for 15 minutes to firm up again.

7. **Bake the cookies.** Bake each batch of cookies for 15 minutes or until lightly golden (don't let them get too dark on the tops or the bottoms). Allow the cookies to cool on the baking sheets.

8. **Assemble the Linzer cookies.** Put 1 teaspoon of jam onto each Linzer cookie base. Gently press the lid on top of the jam.

9. **Assemble the chocolate sugar cookies.** Put 1 teaspoon of chocolate ganache or Nutella onto each cookie base. Gently press the lid on top of the ganache.

10. **Assemble the cookie boxes.** Arrange the cookies in the presentation boxes.

VARIATIONS

You can make variations of these cookies by drizzling them with melted chocolate or decorating them with royal icing. Make the vanilla sugar cookies extra festive by adding a drop of red gel food coloring to the cookie dough. Make a variety of sandwich cookies using a filling of melted chocolate, chocolate ganache (page 211), or buttercream (page 208).

Multipurpose Party Dough

ONE DOUGH, ENDLESS POSSIBILITIES

PREP: 20 minutes, plus 2 hours to rise // **COOK:** 20 minutes // **YIELD:** 48 pieces

INGREDIENTS

FOR THE DOUGH

1⅓ cups (320g) whole milk

1 large egg, at room temperature

2 tsp (7g) active dry yeast

4¼ cups (600g) all-purpose flour

1 tbsp salt

4 tbsp (60g) unsalted butter, melted

Olive oil, for greasing

SPECIAL EQUIPMENT

Stand mixer with dough hook attachment (recommended but not required)

2½-inch (6cm) round cookie cutter

VARIATIONS

Donut holes. Deep fry small balls of the dough and toss them in sugar immediately after frying.

Pretzel balls. Boil balls of the dough in water with baking soda added, then bake them off to make pretzel bites (see page 142). Toss in cinnamon sugar for cinnamon sugar pretzel bites.

Mini chocolate crescent rolls. Roll out the dough thinly and cut out tall triangles. Put a small piece of chocolate on the bases, then roll them up, almost as if you were making croissants (see page 130).

Whether you're hosting a holiday party or just getting together to watch the game, a tasty snack or appetizer is always a hit. This amazingly versatile dough can serve as the base for an endless variety of dishes. So, forget that store-bought dough that comes in a tube—this is so much softer and more delicious! I've included instructions for four crowd-pleasers—mini pizzas, garlic knots, pigs in a blanket, and stuffed buns—as well as a few ideas in the variations to spark your creativity.

FOR THE DOUGH

1. **Activate the yeast.** In a microwave-safe bowl, microwave the milk until lukewarm—about 30 to 40 seconds (don't let it get hot). Incorporate the egg and yeast and allow this mixture to sit for 5 minutes (see page 18).

2. **Mix the dry ingredients.** In a stand mixer or large mixing bowl, whisk together the flour and salt.

3. **Combine and knead the dough.** Using the dough hook attachment of the stand mixer, combine the dry ingredients with the wet ingredients and melted butter on medium-low speed until the dough comes together. If it seems dry at this stage, add an extra tablespoon of milk and knead until it's incorporated. Increase the speed to high and continue kneading the dough for another 8 minutes. After 8 minutes the dough should feel tacky to the touch and look smooth. (Alternatively, you can also make the dough by hand, but it requires arm muscle; see page 19.)

4. **Let the dough rise.** Using wet hands shape the dough into a ball. Lightly grease your bowl with ½ tablespoon of oil and place the dough back into the bowl. Cover with a damp kitchen towel or with plastic wrap and allow the dough to rise for 2 hours at room temperature, or until doubled in size.

5. **Shape as desired.** Follow the recipes on pages 252 and 253 to make garlic knots, stuffed buns, pigs in a blanket, or mini pizzas. Or come up with your own creation!

MAKE AHEAD
You can make the dough the day before. After letting it rise, store in the fridge covered overnight. Take the dough out of the fridge 90 minutes before you want to use it.

MAKING THE APPETIZERS

FOR THE EGG WASH

1 large egg, beaten

2 tbsp whole milk

Use the Multipurpose Party Dough (page 251) to make all four of these appetizers—a dozen of each type. Feel free to adjust the quantities to make as many or as few of each as you like. This is a big batch of dough, and should be kept covered until use. As you prepare one of the recipes, keep the rest of the dough covered. Share the egg wash across recipes, except the mini pizzas.

GARLIC KNOTS

INGREDIENTS

10oz (280g) Multipurpose Party Dough (page 251)

Egg wash

4 tbsp (60g) unsalted butter, melted

2 garlic cloves, minced

¼ teaspoon salt

¼ cup Parmesan cheese, grated

1. **Prepare baking sheet.** Line a baking sheet with parchment paper.

2. **Make the dough balls.** Divide into 12 equal portions and roll into balls.

3. **Prepare the garlic knots.** Take one of the garlic knot dough balls. On a work surface, using your hands, roll the ball out into a rope about 7 inches (18cm) long. Tie the rope into a knot, and place on a prepared baking sheet. Repeat for all 12 garlic knots, leaving space between each knot. Cover the baking sheet with plastic wrap and set aside to rise for 45 minutes. (Tip: While the garlic knots are rising, you could prepare the mini pizzas and/or pigs in a blanket.)

4. **Preheat the oven.** Preheat the oven to 350°F (180°C).

5. **Bake the garlic knots.** Remove the plastic wrap from the baking sheets and brush knots with egg wash. Then bake for 8 to 12 minutes until lightly golden.

6. **Finish the garlic knots.** In a large bowl, combine the hot butter, minced garlic, and salt. Toss the knots in the butter/garlic/salt mixture. Then sprinkle with the grated Parmesan cheese.

STUFFED BUNS

INGREDIENTS

12½oz (350g) Multipurpose Party Dough (page 251)

Cubed low-moisture mozzarella (enough for stuffing to your liking)

Cubed cooked ham (optional)

Egg wash

2 tbsp (30g) unsalted butter, melted

1. **Prepare baking sheet.** Line a baking sheet with parchment paper.

2. **Make the dough balls.** Divide into 12 equal portions and roll into balls.

3. **Prepare the buns.** Take each bun dough ball, and using your thumb, make an indentation. Put a small piece of cheese and/or ham in the indentation. Then pinch the dough around the filling so that it's completely enclosed in the dough. Roll into a ball shape and place on a prepared baking sheet. Repeat for all 12 buns, leaving space between each bun. Cover the baking sheet with plastic wrap and set aside to rise for 45 minutes. (Tip: While the buns are rising, you could prepare the mini pizzas and/or pigs in a blanket.)

4. **Preheat the oven.** Preheat the oven to 350°F (180°C).

5. **Bake the buns.** Remove the plastic wrap from the baking sheets and brush the buns with egg wash. Then bake for 8 to 12 minutes until lightly golden.

6. **Finish the buns.** Brush the stuffed buns with melted butter.

PIGS IN A BLANKET

INGREDIENTS

6½oz (180g) Multipurpose
  Party Dough (page 251)

12 mini cocktail wieners

Egg wash

Finishing salt, for sprinkling

2 tbsp (30g) unsalted butter,
  melted

1. **Preheat the oven and prepare the baking sheet.** Preheat the oven to 350°F (180°C). Line a baking sheet with parchment paper.

2. **Prepare the pigs in a blanket.** Divide the dough into 12 equal portions. Take a piece of dough, and using your hands, roll it into a thin rope about 5 inches (12cm) long. Wind the rope around a mini wiener and place on a prepared baking sheet. Repeat for all 12 pigs in a blanket. Brush the "blankets" with egg wash. Sprinkle with salt.

3. **Bake the pigs in a blanket.** Bake for 8 to 12 minutes until lightly golden.

4. **Finish the pigs in blankets.** Brush the pigs in blankets with melted butter.

MINI PIZZAS

INGREDIENTS

8½oz (240g) Multipurpose
  Party Dough (page 251)

12 tsp seasoned pizza sauce

Toppings of choice, such
  as shredded mozzarella,
  Parmesan, pepperoni,
  olives, green peppers,
  cooked sausage/bacon,
  onions, or mushrooms

1. **Preheat the oven and prepare the baking sheet.** Preheat the oven to 350°F (180°C). Line a baking sheet with parchment paper.

2. **Prepare the mini pizzas.** Roll out the dough on a work surface to a thickness of about ⅛ inch (3mm). Cut out the bases using a 2½-inch (6cm) round cookie cutter. Cut out as many bases as you can, then gather the scraps and re-roll the dough (see page 19) to cut out more bases. Place the bases on the prepared baking sheet. Spread a teaspoon of pizza sauce to the edges of each base and add toppings to each pizza. (Less is more when it comes to pizza toppings, so don't overload the pizzas).

3. **Bake the pizzas.** Bake for 6 to 8 minutes until the edges of the bases are light golden brown and the cheese has melted to your liking.

Three-Ingredient Shortbread

PREP: 10 minutes, plus 20 minutes to chill // **COOK:** 12 minutes, plus 30 minutes to cool // **YIELD:** 20 cookies

INGREDIENTS

8 tbsp (1 stick / 115g) salted butter, at room temperature

½ cup (60g) powdered sugar

1¼ cups (175g) all-purpose flour

SPECIAL EQUIPMENT

Stand mixer (recommended but not required)

Embossed rolling pin (optional)

Cookie cutters (optional)

Shortbread cookies are one of the most delicious holiday cookies, and they're also probably the easiest to make! The base recipe only has three ingredients, and the recipe is so flexible, it's easy to get creative with different mix-ins—from lemon zest to chocolate chips or nuts.

1. **Prepare the baking sheet.** Line a baking sheet with parchment paper.

2. **Combine the ingredients.** To a stand mixer with a paddle attachment, add the soft, room-temperature butter and the powdered sugar. Beat until the mixture is smooth. Add the flour and mix to combine. The dough will seem dry at first but keep mixing; eventually the dough will come together. Stop mixing when there are no more spots of flour, and the dough is smooth. (Alternatively, you can make the dough using a rubber spatula and your hands.)

3. **Roll out the shortbread.** Gather and transfer the dough to a lightly floured work surface, and using a rolling pin, roll out the dough to about ½-inch (1.25cm) thickness. (I like to use an embossed rolling pin, but it's not necessary.) Cut into whatever shapes you prefer—I like circles and rectangles—and transfer the cookies to the prepared baking sheet. Chill the cookies in the fridge for at least 45 minutes or in the freezer for 20 minutes.

4. **Preheat the oven.** Preheat the oven to 350°F (180°C).

5. **Bake the shortbread.** Bake for 12 to 15 minutes or until lightly golden. Remove from the oven and let them rest on the baking sheet for 15 minutes before transferring to a wire rack and allowing them to cool completely.

MAKE AHEAD
When cool, store the shortbread in an airtight container at room temperature for up to 5 days.

Ultimate Quick Panettone

PREP: 40 minutes, plus 5½ hours to rise // **COOK:** 1 hour, plus 2 hours to cool // **YIELD:** 1 panettone; serves 8 to 10

INGREDIENTS

FOR THE DRIED FRUIT
1–1¼ cups (200–250g) mixed chopped dried fruit, raisins, and candied citrus peel

2 cups boiling water

FOR THE DOUGH
½ cup + 1 tbsp (130g) whole milk

½ cup + 1 tbsp (130g) water

2 tsp (7g) active dry yeast

4½ cups (600g) all-purpose flour, divided

¾ cup (150g) granulated white sugar

Zest of 1 large orange

Zest of 1 large lemon

1½ tsp salt

3 large egg yolks

½ tbsp vanilla extract

8 tbsp (1 stick / 115g) unsalted butter, at room temperature

FOR THE EGG WASH
1 large egg

1 tbsp whole milk

FOR THE TOPPING (OPTIONAL)
20 whole raw almonds, roughly chopped

2–3 tbsp pearl sugar

SPECIAL EQUIPMENT

Stand mixer with dough hook (required)

Paper panettone mold, about 4½ inches (11cm) high and 6¾ inches (17cm) wide (available online)

Panettone is the most iconic Italian Christmas pastry. It's a super soft, light, and airy sweet bread, a little like brioche, scented with citrus and studded with dried fruit. Homemade panettone is nothing like the store-bought version, but it traditionally takes up to three days to make. This delicious shortcut version is ready in one day, and the texture and flavor are so much better than the store-bought.

1. **Soak the dried fruit.** To a medium bowl, add the dried fruit and cover with the hot water. Add enough water to cover the fruit. Set aside for 10 minutes.

2. **Activate the yeast.** In a medium microwave-safe bowl, heat the milk and water for 30 seconds until just warm (not hot). Add the yeast and stir to combine. Set aside for 10 minutes or until the mixture begins to foam.

3. **Make the dough.** To the bowl of a stand mixer, add 3 cups (400g) flour, the sugar, orange zest, lemon zest, and salt. (You only add part of the flour at this stage, to avoid overloading the motor of the stand mixer.) Using the dough hook attachment, mix to combine. Add the yeast mixture, egg yolks, and vanilla. Knead on medium speed until the dough comes together. Once the dough comes together, increase the speed to high and continue kneading for 8 minutes more.

4. **Add the butter.** While continuing to knead, gradually add the butter 1 tablespoon at a time, and fully incorporate before adding the next tablespoon. Once all the butter is incorporated, continue kneading for another 3 minutes. At this stage, the dough should be loose and very smooth. Add the remaining 1½ cups (200g) of flour and mix on medium/high speed for 2 to 3 minutes.

5. **Add the dried fruit.** Drain the soaked dried fruit (squeeze out any excess water) and add to the dough. Mix for 1 minute until the fruit is evenly distributed through the dough.

>> *Recipe continues on next page.*

// NOTE

In recent years, some people have come to believe that "true" panettone requires a sourdough starter. This is mistaken. The flavor and texture of panettone derives from the enriched dough (a little like brioche), and the light, aerated texture. People have confused the trend for sourdough with the long ferments that used to be required to make enriched doughs. Today, with modern yeasts, we don't need those slow ferments (although you can achieve great flavor by using them).

VARIATION

For a boozy variation, soak the dry fruit in alcohol instead of water the night before you want to make the panettone. To a small saucepan, add the dried fruit and ½ cup (120g) of your chosen alcohol, such as dark rum, cognac, or bourbon. Carefully bring the mixture to a simmer over medium-low heat. Reduce the heat to low, cover with a lid, and continue to heat for 10 minutes. Remove from the heat and pour the fruit and liquid into a heat-safe bowl. Cover with plastic wrap and let soak overnight at room temperature. The next day, prepare the panettone as directed.

6. **Fold the dough during the first rise.** Transfer the dough onto a buttered or oiled work surface and flatten it into a square shape with a thickness of about ½ inch (1.25cm). Fold in half, and in half again. Transfer the dough to a large greased bowl. Cover with a damp towel or plastic wrap and allow the dough to rise at room temperature. After 30 minutes, using wet hands, gently add more folds and cover again with plastic wrap (see photos). These folds give the finished panettone its light texture. Repeat this folding process four more times at 30-minute intervals. (The total time for the first rise is 2½ hours.)

7. **Prepare the mold.** Place the panettone mold on a baking sheet. Later, this will allow you to transfer the delicate panettone into the oven without having to directly touch the paper mold, which may deflate the panettone.

8. **Transfer the dough to the mold.** Using wet hands, gently transfer the dough into the mold (with the rough side facing down, leaving a smooth surface on top of the ball), being careful to retain as much air in the dough as you can. Lightly grease the top of the panettone with oil and cover it with plastic wrap, pressing it down gently onto the top surface (don't deflate it!) The oil will prevent the plastic wrap from sticking to the dough. Make sure the top surface of the dough is completely covered with the plastic wrap to prevent the panettone from drying out.

9. **Rise again.** Allow the dough to rise until it reaches the top of the mold, about 2 to 3 hours. Don't proceed with the recipe until the dough has risen to the top of the mold.

10. **Preheat the oven.** Preheat the oven to 350°F (180°C).

11. **Apply the egg wash.** In a small bowl, whisk 1 egg with 1 tablespoon of milk until well combined. Gently remove the plastic wrap from the panettone and brush the top with the egg wash. Add the almond and pearl sugar topping, if using.

12. **Bake the panettone.** Place the panettone on the bottom rack of the oven, away from the heat source. Bake for 20 minutes. After 20 minutes, quickly but carefully open the oven and place a sheet of aluminum foil on top of the panettone. This will prevent the top from burning. Continue baking for 30 to 40 minutes more. The total baking time should be 50 minutes to 1 hour. After 50 minutes, using a long skewer inserted to the center of the panettone, do the "toothpick test" (see page 15). If there's no wet dough stuck to the skewer, the panettone is ready. Keep baking until it's ready—it might take an additional 10 minutes, depending on your oven.

13. **Allow the panettone to cool.** Leave the panettone in the paper mold (but remove it from the baking sheet) and place it on a rack and allow to cool for at least 2 hours before serving.

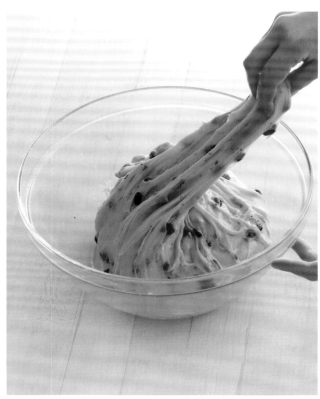

Hot Chocolate

ITALIAN VS. AMERICAN

PREP: 5 minutes // **COOK:** 5 minutes // **YIELD:** 2 servings of each hot chocolate

Hot chocolate is a must for the holidays. Growing up, I couldn't help but notice Italians loved their thick, indulgently textured *cioccolata calda,* whereas in the United States, people are used to a much thinner hot cocoa. I can't choose between them, so I'm giving you both!

ITALIAN HOT CHOCOLATE

INGREDIENTS

1½ cups (375g) whole milk

2½ tbsp (30g) granulated white sugar

2 tbsp (14g) Dutch-process cocoa powder

1 tbsp (8g) cornstarch

3½oz (100g) dark chocolate, chopped into small pieces

¼ tsp salt

2 tbsp softly whipped cream, for topping

1. **Heat the milk.** In a small saucepan over medium-low heat, combine and heat the milk and sugar.

2. **Bloom the cocoa powder.** In a small bowl, combine the cocoa powder, cornstarch, and 2 to 3 tablespoons of the warm milk until creamy and there are no lumps.

3. **Bring to a boil.** Add the cocoa powder mixture to the saucepan with the milk and continue heating until it comes to a gentle simmer and the mixture thickens. For the mixture to thicken, it will need to boil.

4. **Add the chocolate.** As soon as the mixture thickens, turn off the heat. Whisk in the chopped dark chocolate and salt until the chocolate has melted. Scrape the bottom and sides of the pan to make sure everything has fully incorporated.

5. **Serve.** Serve topped with a few spoonfuls of softly whipped cream. Eat using a spoon—the texture is like a thin pudding.

AMERICAN HOT CHOCOLATE

INGREDIENTS

1½ cups (375g) whole milk

2½ tbsp (30g) granulated white sugar

1 tbsp (7g) Dutch-process cocoa powder

2oz (50g) dark chocolate, chopped into small pieces

¼ tsp salt

Marshmallows (homemade, page 234, or store-bought), for topping

1. **Heat the milk.** In a small saucepan over medium-low heat, combine and heat the milk and sugar.

2. **Add the cocoa and simmer.** Whisk in the cocoa powder until no lumps remain and the mixture is piping hot.

3. **Add the chocolate.** As soon as the mixture starts to boil, turn off the heat. Whisk in the chopped dark chocolate and salt until the chocolate has melted.

4. **Serve.** Serve topped with marshmallows.

Easy Fancy Apple Pie

PREP: 1 hour, plus 30 minutes to chill // **COOK:** 45 minutes, plus 4 hours to cool // **YIELD:** 1 pie; serves 8

INGREDIENTS

FOR THE CRUST

1¾ cups (250g) all-purpose flour, plus more for dusting

10 tbsp (150g) unsalted butter, very cold, cut into pieces

3 tbsp (50g) granulated white sugar, plus more for dusting

¼ tsp salt

2 large egg yolks

1 tsp apple cider vinegar

FOR THE FILLING

½ cup (100g) + 2 tsp granulated white sugar, divided

4 tbsp (30g) + 2 tsp all-purpose flour, divided

½ tbsp ground cinnamon

½ tsp salt

7–8 medium apples, peeled, cored, and chopped into 1¼-inch (3cm) pieces (about 25oz / 700g in total once peeled and cored; I like to use Granny Smith apples.)

SPECIAL EQUIPMENT

Food processor

8- or 9-inch (20–23cm) pie dish, about 2 inches (5cm) deep

MAKE AHEAD

Pie crust dough can be made ahead and wrapped tightly in plastic wrap. Store in fridge for 1 week or in the freezer for up to 3 months.

I know, I know. You already have your own family apple pie recipe. Does the world really need another one? Of course not! However, I came up with this easy decoration concept many years ago, and it proved so popular that I had to include it. And for those of you who are looking for an apple pie recipe—this one is amazing!

1. **Make the pie crust dough.** To a food processor, add the flour, butter, sugar, and salt. Process until the mixture has the texture of fine breadcrumbs—this should take only a few seconds. Add the egg yolks and apple cider vinegar. Pulse until the dough comes together. Bring the dough together with your hands and divide into two equal portions. Flatten each portion so it's about ¾ inch (2cm) thick. (This will help the dough chill quickly). Wrap in plastic wrap and refrigerate for at least 1 hour.

2. **Prepare the pie dish.** Butter and flour an 8- or 9-inch (20–23cm) pie dish.

3. **Prepare the bottom crust.** On a floured work surface, roll out one portion of dough to a thickness of about ¼ inch (6mm). Flour the bottom and top of the dough to make sure nothing sticks. Transfer the rolled-out crust to the prepared pie dish. Gently push the dough into all the edges of the dish and patch any holes with pieces of excess dough from around the edge of the dish. Using a knife, cut off any excess dough overhanging the edge of the dish. Put the pie dish in the fridge to chill.

4. **Prepare the top crust.** On a floured work surface, roll out the second portion of dough to a thickness of just over ⅛ inch (3mm). (The dough needs to be quite thin, otherwise the leaves will look weirdly thick.) Using a sharp knife, cut out leaf shapes in different sizes. Make your leaves about 2 inches (5cm) long on average, with some shorter and some longer. Using the knife, gently mark the central and side veins of each leaf. Making all the leaves will only take about 10 minutes.

5. **Make the filling.** In a large bowl, whisk together the sugar, flour, cinnamon, and salt. Add the apples and mix using your hands until each piece of apple is well coated.

6. **Assemble the pie.** In a small bowl, mix together 2 teaspoons of granulated sugar and 2 teaspoons of flour. Sprinkle this mixture evenly over the bottom crust. (This will help prevent a soggy crust.) Distribute the apple filling evenly over the bottom crust. To make the top crust, wet the edges of the bottom crust and arrange the leaves over the top of the pie, covering the entire surface with the leaves overlapping a little. The small gaps between the leaves will allow steam to escape as the pie bakes.

7. **Chill the pie and preheat the oven.** Place the pie in the freezer for 30 minutes. (This will help the leaves keep their shape while baking.) Preheat the oven to 350°F (180°C).

8. **Bake the pie.** Bake for 45 minutes to 1 hour, until the pastry is golden brown.

9. **Serve.** Allow the pie to cool for at least 4 hours before you cut into it.

Apple Cinnamon Snacking Cake

PREP: 30 minutes // **COOK:** 45 minutes, plus 1 hour to cool // **YIELD:** 1 cake; serves 10

INGREDIENTS

FOR THE CAKE

1½ cups (210g) all-purpose flour, sifted

1 tsp baking powder

½ tsp salt

1 large Pink Lady apple or an apple of your choice, about 5½oz (150g)

8 tbsp (1 stick / 115g) unsalted butter, softened

¾ cup (150g) granulated white sugar

1 tsp vanilla extract

2 large eggs, at room temperature

⅓ cup + 2 tbsp (100g) plain Greek yogurt

¼ cup (60g) whole milk

1 tsp ground cinnamon

FOR THE CARAMEL WHIPPED CREAM (OPTIONAL)

1 cup (250g) heavy cream

5–6 tbsp Italian Salted Caramel (page 217), plus more for drizzling

SPECIAL EQUIPMENT

8 × 4-inch (10 × 20cm) loaf pan

Handheld or stand mixer

Food processor

Incredibly simple and comforting, this cake captures all the flavors of fall. It's so easy to make, and requires only one apple. Less peeling, less chopping, but still packed with apple flavor.

1. **Preheat the oven and prepare the pan.** Preheat the oven to 350°F (180°C). Grease and flour the loaf pan. Line the bottom of the pan with parchment paper, leaving some overhang to make it easy to lift the cake out of the tin. Grease and flour the parchment paper as well.

2. **Mix the dry ingredients.** In a medium bowl, mix the flour, baking powder, and salt. Set aside.

3. **Prepare the apple.** Peel and core the apple and chop into small chunks. Place the chunks in the bowl of the food processor along with the milk and ground cinnamon. Pulse the mixture a few times until the apple is finely chopped into tiny pieces. (Alternatively, you can use a grater to grate the apple.)

4. **Mix the wet ingredients.** In a stand mixer with a paddle attachment (or in a large bowl, if using a handheld mixer), cream together the butter, sugar, and vanilla. Beat for 1 minute to incorporate air into the mixture. Add the eggs one at a time and beat until incorporated. Add the yogurt and beat to incorporate it. Don't worry if the mixture curdles at this point—it will come back together in the next step.

5. **Finish the batter.** Add the apple mixture into the bowl with the wet ingredients and mix to combine. While continuing to mix, add the dry ingredients. Stop mixing when the dry ingredients are almost combined. Using a rubber spatula, scrape the sides and bottom of the bowl to finish combining the ingredients. As soon as there are no more visible spots of flour, it's ready. Your batter should be quite thick.

6. **Bake the apple cake.** Transfer the cake batter to the loaf pan and spread it out as evenly as you can. Tap the pan on the countertop a few times to level out the batter. Bake for 45 minutes to 1 hour. After 45 minutes, do the toothpick test (page 15). When the toothpick comes out clean, the cake is ready. Cool the cake in its pan for 10 minutes, then transfer to a wire rack to cool completely.

7. **Make the caramel whipped cream.** In a stand mixer (or in a medium bowl, if using a handheld mixer), whip the heavy cream and salted caramel until soft peaks form.

8. **Serve.** Cut the loaf cake into slices and serve with a generous dollop of caramel whipped cream and a drizzle of the salted caramel, if desired.

MAKE AHEAD & FREEZE

When cool, store the apple cake in an airtight container or a zip-top bag at room temperature for up to 3 days.

To freeze, wrap tightly in plastic wrap and store in the freezer for up to 1 month.

Fresh Pumpkin Layer Cake

PREP: 30 minutes // **COOK:** 20 minutes, plus 1 hour to cool // **YIELD:** 1 cake; serves 10

INGREDIENTS

FOR THE CAKE

1⅓ cups (190g) all-purpose flour

1½ tsp baking powder

½ tsp baking soda

1 tsp ground cinnamon

½ tsp ground ginger

½ tsp salt

⅛ tsp ground nutmeg

3–4oz (about 100g) peeled raw pumpkin or butternut squash, cut into chunks

8 tbsp (1 stick / 115g) unsalted butter, at room temperature

¾ cup (150g) light brown sugar

3 large eggs

FOR THE FROSTING AND DECORATION

1 batch Cream Cheese Frosting (page 209)

1 tbsp ground cinnamon (to stir into the frosting; optional)

Cinnamon sticks (optional)

Pumpkin seeds (optional)

Mini fondant pumpkins (optional)

SPECIAL EQUIPMENT

Two 7-inch (18cm) round cake pans

Food processor

Handheld mixer or stand mixer

Nothing beats fresh pumpkin in a pumpkin cake! Instead of using canned pumpkin, you can take the same approach used for carrot cake and add freshly grated raw pumpkin (or butternut squash) to the batter—it's always better to use fresh ingredients when in season.

1. **Preheat the oven and prepare the pans.** Preheat the oven to 350°F (180°C). Grease and flour two 7-inch (18cm) cake pans and line the bases with parchment paper.

2. **Combine the dry ingredients.** Using a fine mesh sieve, sift together into a large bowl the flour, baking powder, baking soda, cinnamon, ginger, salt, and nutmeg. Set aside.

3. **Make the pumpkin butter.** In a food processor, pulse the pumpkin until finely shredded. Add the butter and pulse until the mixture reaches an almost uniform texture. It won't be completely smooth, but the pumpkin should be in tiny pieces.

4. **Combine the wet ingredients.** In a stand mixer with a paddle attachment (or a large bowl, if using a hand mixer), cream together the pumpkin butter and brown sugar. Don't mix for more than 30 seconds. Add the eggs one at a time, beating well to fully incorporate them. The batter might look like it's split at this stage, but don't worry.

5. **Combine the wet and dry ingredients.** Add the dry ingredients to the wet and mix to combine. As soon as there are no more clumps of flour, stop mixing.

6. **Bake the cake.** Divide the batter evenly between the prepared cake pans and bake for 20 to 25 minutes. Check the cakes after 20 minutes and do the toothpick test (see page 15). When the toothpick comes out clean, the cakes are ready. (The cake layers will be thin and have no doming).

7. **Cool the cake.** Allow the cakes to sit in the pans for 5 minutes, then gently invert onto a cooling rack, remove the parchment paper, and allow to cool completely.

8. **Assemble and frost the cake.** When the cake layers have cooled completely, assemble and frost the cake as desired. (See page 17 for guidance on frosting.) To enhance the fall feel of the cake, decorate it with pumpkin seeds, cinnamon sticks, and mini fondant pumpkins, if desired.

MAKE AHEAD & FREEZE

This cake is best eaten freshly made but it will keep covered for 24 to 48 hours.

The unfrosted cake layers can be made ahead, tightly wrapped in plastic wrap, and frozen for up to 4 weeks (see page 14).

No-Spread Cutout Sugar Cookies

PREP: 30 minutes // **COOK:** 10 minutes, plus 20 minutes to cool // **YIELD:** 20 to 25 cookies

INGREDIENTS

1¾ cups (250g) all-purpose flour, plus more for dusting

1¼ cups (150g) powdered sugar

¼ tsp salt

10½ tbsp (150g) unsalted butter, very cold, cut into small pieces

1 tsp vanilla extract

2 tbsp whole milk

Royal Icing (optional, page 215), to decorate

SPECIAL EQUIPMENT

Food processor

Cookie cutters

You can't have the holidays without sugar cookies! Cutout sugar cookies should hold their shape perfectly when they bake—with no spreading, bubbling up, or collapsed edges. There are so many cutout cookie recipes that don't deliver, so I want to share my foolproof recipe and method. The secret to these cookies is the dough contains no egg or raising agent and the butter is cold.

1. **Prepare the baking sheet.** Line a baking sheet with parchment paper.

2. **Combine the dry ingredients.** In a large food processor, pulse together the flour, powdered sugar, salt, butter, and vanilla until the mixture has a sandy texture.

3. **Add the wet ingredients.** Add the milk to the food processor. Pulse until the cookie dough comes together. Don't overprocess. (If you don't have a food processor, you can easily make this dough using your hands.)

4. **Rest the dough.** Transfer the dough to a work surface and finish bringing it together with your hands until the flour has fully incorporated. Roll out the dough to about ¾ inch (2cm) thick. (This will make it easier to finish making the cookies later.) Wrap with plastic wrap and refrigerate for about 20 minutes. (This allows the butter to begin to resolidify and the flour to hydrate.)

5. **Roll and cut the cookies**. On a lightly floured work surface, roll out the cookie dough to about ¼ inch (6mm) thick and cut out different shapes using cookie cutters. If the dough sticks to the cutters, dip the cutters in flour. You can re-roll the dough as many times as you need so you use it all up. If the dough starts to become soft, refrigerate for 10 minutes to firm up. Place each cookie on the prepared baking sheet. Put the cookies in the freezer for 10 minutes.

6. **Preheat the oven.** While the cookies chill, preheat the oven to 350°F (180°C).

7. **Bake the cookies.** Bake for 10 to 15 minutes or until they're just baked through. (The timing will depend on the size of the cookies.) They should have a light golden color. Allow the cookies to cool on the baking sheet for 10 minutes, then transfer to a wire rack to cool completely.

8. **Serve.** Enjoy these cookies as they are or decorate them with royal icing once fully cool.

> **MAKE AHEAD**
> The cookie dough can be made in advance and baked in batches whenever you want them. Store the dough in a zip-top bag in the fridge for up to 1 week.

Quick Gingerbread Cookies

PREP: 10 minutes // COOK: 10 minutes, plus 15 minutes to cool // YIELD: 20 to 30 cookies

INGREDIENTS

1¾ cups (250g) all-purpose flour

½ cup (100g) granulated white sugar

8 tbsp (1 stick / 115g) unsalted butter, very cold, cut into 8 to 10 pieces

1½ tsp ground ginger

1½ tsp ground cinnamon

1 tsp unsweetened cocoa powder

¼ tsp salt

⅓ cup (100g) honey

1 egg yolk

1 tsp vanilla extract

SPECIAL EQUIPMENT

Food processor

Gingerbread man cookie cutter

VARIATION

To make in an air fryer, follow steps 1 to 4 to make and shape the cookies. It's best to make small cookies for air frying because you can fit more in the basket. Lightly oil and flour the air fryer basket, and then place the cookies directly into the basket. Bake in a preheated air fryer at 350°F (180°C) for 5 to 6 minutes or until just cooked.

Gingerbread cookies are possibly the most iconic of all holiday cookies, and these are great because they come together super quickly. So, if you have unexpected guests, you can whip up a batch of these from scratch in half an hour. I've given you two methods to bake these—one for a regular oven and one for an air fryer. This recipe is also perfect for making a gingerbread house!

1. **Preheat the oven and prepare the baking sheet.** Preheat the oven to 350°F (180°C). Line two baking sheets with parchment paper.

2. **Combine the dry ingredients.** To a food processor, add the flour, sugar, butter, ginger, cinnamon, cocoa powder, and salt. Pulse until the mixture has a sandy texture.

3. **Add the wet ingredients.** Add the honey, egg yolk, and vanilla. Pulse until a dough starts to form. As soon as the dough begins to come together, transfer it to a lightly floured work surface, and finish working the dough with your hands until it looks uniform with no visible spots of flour. Try not to add too much flour to the dough as you work it.

4. **Roll and cut the cookies.** Roll out the cookie dough to about ¼ inch (5mm) thickness and cut out the cookies using a cookie cutter. You can re-roll the dough as many times as you need to use it all up. Place each cookie on the prepared baking sheet.

5. **Bake the cookies.** Bake for 10 to 15 minutes until they're just cooked. (The bake time will depend on the size of the cookies.) The cookies are done when they've lost their shine and have a dull surface. Allow them to cool on the baking sheet for 10 minutes. Transfer to a wire ack to cool completely.

6. **Serve.** Enjoy these cookies as they are, or decorate with Royal Icing (page 215).

MAKE AHEAD
The cookie dough can be made in advance and baked as needed. The dough can be stored in a zip-top bag in the fridge for up to 1 week.

MAKE AHEAD

This cake will last 24 to 48 hours. If you're not eating the whole cake right away, omit the rosemary. It will impart a flavor to the frosting if you leave it for any length of time.

Unfrosted cake layers can be wrapped tightly in plastic wrap and kept at room temperature for up to 1 day or frozen for up to 4 weeks.

White Christmas Cake

PREP: 30 minutes // COOK: 20 minutes, plus 1 hour to cool // YIELD: One 3-layer cake; serves 10 to 12

INGREDIENTS

FOR THE CAKE

1½ cups (210g) all-purpose flour

½ cup (50g) almond flour

3 tsp baking powder

½ tsp salt

3 large egg whites

¾ cup (150g) granulated white sugar, divided

1 stick (115g) unsalted butter, at room temperature

3 tbsp (40g) vegetable oil

½ tsp vanilla extract

¼ tsp almond extract

½ cup (125g) plain yogurt

½ cup (120g) whole milk

FOR THE FROSTING AND DECORATION

1 batch Stabilized Whipped Cream (page 213)

Red berries or fruit, such as red currants, raspberries, or pomegranate seeds

Small handful of flaked almonds

4 small sprigs of fresh rosemary

½ tbsp powdered sugar

SPECIAL EQUIPMENT

Three 7-inch (18cm) round cake pans

Handheld mixer or stand mixer

This white Christmas cake has a delicate almond flavor and a melt-in-your-mouth texture thanks to the almond flour and whipped egg whites. With its winter landscape-inspired decoration, it's a perfect centerpiece for your holiday table.

1. **Preheat the oven and prepare the cake pans.** Preheat the oven to 320°F (160°C). Grease and flour the three cake pans and line the bases with parchment paper.

2. **Mix the dry ingredients.** In a medium bowl, whisk together the flour, almond flour, baking powder, and salt. (Make sure there are no lumps.) Set aside.

3. **Make the meringue.** In the bowl of a stand mixer (or in a medium bowl if using a hand mixer), whip the egg whites until they start to foam. With the mixer running, add half the sugar (75g) a little at a time, until it's fully incorporated and the mixture has reached the soft to medium peak stage (see page 23). Set aside.

4. **Mix the wet ingredients.** To a large bowl, add the butter, oil, the remaining half of the sugar (75g), and the vanilla and almond extracts. Using a whisk, cream together the ingredients. Add the yogurt. Mix to incorporate.

5. **Combine the wet and dry ingredients.** To the yogurt mixture, add the flour mixture and the milk. Using a rubber spatula, mix until all the flour is incorporated. At this stage, the batter will seem stiff. Fold in the egg whites (see page 25). Take your time and make sure the egg whites are fully incorporated into the batter. The final batter will be thick; don't be tempted to add extra liquid.

6. **Bake the cakes.** Divide the batter evenly among the three cake pans and level out using a spoon or offset spatula. Bake for about 20 minutes. After 18 minutes, do the toothpick test (see page 15) to check for doneness. The cakes should be light in color with very little, if any, browning. The cake layers should be thin and will not rise a lot during baking.

7. **Cool the cakes.** Allow the cakes to sit in the pans for 5 minutes, then gently turn them out onto a wire rack. Remove the parchment paper and allow to cool completely.

8. **Assemble the cake.** When the cake layers have cooled completely, assemble and frost the cake as desired. (See page 17 for guidance on frosting.) I like a semi-nude frosting for this cake.

9. **Decorate just before serving.** Transfer the cake to a serving plate. Arrange the red fruit, rosemary sprigs, and nuts in a half-moon shape on one side of the cake. Dust with the powdered sugar. Add the rosemary at the last minute, just before serving, otherwise it will flavor the frosting.

Snowy Chocolate Cake

PREP: 40 minutes // **COOK:** 30 minutes, plus 1 hour to cool // **YIELD:** 1 cake; 10 servings

INGREDIENTS

FOR THE CAKE

1 cup (140g) all-purpose flour

1 tsp baking soda

¼ tsp salt

1 cup (240g) milk

1 stick (115g) unsalted butter, cut into 4 pieces

1 cup (100g) unsweetened cocoa powder

2 tbsp freshly brewed coffee

¾ cup (180g) sour cream

1½ cups (300g) granulated white sugar

2 eggs, at room temperature

FOR THE FROSTING AND DECORATION

14oz (400g) good quality white chocolate, finely chopped

1 cup (240g) heavy cream

Coconut extract (optional)

Coconut flakes

SPECIAL EQUIPMENT

Two 7-inch (18cm) round cake pans

Handheld mixer or stand mixer

MAKE AHEAD

Store the cake covered at room temperature for 1 to 2 days.

If you're looking for a different spin on the classic yule log, look no further. This cake combines a moist chocolate cake with a delicious white chocolate frosting and coconut coating. If you love chocolate cake, this "snowy" version is perfect for any festive winter celebration!

1. **Preheat the oven and prepare the pans.** Preheat the oven to 320°F (160°C). Grease and flour two 7-inch (18cm) cake pans and line the bottoms with parchment paper.

2. **Combine the dry ingredients.** In a large bowl, mix the flour, baking soda, and salt. Set aside.

3. **Combine the wet ingredients.** In a large deep saucepan, heat the milk and butter over medium heat until the butter has melted and the mixture is warm. Do not bring to a boil. Remove from the heat and, using a silicone whisk, whisk in the cocoa powder. Add the coffee and sour cream and whisk until fully incorporated. Mix in the sugar until well combined and then whisk in the eggs.

4. **Add the dry ingredients to the wet.** Whisk the dry ingredients into the wet ingredients until there are no more visible spots of flour. Using a rubber spatula, scrape the bottom and sides of the pan.

5. **Bake the cakes.** Divide the cake batter evenly between the prepared cake pans and bake for 30 to 35 minutes. Do the toothpick test (see page 15). If it comes out clean, the cakes are ready.

6. **Cool.** Allow the cakes to cool in their pans for 5 minutes, then invert onto a cooling rack. Remove the parchment paper and allow the cakes to cool completely.

7. **Make the ganache.** To a medium bowl, add the chopped white chocolate and set aside. In a small saucepan, heat the cream over medium heat until it comes to a gentle simmer (do not boil). When simmering, quickly pour the cream over the chopped chocolate, and let sit for 2 minutes. Add a few drops of coconut extract, if using. Using a rubber spatula, mix the cream and chocolate together until well combined and smooth. If there are some pieces of chocolate that haven't melted, pop the bowl in the microwave, stirring every 20 to 30 seconds until fully melted.

8. **Whip the ganache.** Refrigerate the ganache for 45 minutes, stirring every 10 minutes. When cool, use a hand mixer to whip the ganache until it's lightened in color and fluffy, about 2 minutes. Don't overwhip.

9. **Assemble the cake.** Place one of the cakes on a flat surface. Add a good dollop of whipped ganache frosting to the top of the cake and spread out evenly using an offset spatula. Place the second cake layer on top. Apply a crumb coat of frosting and then a thin, final layer of frosting. (See frosting techniques, page 17). Cover the cake with coconut flakes.

Gingerbread Donuts

PREP: 30 minutes, plus 3 hours to rise // **COOK:** 3 minutes, plus 5 minutes to cool // **YIELD:** 15 large or 25 small donuts

INGREDIENTS

FOR THE DOUGH

1 cup (240g) whole milk

2 medium eggs, at room temperature

2 tsp (7g) active dry yeast

4 cups (550g) all-purpose flour

½ cup (100g) granulated white sugar

2 tbsp ground ginger

2 tbsp ground cinnamon

1 tsp salt

½ tsp ground nutmeg

6 tbsp (85g) unsalted butter, melted and cooled slightly

Neutral cooking oil, for frying and greasing

FOR THE GLAZE

5 tbsp (75g) unsalted butter

3 tbsp (45g) whole milk, at room temperature

1 tsp vanilla extract

2 cups (250g) powdered sugar

SPECIAL EQUIPMENT

Stand mixer (recommended but not required)

Dutch oven or heavy-bottomed pot

Instant-read thermometer

Large gingerbread man cookie cutter or a regular donut cutter

MAKE AHEAD
Donuts are best eaten fresh! However, you can store donuts in an airtight container for up to 1 day. Reheat in the microwave for 20 seconds.

What could be better than incorporating some holiday flavors and decorations into donuts? These gingerbread donuts feature warm spices and are super fun to make and decorate.

1. **Activate the yeast.** In a small microwave-safe bowl or glass measuring cup, microwave the milk until lukewarm, about 30 seconds (don't let it get hot). Incorporate the eggs into the milk and add the yeast. Let sit for 5 minutes.

2. **Mix the dry ingredients.** In the bowl of a stand mixer or in a large bowl, whisk together the flour, sugar, ginger, cinnamon, salt, and nutmeg.

3. **Combine and knead the dough.** To the dry ingredients, add the melted butter and milk/yeast mixture. Using the dough hook attachment, knead the dough on medium-low speed until it comes together, then increase the speed to medium-high and continue kneading the dough for another 10 minutes. After 10 minutes the dough should feel tacky to the touch and look smooth.

4. **Let dough rise.** Remove the dough from the bowl, and using wet hands, shape the dough into a ball. Lightly grease the bowl with ½ tablespoon of oil and place the dough back in the bowl. Cover with a damp kitchen towel or with plastic wrap and allow the dough to rise for 2 to 3 hours at room temperature, until tripled in size.

5. **Roll and cut the donuts.** When the dough has tripled in size, turn it out onto a lightly floured work surface. Gently press the dough down using your hands (do not knead the dough) and using a rolling pin, roll out to ½ inch (1.25cm) thick. Using a gingerbread man cookie cutter, cut out the donuts. Place the donuts onto a lightly floured baking sheet. (A good tip is to put each donut on a square of parchment paper; see page 19.) You can re-roll the scraps and cut out more donuts (see page 19). If the dough pulls back, wrap the dough in plastic wrap and allow to rest for 30 minutes. Then roll the dough out and make more donuts.

6. **Let the dough rise for a second time.** Cover the donuts with a clean kitchen towel and allow to rise for 45 minutes to 1 hour at room temperature.

7. **Fry the donuts.** In a large Dutch oven or heavy-bottomed pot over medium heat, heat 3 inches (7.5cm) of oil to 350°F (180°C). When this temperature is reached, reduce the heat slightly to maintain the temperature (see Deep Frying, page 25). Working in batches, fry the donuts until golden brown, about 1 to 2 minutes on each side. Transfer the donuts onto paper towels and set aside.

8. **Make the glaze and glaze the donuts.** Place the butter in a large bowl and microwave until fully melted. Add the milk, vanilla, and powdered sugar and mix to combine. The glaze should be smooth and loose. If it seems too thick, mix in an additional tablespoon of milk. While the donuts are still warm, toss them in the glaze. Place on a cooling rack for 10 minutes. When the glaze has set, decorate with Royal Icing (page 215), if desired.

Two-Ingredient Chocolate Fudge

PREP: 5 minutes // **COOK:** 5 minutes, plus 2 hours to cool // **YIELD:** 25 pieces

INGREDIENTS

14oz (400g) 70% cocoa dark chocolate, cut into small pieces

14oz (400g) Nutella or any nut butter, at room temperature

SPECIAL EQUIPMENT

8-inch (20cm) square cake pan

VARIATIONS

Add chopped dried fruit or nuts to the fudge mixture before transferring to the cake pan.

There's something so comforting about homemade fudge. It's a must for the holidays, and it makes a great gift. The traditional way of making fudge can be a bit tricky and requires special equipment, but this shortcut method couldn't be easier and comes together in less than 10 minutes.

1. **Prepare the cake pan.** Grease and line the cake pan with parchment paper, leaving a 2-inch (5cm) overhang.

2. **Combine the ingredients.** In a large microwave-safe bowl, microwave the chocolate, stopping to stir well every 20 to 30 seconds. When all the chocolate has melted, add the soft, room-temperature Nutella. Heat the mixture, stirring every 20 seconds, until it's silky smooth. (This should take less than 1 minute.)

3. **Chill.** Transfer the mixture to the prepared pan, and smooth over with an offset spatula or a spoon. Cover with a plate and refrigerate for 2 hours or until set.

4. **Serve.** Remove the fudge from the cake pan, remove the parchment paper, and cut into approximately 1½-inch (4cm) squares. If the fudge is too hard, heat the blade of your knife in hot water to get a clean cut.

MAKE AHEAD
Store fudge in an airtight container at room temperature for up to 2 weeks. If your kitchen is warm, store it in the fridge.

Snickerdoodles

PREP: 15 minutes // **COOK:** 10 minutes, plus 10 minutes to cool // **YIELD:** 10 cookies

INGREDIENTS

FOR THE DOUGH

8 tbsp (1 stick / 115g) unsalted butter

¾ cup (150g) brown sugar (light or dark)

2 egg yolks, at room temperature

1 tsp pure vanilla extract

½ tsp salt

½ tsp baking powder

1¼ cups (175g) all-purpose flour

FOR THE COATING

¼ cup (50g) granulated white sugar

2 tsp ground cinnamon

I've no idea why these cookies are called snickerdoodles, but I absolutely love them—and I bet you will too. For me, snickerdoodles should have crispy edges, chewy middles, and a crunchy, spiced sugar coating—and that's what this recipe delivers.

1. **Preheat the oven and prepare the baking sheet.** Preheat the oven to 350°F (180°C). Line a baking sheet with parchment paper.

2. **Prepare the wet ingredients.** In a microwave-safe bowl, microwave the butter until melted (page 25). Allow the butter to cool for 5 minutes, then add the sugar, egg yolks, and vanilla. Mix well to combine.

3. **Add the dry ingredients.** Add the salt and baking powder. Stir well with a wooden spoon. Add the flour and mix well to combine all the ingredients.

4. **Prepare the coating.** In a small bowl, combine the sugar and cinnamon. Mix well.

5. **Shape the cookies.** Divide the dough into 10 equal portions. Using your hands, roll each portion into a ball, then dip into the cinnamon sugar, coating it completely. Place each ball on the prepared baking sheet.

6. **Bake the cookies.** Bake for 10 minutes. They should still be very soft in the middle when you take them out of the oven. They'll continue to cook after they come out of the oven, so expect them to look underdone at this point. Allow them to cool on the baking sheet for 10 minutes, then very gently transfer them to a wire rack to cool completely.

7. **Serve.** Wait at least 10 minutes after they come out of the oven before eating. This will allow the cookies to set up enough for you to pick them up without them breaking.

> **MAKE AHEAD & FREEZE**
>
> Unbaked cookie dough can be shaped in advance and baked whenever you want cookies. Store the cookie dough balls in a zip-top bag in the fridge for up to 1 week or in the freezer for up to 3 months.
>
> To bake from frozen, place on a parchment-lined baking sheet and bake at 350°F (180°C) for 10 to 12 minutes.

Acknowledgments

First, and most importantly, if you've enjoyed my work on YouTube, Instagram, and Facebook over the years, thank you—I wrote this book for you. If you wondered why I disappeared for so long, this is the reason (it took so much longer than I expected!). Still, I wanted to take the time needed for this book to be personal and authentically me. So, this is all me, from the words to the food styling to the photography. I really hope you like it!

Thank you to all my family and friends, especially Dodo, for the incredible moral support on this project.

Special thanks to Simon for always being there for me as I wrote the book. I couldn't have done this without you. Thank you, Mark (aka Sauce Stache), and Carlo for making me laugh when I needed cheering up.

Thanks to my amazing brand-relations manager, Colin, for sticking with me while I took time out. I know it took a while, but I can finally get back to work now!

Finally, thank you to everyone on the DK and Penguin Random House teams for being so great to work with. From creative to finance and admin, you made it easy to collaborate across continents. Special thanks to my editor, Ann, and my designer, Jessica, for supporting my vision for this book (I know this wasn't an easy one!); and also, to Julie for her fantastic feedback during recipe testing. I couldn't have wished for a better team!

Index

Emma Fontanella is a professional pastry chef and the creator of the YouTube channel Emma's Goodies. She is passionate about developing recipes that are quick and easy for anyone to make at home without compromising on flavor. People from around the world regularly recreate her recipes and share their results across social media. Emma is based in Rome, Italy and splits her time between Rome and New York.